The Psycholinguistics
of Bilingualism

The Psycholinguistics of Bilingualism

François Grosjean and Ping Li
Primary Authors

With contributions from

Ellen Bialystok and Raluca Barac
Annette M.B. de Groot
Rosa M. Manchón
Virginia Yip

WILEY-BLACKWELL

A John Wiley & Sons, Ltd., Publication

This edition first published 2013
© 2013 Blackwell Publishing, Ltd with the exceptions of Chapter 1, Chapter 2, Chapter 3, Chapter 7, Chapter 10 © 2013 François Grosjean and Ping Li

Blackwell Publishing was acquired by John Wiley & Sons in February 2007. Blackwell's publishing program has been merged with Wiley's global Scientific, Technical, and Medical business to form Wiley-Blackwell.

Registered Office
John Wiley & Sons Ltd, The Atrium, Southern Gate, Chichester, West Sussex, PO19 8SQ, UK

Editorial Offices
350 Main Street, Malden, MA 02148-5020, USA
9600 Garsington Road, Oxford, OX4 2DQ, UK
The Atrium, Southern Gate, Chichester, West Sussex, PO19 8SQ, UK

For details of our global editorial offices, for customer services, and for information about how to apply for permission to reuse the copyright material in this book please see our website at www.wiley.com/wiley-blackwell.

The right of François Grosjean, Ping Li, Ellen Bialystok, Raluca Barac, Annette M.B. de Groot, Rosa M. Manchón, and Virginia Yip to be identified as the authors of this work has been asserted in accordance with the UK Copyright, Designs and Patents Act 1988.

Library of Congress Cataloging-in-Publication Data
Grosjean, François.
    The psycholinguistics of bilingualism / François Grosjean and Ping Li , Primary Authors; with contributions from Ellen Bialystok ... [et al.].
        p. cm. Includes index.
    ISBN 978-1-4443-3278-0 (cloth) – ISBN 978-1-4443-3279-7 (pbk.)   1. Bilingualism–Psychological aspects.   2. Cognition.   3. Memory.   4. Psycholinguistics.   I. Li, Ping, 1962–   II. Bialystok, Ellen.
P115.4.G77 2013
404′.2019–dc23

                                                                                          2012022088

A catalogue record for this book is available from the British Library.

Cover image: © Rosanne Olson/Science Faction/Corbis
Cover design by Design Deluxe

Set in 10.5/13 pt Minion by Toppan Best-set Premedia Limited

Printed in Malaysia by Ho Printing (M) Sdn Bhd

3   2014

Contents

Author Biographies

Primary authors

François Grosjean is Professor Emeritus of Psycholinguistics at Neuchâtel University, Switzerland. His many publications on bilingualism include three books: *Life with Two Languages: An Introduction to Bilingualism* (1982), *Studying Bilinguals* (2008), and *Bilingual: Life and Reality* (2010). The latter was selected as a Choice Outstanding Academic Title. He is a Founding Editor of the journal *Bilingualism: Language and Cognition* and was its first Coordinating Editor.

Ping Li is Professor of Psychology, Linguistics, and Information Sciences and Technology at Pennsylvania State University. His books include *The Handbook of East Asian Psycholinguistics* (Volumes 1–3; General Editor; 2006), and *The Acquisition of Lexical and Grammatical Aspect* (co-authored with Y. Shirai, 2000). He is Editor of the journal *Bilingualism: Language and Cognition*, and Associate Editor of *Frontiers in Language Sciences*.

Guest authors

Ellen Bialystok is Distinguished Research Professor at York University in Canada. She has published extensively on bilingualism and its cognitive effects across the lifespan. Her books include *Bilingualism in Development* (2001) and *Lifespan Cognition: Mechanisms of Change* (2006) (co-edited with Fergus I.M. Craik). She is a fellow of the Royal Society of Canada and her research has been recognized with numerous awards, including the 2010 Killam Prize in the Social Sciences.

Raluca Barac, PhD, is a research manager at the Hospital for Sick Children in Toronto, Canada.

Annette de Groot is Professor of Experimental Psycholinguistics at the University of Amsterdam. She is the author of *Language and Cognition in Bilinguals and*

Multilinguals: An Introduction (2011), and with Judith Kroll she edited *Tutorials in Bilingualism: Psycholinguistic Perspectives* (1997) and the *Handbook of Bilingualism: Psycholinguistic Approaches* (2005). She is a member of the editorial board of *Bilingualism: Language and Cognition*.

Rosa Manchón is Professor of Applied Linguistics at the University of Murcia, Spain. Her books include *Writing in Foreign Language Contexts: Learning, Teaching, and Research* (2007), *Learning-to-Write and Writing-to-Learn in an Additional Language* (2011), and *L2 Writing Development: Multiple Perspectives* (2012). Together with Chris Tardy, she edits the *Journal of Second Language Writing*.

Virginia Yip is Professor and Chairperson of Linguistics and Modern Languages as well as Director of the Childhood Bilingualism Research Centre at The Chinese University of Hong Kong. Her books include *Interlanguage and Learnability* (1995) and *The Bilingual Child: Early Development and Language Contact* (co-authored with Stephen Matthews, 2007), which received the Linguistic Society of America's Leonard Bloomfield Book Award. She has also co-authored a series of books on Cantonese grammar.

Introduction

In the last 25 years, the field of bilingualism has grown tremendously, as can be seen by the presence of numerous introductory books on the topic, the publication of edited and more specialized monographs, the emergence of encyclopedias and new academic journals, not to mention numerous websites and blogs dedicated to the subject.

One of the most dynamic areas of bilingualism research involves the psycholinguistic study of both adults and children. Most books usually concentrate on particular domains such as language processing and representation in adult bilinguals, bilingual child language acquisition, the cognitive aspects of bilingualism, the bilingual brain, and so on. Few books cover all these domains at once. In addition, most are aimed at advanced students and specialists or at those who have a solid background in cognitive psychology, psycholinguistics or applied linguistics.

This book on the psycholinguistics of bilingualism is a general introduction to the field rather than a comprehensive survey. Among its different aims, the first is to present the most important aspects of the area in a clear, informative and pedagogical manner. To do so, the main authors have benefited from the collaboration of guest authors, who are experts in their own fields – Ellen Bialystok and Raluca Barac, Annette de Groot, Rosa Manchón and Virginia Yip. The second aim is to make the issues discussed accessible to non-specialists, most notably undergraduates and masters students with little previous exposure to the field of bilingualism and, sometimes, limited knowledge of psycholinguistics and cognitive psychology. The third aim is to give the various areas of the psycholinguistics of bilingualism equal weight, even though some are investigated more extensively by today's researchers. For example, written language processing has received much more attention than spoken language processing in recent years even though bilingualism primarily involves spoken languages. The final aim is to introduce readers to the approaches and methodology used in the field, most

The Psycholinguistics of Bilingualism, First Edition. François Grosjean and Ping Li.
© 2013 Blackwell Publishing Ltd with the exceptions of Chapter 1, Chapter 2, Chapter 3, Chapter 7, Chapter 10 © 2013 François Grosjean and Ping Li. Published 2013 by Blackwell Publishing Ltd.

notably observation, experimentation, verbal and computational modeling, as well as brain imaging.

The book begins with a short introductory chapter on bilingualism and bilinguals (Chapter 1). It presents a number of basic concepts and clarifies some misconceptions. Since bilingual participants in studies bring specific language knowledge and use to the research environment, it is important to understand these phenomena as reflected in the participants themselves so as to be able to make better sense of the data obtained.

The book is then organized into four parts. Part I concerns spoken language processing. Chapter 2 is dedicated to speech perception and comprehension and examines how bilinguals process just one language when no elements of the other language(s) are present. It then considers how bilinguals perceive and comprehend speech that contains code-switches and borrowings. Chapter 3 examines speech production and shows how it is a dynamic process, sometimes language selective and sometimes language independent. In addition it studies the time course of language switching, how it is constrained by syntactic considerations, and its impact on the phonetics of the utterance.

Part II is concerned with written language processing. It contains two chapters, one on reading and one on writing (this latter topic is relatively rare in the literature). Chapter 4, written by Annette de Groot, examines whether visual word recognition in bilinguals is restricted to the contextually appropriate language or whether the other language is also involved. Both experimental studies and models are called upon to provide an answer. It then discusses how bilingual readers resolve syntactic ambiguities and how they process semantic and syntactic anomalies. Chapter 5, authored by Rosa Manchón, considers the processing features of bilingual text production including the strategic role of the stronger language when the less dominant language is being written. It also investigates the interplay between writing expertise and linguistic ability, and discusses the transfer of writing knowledge and skills across languages.

Part III is dedicated to language acquisition in bilinguals. Chapter 6, written by Virginia Yip, deals with simultaneous language acquisition and discusses such issues as balanced vs. unbalanced development and whether the latter takes place separately for each language or not. It also examines language differentiation in the early stages of acquisition and looks into cross-linguistic influences, code-mixing, as well as trilingual acquisition and language development in children with language disorders. Chapter 7 is concerned with successive language acquisition. It provides a review of the contentious critical period hypothesis and the theoretical perspectives that accompany it. It then examines speech learning and the variables that may influence its success. It ends with an examination of how the two languages influence one another and suggests that even a native language is susceptible to change as proficiency and use increase in the other language.

The final part, Part IV, covers cognition and the bilingual brain. Chapter 8, authored by Annette de Groot, examines bilingual memory and presents various models of the organization of lexical word forms and their conceptual representations in the bilingual mental lexicon. It then looks at whether, how, and why L1 and L2 concepts differ from one another and from those of monolinguals. It ends with a discussion of bilingual episodic/autobiographical memory and asks whether one's memory encodes the language used in a past event, and what this implies for later retrieval. Chapter 9, written by Ellen Bialystok and Raluca Barac, is dedicated to the cognitive effects of bilingualism. It begins by describing the verbal abilities of bilingual children and adults in terms of vocabulary size, metalinguistic awareness and learning to read. It continues with an overview of the nonverbal consequences of being bilingual, primarily changes in executive function abilities during childhood and adulthood, and what this means for the aging brain. The last chapter of the book, Chapter 10, investigates neurolinguistic and neurocomputational models that pertain to bilingualism. It offers an overview of a number of neurolinguistic traditions and debates, and then examines the cognitive neuroscience of bilingualism. This is accompanied by a brief guide to relevant neuroimaging methodologies. The chapter ends by showing how neurolinguistic computational modeling complements behavioral and neuroimaging studies.

A few additional points need to be made. First, all authors in their respective chapters attempt to present the approaches and methodology used in their domains by taking illustrative studies or models and describing them in some detail. Thus readers will normally find an in-depth discussion of a few studies instead of a comprehensive review of numerous studies. Second, even though some references are made to monolinguals, in particular with regard to language processes and representation as well as cognitive effects, the aim is not to compare monolinguals and bilinguals. This is a delicate issue, especially for those who espouse a holistic view of bilingualism whereby the bilingual person is not considered as two separate monolinguals. For the time being, we have decided to leave this issue aside. Third, the book has been written with pedagogical considerations in mind. Thus, for instance, each chapter ends with research questions and further readings.

This book can be used for courses in psycholinguistics, linguistics, cognitive sciences, speech and language pathology, bilingualism, applied linguistics, and first and second language acquisition. It is ideal for upper level BA and BS courses, first- and second-year graduate studies, as well as for lay persons who wish to find out about the psycholinguistics of bilingualism.

We would like to end by thanking our guest authors who very kindly accepted to take part in this book project and write chapters for the level of reader at which the book is aimed. They have done a wonderful job in putting this into practice as well as integrating their chapters into the book as a whole, and for this we are grateful to them. Our thanks also go to Professor John Field, with whom this book was discussed at the very outset, to Danielle Descoteaux, Acquisitions Editor at Wiley-Blackwell, who made the project possible and who has accompanied us in such a supportive way from the very beginning, as well as to Julia Kirk, Project Editor,

Fiona Screen, Copy Editor, and Allison Medoff, Editorial Assistant, for their kind help. Finally, we wish to thank our respective families for their unwavering and loving support. We dedicate this book to them.

François Grosjean and Ping Li
March 2012

Chapter 1

Bilingualism: A Short Introduction

François Grosjean

The words "bilingual" and "bilingualism" have many different meanings depending on the context they are used in. They can include the knowledge and use of two or more languages, the presentation of information in two languages, the need for two languages, the recognition of two or more languages, and so on. Since this book focuses on the psycholinguistics of bilingual adults and children, we will define bilingualism, and indeed multilingualism, as the use of two or more languages (or dialects) in everyday life.

This chapter has several aims. The first is to introduce readers to basic concepts concerning bilingualism and bilinguals so as to help them understand more specialized chapters later in the book. Readers bring with them knowledge of language and cognition but they may know less about bilingualism. Hopefully this chapter will help fill this gap. The second aim is to describe what it is that bilingual participants bring to the studies they take part in. In everyday life, they are "regular bilinguals" with specific language knowledge and language use which they bring to this research as participants. Some of the aspects that will be mentioned are studied specifically or manipulated directly by psycholinguists whilst others simply accompany bilingual participants into the research environment. We need to understand these phenomena so as to be able to make sense of the data that are obtained.

A third aim, which is not restricted to this chapter alone, will be to clarify some misconceptions that surround bilingualism and bilinguals, such as that bilinguals have equal and perfect knowledge of their two or more languages, that they have no accent in any of their languages, that they acquired their languages in childhood, that they are all competent translators, and so on. When it comes to children, we hear that bilingualism will delay their language acquisition, that children will invariably mix their languages, and that being bilingual will have negative effects on their development (see Grosjean, 2010, for a discussion of many of these misconceptions). Some of these will be dispelled in this chapter and others in later chapters.

The Psycholinguistics of Bilingualism, First Edition. François Grosjean and Ping Li.
© 2013 Blackwell Publishing Ltd with the exceptions of Chapter 1, Chapter 2, Chapter 3, Chapter 7, Chapter 10 © 2013 François Grosjean and Ping Li. Published 2013 by Blackwell Publishing Ltd.

We will begin with a description of the extent of bilingualism and the reasons that underlie it. Next, we will describe bilinguals in terms of language use and language fluency, and show how these factors can change over time; we will call this the wax and wane of languages. This will be followed by a discussion of the functions of languages, which will revolve around what is now known as the Complementarity Principle. We will then describe what happens when bilinguals are interacting with other bilinguals who share their languages and how this is different from when they are addressing monolinguals; we will do this by means of the language mode concept. We will end with a discussion of biculturalism in bilinguals and the impact it has on bilingual language knowledge and language processing.

1.1   The Extent of Bilingualism

Researchers on bilingualism have repeated over the years that half of the world's population, if not more, is bilingual. Unfortunately, there are no clear data for the whole world but it is clear that bilingualism is found in all age groups, in all levels of society, and in most countries. For example, a European Commission report (2006) showed that some 56% of the inhabitants of 25 European countries speak a second language well enough to have a conversation in it. They may not all lead their lives with two or more languages but the percentage gives an idea of how extensive bilingualism can be. In North America, some 35% of the population of Canada is bilingual. The percentage is smaller in the United States (around 18–20%) but this still amounts to some 55 million inhabitants. The proportion of bilinguals is much higher in other parts of the world such as Asia and Africa where it is normal to know and use several languages in one's everyday life.

How can we explain the extent of bilingualism? First, there are many more languages (some 7000 according to Gordon, 2005) than there are countries (193 in 2011). Some countries house numerous languages and this leads to language contact between the inhabitants, and hence bilingualism. For example, there are 516 languages in Nigeria, 427 in India, 200 in Brazil, and so on. Most such countries have one or two languages of communication (lingua francas) which people use along with their more local language, hence the presence of bi- or multilingualism. A second reason, which goes back to the origins of mankind, is that people have always traveled for trade, commerce, business, employment, religion, politics, conflicts, and so on. The populations of many countries today are the result of immigration – examples are the United States, Canada, Australia, and many South American nations. Other countries, which witnessed the emigration of its populations some while back, are now seeing the influx of new immigrants. In the majority of cases, migrants acquire the language of the host country and hence become bilingual; there are also many cases where the original inhabitants adopt the new language, such as with American Indians in North America.

Another important reason for the extent of bilingualism is education and culture. Many students pursue their studies in a region or country with a different language to their own and hence become bilingual. Other events such as intermarriage or professional opportunities – diplomacy, business, foreign journalism, language teaching, and so on – lead to the development of language contact. The phenomenon is far more frequent than one imagines at first and it is only natural, therefore, that the language sciences have given bilingual studies much more room in recent years.

1.2 Describing Bilinguals

In this part, we will first examine two important defining factors of bilingualism – language fluency and language use – and we will then observe how the languages of bilinguals can wax and wane over time.

1.2.1 Language fluency and language use

A common misconception is that bilinguals master two languages fluently. Some will then add that bilinguals do not have an accent in either language and others will propose that they must have learned their languages in childhood. In a sense, bilinguals are seen as two monolinguals in one person. In fact, the majority of bilinguals do not have equal fluency in their languages, many have an accent in at least one of their languages, and many acquired their other language(s) when they were adolescents or adults. As we will see, bilinguals use their languages for different purposes, in different domains of life, to accomplish different things. Their level of fluency in a language depends on their need for that language. Hence many bilinguals are more fluent in a given language, and some cannot read or write one of their languages.

To get around the problem of fluency as a defining criterion (how fluent does one have to be in one's languages to be bilingual?), many researchers, starting with Weinreich (1968) and Mackey (2000), have put the stress on language use as the defining factor. This explains the definition given at the beginning of this chapter: bilingualism is the use of two or more languages (or dialects) in everyday life. Note that this definition includes dialects, and encompasses two or more languages (covering trilingualism, quadrilingualism, etc.). This definition accounts for many more speakers of languages than one based on fluency alone – especially if balanced fluency in the two languages is required – and hence is more realistic.

This said, it is important to also take into account the level of fluency in the bilinguals' different languages (and language skills), whatever that level may be. To do so, the grid approach that this author has developed can be helpful. Figure 1.1 presents the bilingualism of a person (MC) at two moments in time: at age 26 and at age 36. Language use is presented along the vertical axis of each grid (Never used to Daily use) and language fluency along the horizontal axis (Low fluency to High fluency).

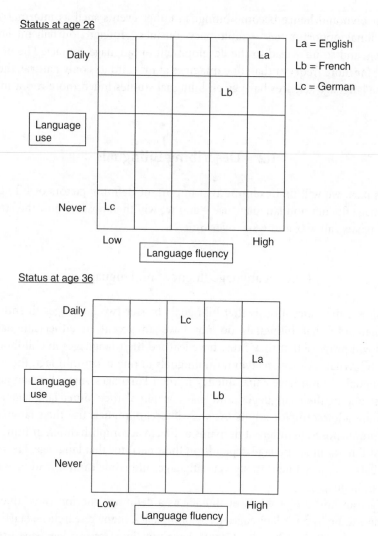

Figure 1.1: Describing a bilingual in terms of language use and language fluency at two moments in time: age 26 and age 36.

We see in the top grid that MC's most used and most fluent language at age 26 was La (English). His other language, Lb (French), was used on a regular basis although slightly less frequently than La; he was also slightly less fluent in it. MC also had some knowledge of a third language he learned at school (Lc; German) but he never used it. Hence, MC was bilingual in English and French, with a slight dominance in English, and had some knowledge of another language. This is frequent in bilinguals who, in addition to the languages they use on a regular basis, know one or two other languages which they employ more rarely. (It should be noted that we use the symbols La, Lb, and Lc for MC's three languages. This is because we are not interested here in pointing out which was his first language [L1], his second language [L2], and his third language [L3]. Both types of symbols will be used in this book).

Of course, this first description of the language status of a bilingual is very general as it does not take into account the domains (situations) in which the languages are used (see Section 1.3) or the modalities of a language (the oral, written or signed modalities). To make the description more complete, this kind of grid can be duplicated and used, for instance, for each of the bilingual's four language skills: speaking, listening, reading, writing. This allows one to delve more deeply into the bilingual's language configuration, as is normally done with a language questionnaire (see, for example, the questionnaire in Li, Sepanski, & Zhao, 2006). One often finds that the proficiency bilinguals have in the four skills is not the same for their different languages: some may have very good oral comprehension of a language but may not speak it very well; others may know how to read and write one of their languages but not the other, and so on.

The grid approach presented here can also encourage us to examine the relationship between the bilingual's languages: some languages can be quite close (e.g., Spanish and Italian) and some quite distant (e.g., English and Chinese). It is a well-known fact that closely related languages will influence one another more than will distant languages.

1.2.2 The wax and wane of languages

If we go back to Figure 1.1 and examine the bottom grid, we see MC's present bilingual configuration (at age 36), that is, 10 years after that of the top grid. We note a striking change: La (English) and Lb (French) are still the best known languages but each one is used slightly less frequently now. Lc (German), however, which was a dormant language acquired in school, has moved up in the grid (it is now used daily) and it has also moved to the right (MC is more fluent in it). The reason is that MC moved to Germany during the 10-year interval and German has become his everyday language, used more frequently than La or Lb. This exemplifies the importance of knowing the language history of bilinguals: which languages are acquired, when and how; what the pattern of fluency and use is over the years; whether some languages go through periods of restructuring under the influence of another, stronger, language, or even become dormant and are slowly forgotten in later years.

Figure 1.2 merges two grids into one and presents the case of a 30-year-old bilingual (EP) who, between the ages of 20 and 30, not only changed his language configuration (as had MC) but, in addition, acquired two new languages. The languages present at age 20 (La: French; Lb: English; Lc: German) are underlined. If they changed position in the 10-year interval this is shown by an arrow going from the original position to the new position. The new languages (Ld: Spanish; Le: Swiss German) are marked (N).

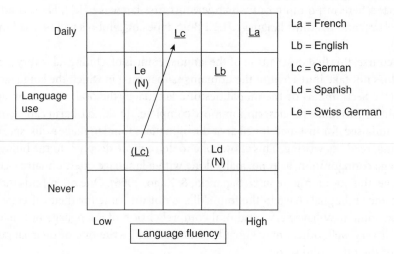

Figure 1.2: A bilingual who, at age 20, knew three languages (La, Lb, Lc) to varying degrees. Between age 20 and 30, two new languages (Ld, Le) were acquired (marked N) and one language (Lc) changed its status (marked by the arrow).

What we observe is that La and Lb have stayed in the same position over the 10-year interval, but Lc is now being used daily and is more fluent. In addition, two new languages have been acquired: Ld (Spanish), which is now known quite well but is not used much, and Le (Swiss German), which is used almost daily but not yet known well. A 1-year stay in another country and then movement within a country (in this case, Switzerland) accounts for these changes.

As illustrated by EP (above), a bilingual's language history can be quite complex due to life events that reduce or increase the importance of a language (e.g., meeting a companion, losing a family member with whom one spoke a language exclusively, moving to another language region or country, and so on). The process is dynamic and leads to a change in a person's language configuration and hence language processing. Thus, a bilingual's languages have moments of stability (the language pattern is relatively stable) and moments of change where one language suddenly acquires new importance and another language may remain stable or have less of a role to play. If one assesses a person's languages (and language skills) or one undertakes a psycholinguistic study, one must keep in mind the transition periods which can last several years. During these periods, the level of communication attained by the bilingual may not be optimal while the languages reorganize themselves. But when stability is attained, the bilingual will usually regain the level of communication achieved before the change, even if the language configuration is now very different.

Although the examples given above do not exemplify it, language forgetting (called "language loss" or "language attrition") can also take place during a bilingual's lifespan. It is a frequent phenomenon, as frequent as language learning, but it has received far less attention (see, for example, Schmid, Köpke, Keijzer, &

Weilemar, 2004). During language forgetting, the domains of use of the language are greatly reduced, or sometimes even disappear, and signs of loss appear over time: language production is filled with word finding problems and hesitations; the person's accent is influenced by the other, stronger, language(s), as is the syntax; the speaker calls on the other language(s) more and more for a word or a phrase, and so on. In addition, bilinguals become very unsure of themselves when they have to use the language and often state that they do not know it any more. Oral comprehension suffers too but less so than production.

In sum, the bilingual's languages will wax and wane over the years and the different stages will have an impact on psycholinguistic processes. Thus, starting with the early years, the age at which a language is acquired, how it is acquired (for example, in a natural setting or more formally such as in school, or a combination of the two), and the amount of use it is given over the years all play a role on how well the language is known, how it is processed, and even on the way the brain stores and deals with it. And, when, with the passing of time, languages are restructured, or even fade away, psycholinguistic and cognitive operations will also be influenced by this.

In the following sections we examine other important characteristics of bilinguals that the student of psycholinguistics should know about.

1.3   The Functions of Languages

Were one to ask a bilingual which languages she uses in different domains of life (e.g., with parents, siblings, relatives, friends, at work, for sport, when going out, when reading a newspaper, when writing reports, etc.), one might obtain the kind of pattern that is shown in Figure 1.3.

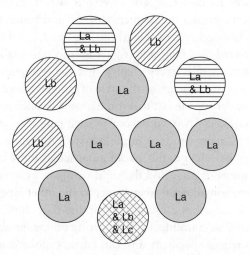

Figure 1.3: The domains covered by a bilingual's three languages (La, Lb, and Lc).

The domains are represented by circles and can be covered by one language (see the circles marked with La or Lb only), two languages (see the two circles marked La & Lb) or even, in this case, three languages (one such circle here). The pattern shown is a visual representation of the Complementarity Principle (Grosjean, 1997), which can be stated as follows:

> Bilinguals usually acquire and use their languages for different purposes, in different domains of life, with different people. Different aspects of life often require different languages.

Thus, in the example above, which only presents a subset of domains, we find that the bilingual in question covers six domains with La only, three domains with Lb, two domains with La and Lb, and one domain with La, Lb, and Lc. A pattern of this type can be drawn up for any bilingual. Rare are the bilinguals who cover all their domains of life with all their languages. If that were the case, there would be little reason to be bilingual as one language would suffice. It should be noted that diglossia is a form of societal bilingualism where two languages or two varieties of a language have very precise domains of use. Thus the principle stated above is rigidified in diglossia – very few (if any) domains are covered by two or more languages.

The Complementarity Principle refers to what has been known for many years as the functions of languages (see Mackey, 2000, for example) and it explains a number of interesting phenomena in the linguistics and psycholinguistics of bilingualism. The first concerns a bilingual's level of fluency and use of a language. Although the fluency/use grid presented earlier is different from the language domain pattern shown here, there is a close link between the two. When a language is used in a very restricted number of domains, then there is every chance that it will be used less frequently and that it will have a lower fluency (bottom left-hand area of the grid in Figures 1.1 and 1.2). The reverse is also true: the more domains a language is used in, the greater the frequency of use and hence, usually, the greater the fluency (top right-hand area of the grid in Figures 1.1 and 1.2). In addition, if a domain is not covered by a language (e.g., a person never talks about work in a given language), then there is every chance that the bilingual will not have the vocabulary, the variety of language, or the style of language needed for that specific domain. (This is true despite the fact that some people still believe that for any given concept, all bilinguals know two words, one in each language, and hence that they have roughly twice as many words as monolinguals). All bilinguals have been in a situation where they have had to talk about a particular topic in the "wrong" language. They don't know or can't find the right words or expressions, they hesitate a lot, and, if the situation allows it, they resort to the other language to help them out (Grosjean, 2008, describes a number of studies that show this clearly). Well-learned behaviors such as counting, praying, giving phone numbers, and so on, are extreme cases of language specificity and can create problems when conducted in the wrong language.

The Complementarity Principle can also explain the phenomenon of language dominance, in part at least. If we examine Figure 1.3 again, we see that the bilingual in question is dominant in La. Not only is it the sole language of six domains but it also covers another three domains, two with Lb and one with Lb and Lc, for a total of nine domains. The other languages cover fewer domains: Lb, by itself or with other languages, covers six domains and Lc just one domain (along with La and Lb). Thus one could say that the bilingual in question is dominant in La. Care should be taken, though, when using only a global measure of dominance such as counting domains of use. This is because for some domains the "non dominant" language can be the sole language and it is, de facto, the dominant language for that particular domain. In what is a rather old study now, Cooper (1971) showed that Spanish-English bilinguals had very different word naming scores depending on the domain referred to (family, neighborhood, school, religion, etc.). In some, they showed balance (they did as well in Spanish as in English) whereas in others they showed dominance in one language. Close to 40 years later, some aspects of the results of word naming studies in psycholinguistics, among other experimental studies, may be explained by the Complementarity Principle (a point also made by Ivanova & Costa, 2008).

At this point, it is important to note that language dominance in a bilingual (measured in terms of overall use of a language, overall fluency, domains covered by a language, or a combination of all of these) can change over time. Thus, a person's first language may not always be his or her dominant language. Grosjean (2010) describes a person whose dominance has changed four times over a stretch of some 50 years, with two periods, both some 10 years long, where the second language was the person's dominant language. One should be careful, therefore, not to assume that a person's first language or "mother tongue" is automatically their dominant language. Personal language history may show quite different bilingual configurations at different moments in time.

Two additional impacts of the Complementarity Principle should be mentioned. The first concerns translation. Even though bilinguals are thought to be natural translators (yet one more myth that surrounds bilingualism), they often have difficulties translating when the domains are specialized. This makes a lot of sense since their two or more languages do not cover all domains of life. Hence, bilinguals often find themselves doing less well than second language learners who have systematically learned the translation equivalents of words and expressions in their second language. Of course, bilinguals are no less bilingual for this; they are simply reflecting the fact that their languages are distributed across different domains. The second impact concerns memory of events. Marian and Neisser (2000) showed in an experimental study that events are better recalled if the language used to recall them is the language in which the event took place (see Chapter 8 for a description of the study). They called this "language-dependent" recall. They illustrated it with a real-life example reported by Aneta Pavlenko, a multilingual researcher in this field. When she was asked, in Russian, for the number of her apartment in the United States, she gave the number of her former apartment in her native European country, which she knew in Russian!

In sum, the Complementarity Principle is an important part of a bilingual's life. It is present at all times and it can explain many aspects of a bilingual's language knowledge and language processing.

1.4   Language Mode

When interacting with an interlocutor but also when using language in other situations (e.g., writing to someone, reading a book, doing a language task in a laboratory, etc.), bilinguals have to ask themselves two questions, most of the time subconsciously: Which language should be used? and Should the other language be brought in? Figure 1.4 takes up these questions and shows the consequences they have on the bilingual's languages and processing mechanisms.

In the figure, which, to simplify things, covers just two languages (though the same applies to three or more languages), we see that the bilingual has to choose between language a (La) and language b (Lb). Both are inactive, or deactivated, at first, and this is represented with squares filled with light diagonal lines. To the first question, "Which language should be used?", the bilingual in our example answers

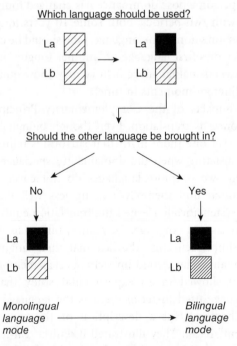

Figure 1.4: The two questions bilinguals have to ask themselves, often subconsciously, when communicating with others.

with La. It becomes activated and the square changes over to black, representing full activation. This first operation is called "language choice" and the language chosen is termed the "base language."

Now comes the second question: "Should the other language be brought in?" If the answer is "no" (imagine that the bilingual is speaking to someone who only knows one of her languages), then the other language remains inactive and only one language will be used. This is called the monolingual mode (represented in the bottom left area of the diagram). Examples of a monolingual mode are reading a book in a particular language, listening to a radio program which only uses one language, speaking to a monolingual adult or child, and so on. In this mode, the bilingual will usually only use one language and deactivate the other (see Section 1.5.2). If the answer to the second question is "yes" (for example, the bilingual is speaking to bilingual friends who share her languages), then the other language is activated, but less so than the base language (compare the two squares on the right), in case the bilingual needs it during the interaction. Here, the bilingual is in a bilingual mode and can bring in elements of the other language (see Section 1.5.1) or even change base language completely. Other examples of a bilingual mode are listening to a conversation between bilinguals where two languages are used interchangeably, doing an experimental study which requires, overtly or covertly, the use of two languages, interpreting from one language to another, and so on.

So far we have accounted for the two endpoints of a continuum – the language mode continuum – which ranges from a monolingual mode to a bilingual mode (see the bottom area of the figure). In fact, in their everyday lives, bilinguals find themselves at various points along the continuum. For example, bilinguals can be in an intermediary language mode – in other words, between the two endpoints. This is the case when they are speaking to a bilingual who shares their languages but who prefers to stick to one language, or when they are speaking about something which really demands the other language (see the discussion of the Complementarity Principle in Section 1.3) but which cannot be used. This may happen, for example, when a French-English bilingual has to speak about a typically American event such as Thanksgiving in French instead of in English.

Language mode can be defined as the state of activation of the bilingual's languages and language processing mechanisms at a given point in time (see Grosjean, 2008, for an extensive review of the concept). Several points can be made about it. First, bilinguals may differ from one another as to how much they move along the language mode continuum. Some, who live in bilingual communities where the two languages are used together extensively, may rarely find themselves at the monolingual end of the continuum. Others, who are surrounded by monolinguals during their everyday activities, may never move to the bilingual endpoint and bring in the other language in their interactions. It is fair to say, though, that many bilinguals navigate along the continuum depending on the person they are speaking to, the situation they are in, the topic of discourse, and so on.

A second point is that movement along the continuum can take place at any time and in any place, and can be very rapid. Thus, one person may start at the bilingual end but realize as the conversation is taking place that his interlocutor, even though she is bilingual, does not seem to accept that he slips into the other language for a word, phrase, or sentence. He will then deactivate the other, unwanted language, and hence move to the monolingual end of the continuum. Similarly, a bilingual may start interacting monolingually with someone but then realize, as the conversation continues, that the person shares the same two languages. This will induce some movement along the continuum in case the bilingual needs the other language in the interaction, even if only to signal, with a few words, that they share the fact of being bilingual. The same is true of a participant in an experiment who suddenly hears or sees a word from the other language; she will immediately activate that language and hence move toward the bilingual end of the continuum (see Chapter 2).

A third point concerns the bilingual mode. Since the other language is also active, but less so than the base language, it can be brought in for a few words, as indicated above, or it can quite simply take over the role of base language (something that simply can't happen in a monolingual mode unless the interlocutor changes, of course). When the base language does change, the activation pattern shown in Figure 1.4 also changes; Lb becomes the most active language and La is less active. Note also that there are cases where both languages can be fully active in a bilingual mode. Two instances come to mind: the first is when a bilingual is listening to two people, each one speaking a different language; the second is when someone is interpreting from one language to another. Here, the person needs both languages, the source language – the language being heard – and the target language – the language being produced (Grosjean, 2008).

A fourth point pertains to the language that is not being used in the monolingual mode. Researchers such as Green (1998) propose that it is inhibited whereas others prefer the notion of deactivation. There are two reasons to lean toward the latter. First, the bilingual language system has to be able to change base languages rapidly; a language that is deactivated will be "on line" more rapidly than if it is inhibited. Second, there is some slippage in the monolingual mode in that the other language can slip through in the form of dynamic interferences (see Section 1.5). This can be explained more readily with the notion of deactivation than with inhibition.

A final point that needs to be mentioned concerns processing. Until very recently, most psycholinguists have claimed that perceptual processing is nonselective, that is, all the bilingual's languages are involved in the processes that take place during the acts of listening to or reading just one language. In terms of language mode, it has been argued that listeners and readers, even though in a monolingual mode, call on their two or more languages to do the task asked of them (see Chapter 2). The same has been said of language production in bilinguals (see Chapter 3). The problem with this view, discussed in Grosjean (1998), is that the only way to study whether processing is nonselective is to put the participants in a truly monolingual mode. (No one would counter the claim that processing is indeed nonselective when bilinguals are hearing or reading two languages in a bilingual mode; processing couldn't take place otherwise). Putting a bilingual in a monolingual mode is relatively easy to do in a natural speaking situation (basically, just make sure that the bilingual's interlocutor does not know the language that is not being used) but it is much more difficult in experimental perception tasks.

Grosjean (1998) reviews two perception studies, among others, that attempted to put their participants in a monolingual mode, but failed to do so (Spivey & Marian, 1999; Dijkstra & Van Hell, 2003). The reason for this failure is that a number of factors invariably push the bilingual toward a bilingual mode. Among them we find: the knowledge the participant has that the study relates to bilingualism; a laboratory that works on bilingual research; a bilingual university environment; the bilingual task that is used and/or the instructions that are bilingual; the presence of elements of the other language in the stimuli (e.g., code-switches); the use of cross-language homophones; a high density of interlingual homographs and/or cognates, and so on (see Grosjean, 2008, for a full discussion). Until these factors have all been controlled for, it appears premature to state categorically that language processing is nonselective when bilinguals are in a monolingual mode. As we will see in the first chapters of this book, notably Chapters 2 and 3, the picture that is emerging is both more subtle and more interesting. Processing can be selective at times and nonselective at other times.

1.5   Interacting with Bilinguals and Monolinguals

The psycholinguistics of bilingualism also studies the processes concerned when bilinguals communicate with one another in a bilingual mode, as well as with monolinguals in a monolingual mode (see Chapters 2 & 3). It is important, there-fore, to survey the many phenomena that are involved, most notably language choice, code-switching, borrowing, and interferences.

1.5.1   Interacting with bilinguals

In this section we will first examine language choice, then discuss code-switching and borrowing. Interferences will be covered in the next section.

Language choice   We saw in Figure 1.4 that the first thing a bilingual has to do during an interaction or a specific task such as reading or writing is to choose a base language. This is a rather simple operation in a monolingual mode (if it is truly monolingual!) but it is much more complex in a bilingual mode. Basically, the ques-tion is which language to use when more than one is possible. Much has been written about language choice and researchers seem to agree that the factors which determine choice can be organized into four main categories: participants, situation, content of discourse, and function of the interaction. Concerning participants, an important factor is the language proficiency of the two or more interlocutors. They will tend to use a language which each commands sufficiently well. There is also the language history between the participants; bilinguals often have a preferred language with a bilingual interactant whom they know. The attitude one has toward a language or a group may also account for language choice; thus, members of stigmatized minorities may refrain from using the minority language with others. Additional factors include age, socio-economic status, the degree of intimacy of the participants, the power relation between the two, and so on.

As concerns situation, the place where the interaction takes place is an important factor. In some countries, such as in Paraguay, for example, a particular language is used in the countryside and another one in the cities. There is also the formality of the situation; some languages are simply not used in very formal surroundings (e.g., Swiss German in Switzerland). The presence of monolinguals will also impact on the language to use; one usually wants to include them, even if momentarily, by choosing the appropriate language. As for content of discourse, we have seen its importance when discussing the Complementarity Principle (see Section 1.3). Some topics are better dealt with in a particular language, and if both speakers share that language, they will slip into it. Finally, the function of the interaction plays a large role in language choice. Depending on what one is trying to achieve (e.g., raise one's status, create a social distance, exclude someone, request something, etc.), one will choose the most suitable language.

Of course, several factors taken together usually explain the final language choice. The decision is rapid and it is usually just right. That said, language accommodation, that is, finding the most appropriate language for all concerned, may not always be achieved. This is the case, for example, when several bilinguals and monolinguals meet and there is no common language. A bilingual may then volunteer to translate so as to include everyone in the interaction.

Code-switching and borrowing When in a bilingual mode, that is, interacting with someone who shares the bilingual's languages, there is always the possibility of bringing in the language, or languages, that have not been chosen as the base language. This happens if the need arises and if the interactants feel comfortable doing so. (Some bilinguals do not resort to the other language(s) and hence the interactants may stick to just one language.) There are two ways of calling in the other, guest, language – through code-switching or through borrowing. Code-switching is the alternate use of two languages, that is, the speaker makes a complete shift to the other language and then reverts back to the base language. Borrowing, on the other hand, is the integration of one language into another. Figure 1.5 illustrates the difference between the two.

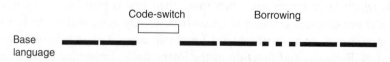

Figure 1.5: The difference between a code-switch (the alternate use of two languages) and a borrowing (the integration of one language into the other).

In the left area of the figure, where a code-switch is depicted, the person speaking the base language shifts over completely to the other language before shifting back to the base language. In the right area, where a borrowing is illustrated, an element from the other language is brought in and integrated into the language being spoken (discontinuous line). It should be noted that in the bilingual child language literature, both code-switching and borrowing are covered by the term "code-mixing" (see Chapter 6). Each type of guest element will be taken up separately in the examples that follow.

Code-switching may involve a word, a phrase or a sentence. Here are two examples taken from Grosjean (1982) where French is the base language and English the guest language:

- Va chercher Marc *and bribe him* avec un chocolat chaud *with cream on top*
  (Go fetch Marc and bribe him with a hot chocolate with cream on top)

- Des *wild guys* à cheval
  (Some wild guys on horseback)

In the next example, taken from Poplack (1980), the base language is English and the guest language is Spanish:

- But I wanted to fight her *con los puños*, you know
  (But I wanted to fight her with my fists, you know)

Even though code-switching has been looked down upon by many (they deplore the mixing of languages, among other things), it is frequently used by bilinguals with one another. In the last 30 years or so, many aspects of code-switching have been studied by linguists, sociolinguists, and psycholinguists (for a review, see Gardner-Chloros, 2009). It is now clear that code-switching is not simply a haphazard behavior due to some form of semilingualism but that it is, instead, a well-governed process used as a communicative stratagem to convey linguistic and social information. The reasons for code-switching are many: using the right word or expression, filling a linguistic need (see the Complementarity Principle among other causes), marking group identity, excluding or including someone, raising your status, and so on.

Borrowing, which involves integrating elements of one language into the other language, can be of two types (see Treffers-Daller, 2007, for a review). In the first – a loanword – both the form and content of a word are borrowed. For example, in the sentence:

- Ca m'étonnerait qu'on ait *code-switché* autant que ça
  (I can't believe we code-switched as often as that)

the English word "code-switch" has been brought in and integrated into the French sentence. A second type of borrowing, called a loanshift, consists in either taking a word in the base language and extending its meaning to correspond to that of a word in the other language, or rearranging words in the base language along a pattern provided by the other language and thus creating a new meaning. An example of the first kind of loanshift would be the use of "humoroso" by Portuguese-Americans to mean "humorous" when the original meaning is "capricious." An example of the second kind is the use of idiomatic expressions that are translated literally from the other language, such as "I put myself to think about it" said by a Spanish-English bilingual, based on "Me puse a pensarlo."

The reasons for borrowing are very similar to those for code-switching. The two most important ones are using the right word and using a word from a domain normally covered by the other, guest, language (the Complementarity Principle is again one of the causes). It is important to distinguish between idiosyncratic loans used on an individual basis by bilinguals, as illustrated above, and words which have become part of a community's vocabulary and which monolinguals also use (the latter are often referred to as "established loans"). Thus, in English, the following words are now well established in the language and yet were originally borrowed from French: "poet," "duke," "paint," "music," "poem," "companion," and so on.

1.5.2   Interacting with monolinguals

We saw in Figure 1.4 that a first decision bilinguals have to make relates to the language to use for the interaction or task at hand. When they are in a monolingual mode, this appears to be a relatively simple task. Basically, the bilingual deactivates other languages, and sticks to the language of the monolingual interlocutor(s) or situation. Bilinguals who speak the language fluently, and have no accent in it, can then pass as monolinguals. It should be noted though that many bilinguals *do* have an accent in at least one of their languages (some of them, in all their languages) and so their bilingual identity often comes through.

If the person being spoken to is monolingual or shares only one language with the bilingual, isn't it always the case that the bilingual stays totally within one language? This is most often the case but there can be some exceptions. First, there is the fact that some minimal code-switching may take place, although it is rare. It can happen for proper nouns, for example, or when bilinguals do not have a word or expression needed in the language they are speaking (see the Complementarity Principle). They may then say the word or expression and add an explanation if their interlocutor does not give them the equivalent in the language being spoken. Second, and more importantly, the other language can seep through in the form of interferences, that is, deviations from the language being spoken (or written) due to the influence of the other language(s). Interferences can occur at all levels of language – from the phonetic to the pragmatic. Here are just a few examples taken from Grosjean (1982):

   – "Look at the *camion*": the form and meaning of French "camion" (truck) are brought in and are pronounced like "canyon."

- "Look at the *corns*": the French meaning of "corne" (horn) has been attached to the English word "corn."

- "On *the* page five," based on the French "Sur la page cinq" (instead of "On page five").

- "I'm telling myself stories": the literal translation of "Je me raconte des histoires" (the equivalent of "I'm kidding myself").

- In writing: "adress" or "apartment," based on the French near homographs "adresse" and "appartement."

Interferences must be distinguished from intra-language deviations such as over-generalizations, simplifications, hypercorrections, the avoidance of words and expressions, and so on. These are often due to a low or medium level of fluency in a language and not to the direct influence of the other language, as in the case of interferences. They must also be distinguished from code-switching and borrowing since the these, especially borrowings, can greatly resemble interferences. Those interested in studying interferences must make sure the bilingual is in a monolingual mode; it is only then, with the absence, or quasi-absence, of code-switches and borrowings, that the interferences will appear – a bit like a landscape emerging when the fog lifts.

Interferences, which are termed "transfers" by many, are of two types. There are static interferences which reflect permanent traces of one language (La) on the other (Lb), such as an accent or the permanent use of a syntactic structure. These interferences are linked to the person's competence in Lb (they are part of language knowledge), and can involve all linguistic levels. It has been proposed recently to reserve the name "transfer" for these static interferences (Grosjean, 2012). The other type of interferences are dynamic interferences, which are the ephemeral intrusions of the other language. These interferences (as opposed to more permanent transfers) can take the form of the accidental slip on the stress pattern of a word because of the stress rules of the other language, the one-time use of a word from the other language (but produced phonetically in the language being spoken), the momentary use of a syntactic structure taken from the other language, and so on. Dynamic interferences are linked to processing and have to be accounted for by encoding mechanisms as studied in psycholinguistics. Bilinguals often report making interferences when they are stressed, tired or emotional. What is normally under control (pronunciation, prosody, lexical access, the choice of syntax, etc.) can break down under certain conditions.

1.6   Biculturalism

If there is one domain that is poorly studied in the large field of bilingualism, it is that of biculturalism. And yet, it has a large impact on bilinguals who are also bicultural, both on a personal level (psychological, cultural) and on their cognition, language knowledge, and language processing.

Biculturals can be characterized in the following way (Grosjean, 2008; see also Nguyen and Benet-Martinez, 2007):

1. They take part, to varying degrees, in the life of two or more cultures.
2. They adapt, in part at least, their attitudes, behaviors, values, languages, etc. to these cultures.
3. They combine and blend aspects of the cultures involved. Some of these come from one or the other culture(s) whereas others are blends of the cultures. Hence, some aspects of the bicultural are adaptable and controllable (this allows the bicultural to adapt to the context and situation) but other aspects are more static; they are blends of the cultures and cannot be adapted as easily.

Bilingualism and biculturalism are not necessarily coextensive. Thus, you often find bilinguals who are not bicultural. They have always lived in one culture but they know and use two or more languages. This is the case, for example, of Swiss Germans who speak both Swiss German and standard German but who are culturally Swiss. You also find biculturals who are not bilinguals such as British expatriates in the United States. And, of course, you find people who are both bicultural and bilingual as in the case of immigrants, many of whom have acquired their second language in their country of adoption and who have acculturated into their new culture.

The psycholinguistics of bilingualism is starting to manipulate or control for the biculturalism of participants in observational and experimental studies. This is because many aspects of cognition and language are influenced by biculturalism. In what follows, we will concentrate on biculturals who are also bilingual (often called bicultural bilinguals) and discuss two aspects of their biculturalism that involve language. The first concerns bicultural behavior. In their everyday lives, bicultural bilinguals find themselves at various points along a continuum – a cultural one this time – marked by two endpoints: a monocultural mode and a bicultural mode. In the first, they are with monoculturals or are with biculturals who share only one of their cultures, and they must deactivate their other culture(s) as best they can. In the second, they find themselves with other biculturals who share their cultures; they will choose a cultural base to interact in and will then bring in the other culture(s) when they need to. This is very similar to the language mode concept discussed in Section 1.4. One main difference with the latter, though, is that certain attitudes, feelings, behaviors, and so on may not be totally adaptable because of the blending component discussed above. Thus, such aspects as body language, distance to leave between interlocutors, the management of time, greeting and leaving behaviors, the way to express emotions, and so on, may not all be as monocultural as the biculturals would like them to be in certain monocultural situations.

This said, bicultural bilinguals manage to adapt their behavior to quite an extent, so much so that when a change of language is also concerned, a myth has developed that changing languages leads to a change in personality (see, for example, Luna, Ringberg, & Peracchio, 2008). Could there be some truth to the Czech proverb, "Learn a new language and get a new soul"? Clearly, this does not concern mono-cultural bilinguals as they remain within one culture. But how about bicultural bilinguals? Although the idea is terribly appealing (see the many bilinguals who report being "different" when speaking the one or the other language), there is a rather simple explanation that has been around for many years (Grosjean, 1982). Basically, what is seen as a change of personality is simply a shift in behavior and attitudes corresponding to a shift in situation or context (a change of cultural base to use an expression employed above). That is, bicultural bilinguals adapt to the cultural context they are in, as do monolinguals with their one language. Different situations and interlocutors may trigger different attitudes, impressions, behaviors but also language in bicultural bilinguals. In sum, it is not language as such that triggers these changes but the context. Another way of seeing this is to look at biculturals who are monolingual. With just one language, they behave like bicultur-als who are bilingual, that is, they adapt to the environment they are in but in their case, a different language is not involved.

We will end this chapter with a few words concerning the bilingual lexicon and the impact biculturalism may have on its organization. Let us take a very simple example, that of English "bread" and French "pain." A bilingual who has only known one type of bread (i.e., a bilingual who is not bicultural) will refer to the same reality when he or she hears, or uses, "pain" and "bread." Since this bilingual has interacted with just one culture, and its various component subcultures, there is every chance that the meaning of the two words will be very similar. A bicultural bilingual, on the other hand, who has lived both in the United States and France, for example, will have very different concepts for these words since the "pain" reality and the "bread" reality is very different ("pain" refers to the baguette type bread in many bicultural bilinguals whereas "bread" refers to a larger loaf baked in a bread pan). The same case can be made for French "café" and English "coffee" – probably very similar meanings in monocultural bilinguals but very different meanings in bicul-tural bilinguals.

This influence of biculturalism on the nature of the bilingual's lexicon was acknowledged by the pioneering bilingualism researcher Uriel Weinreich (1968). He proposed that in coordinative (type A) bilingualism, the meanings of words in the two languages are kept separate, that is, that each word has its own meaning, whereas in compound (type B) bilingualism, the words share a common meaning – they conjure up the same reality. Weinreich also stated that each bilingual (he no doubt meant each bicultural bilingual) could show a combination of the coor-dinative and compound type of bilingualism. (Just to be complete, Weinreich proposed a third type of bilingualism, subordinative bilingualism (type C), where words in the weaker language are interpreted through the words of the stronger language.) Keeping in mind that bilinguals do not reflect just one type of bilingual-ism as defined by Weinreich, it is also true that different cultural realities may be reflected in bicultural bilinguals. Some aspects of life in the one and in the other culture will lead to words referring to meanings with different cultural

underpinnings; other aspects of life will lead to words sharing meaning components or traits; and still other aspects will produce words with totally overlapping
meanings (see Chapter 8).

The message to retain from all of this is that bilinguals who are also bicultural
will differ from bilinguals who are monocultural, both culturally and linguistically.
If we add to this the fact that bilinguals will differ from one another on many other
aspects mentioned in this chapter (languages, language fluency, language use,
language history, language mode, etc.), we can expect the results from the psycholinguistic studies of bilinguals to be both fascinating and diverse – but sometimes also
difficult to interpret, as we will see at various times in the chapters to come.

Research Questions

1. Discuss the aspects of language processing that will be influenced by a bilin-
    gual's language history as described in Section 1.2.
2. It is reported that bilinguals have more word searching (tip of the tongue)
    difficulties than monolinguals. Can this result be explained in part by the
    Complementarity Principle (Section 1.3) which states that different domains
    of life often require different languages? If so, how?
3. What kind of study could be designed to show that language processing is
    sometimes selective despite what is stated by many researchers (see Section 1.4)?
4. Bicultural bilinguals are clearly different from monocultural bilinguals (see
    Section 1.6). Discuss the impact this has on language perception, production,
    and memorization.

Further Readings

Gardner-Chloros, Penelope. 2009. *Code-Switching*. Cambridge: Cambridge University Press.

Grosjean, François. 1998. Studying bilinguals: Methodological and conceptual issues. *Bilingualism: Language and Cognition* 1. 131–149.

Grosjean, François. 2010. *Bilingual: Life and Reality*. Cambridge, MA: Harvard University Press.

Mackey, William. 2000. The description of bilingualism. In Li Wei (ed.), *The Bilingualism Reader* (first edition, pp. 26–54), London: Routledge.

References

Cooper, Robert. 1971. Degree of bilingualism. In Joshua Fishman, Robert Cooper, & Roxana Ma (eds), *Bilingualism in the Barrio*, 273–309. Bloomington, IN: Indiana University Press.

Dijkstra, Ton & Van Hell, Janet (2003). Testing the language mode hypothesis using trilinguals. *International Journal of Bilingual Education and Bilingualism* 6. 2–16.

European Commission (2006). Europeans and their languages. *Special Eurobarometer* 243.

Gardner-Chloros, Penelope. 2009. *Code-Switching*. Cambridge: Cambridge University Press.

Gordon, Raymond (ed.). 2005. *Ethnologue: Languages of the World*. Dallas, TX: SIL International, fifteenth edition. On-line version: http://www.ethnologue.com/ [accessed on-line July 4, 2012].

Green, David. 1998. Mental control of the bilingual lexico-semantic system. *Bilingualism: Language and Cognition* 1. 67–81.

Grosjean, François. 1982. *Life with Two Languages: An Introduction to Bilingualism*. Cambridge, MA: Harvard University Press.

Grosjean, François. 1997. The bilingual individual. *Interpreting* 2(1/2). 163–187.

Grosjean, François. 1998. Studying bilinguals: Methodological and conceptual issues. *Bilingualism: Language and Cognition* 1. 131–149.

Grosjean, François. 2008. *Studying Bilinguals*. Oxford: Oxford University Press.

Grosjean, François. 2010. *Bilingual: Life and Reality*. Cambridge, MA: Harvard University Press.

Grosjean, François. 2012. An attempt to isolate, and then differentiate, transfer and interference. *International Journal of Bilingualism* 16(1). 11–21.

Ivanova, Iva & Costa, Albert. 2008. Does bilingualism hamper lexical access in speech production? *Acta Psychologica* 127. 277–288.

Li, Ping, Sepanski, Sara, & Zhao, Xiaowei. 2006. Language history questionnaire: A web-based interface for bilingual research. *Behavior Research Methods* 38(2). 202–210.

Luna, David, Ringberg, Torsten, & Peracchio, Laura. 2008. One individual, two identities: Frame switching among biculturals. *Journal of Consumer Research* 35. 279–293.

Mackey, William. 2000. The description of bilingualism. In Li Wei (ed.), *The Bilingualism Reader* (1st edition, pp. 26–54), London: Routledge.

Marian, Viorica & Neisser, Ulrich. 2000. Language-dependent recall of autobiographical memories. *Journal of Experimental Psychology: General* 129. 361–368.

Nguyen, Angela-MinhTu & Benet-Martinez, Veronica. 2007. Biculturalism unpacked: Components, measurement, individual differences, and outcomes. *Social and Personality Psychology Compass* 1. 101–114.

Poplack, Shana. 1980. Sometimes I'll start a sentence in Spanish y termino en Espanol: Toward a typology of code-switching. *Linguistics* 18. 581–618.

Schmid, Monika, Köpke, Barbara, Keijzer, Merel, & Weilemar, Lina. 2004. *First Language Attrition: Interdisciplinary Perspectives on Methodological Issues*. Amsterdam/Philadelphia: John Benjamins.

Spivey, Michael & Marian, Viorica. 1999. Cross talk between native and second languages: Partial activation of an irrelevant lexicon. *Psychological Science* 10. 281–284.

Treffers-Daller, Jeanine. 2007. Borrowing. In Jan-Ola Östman, Jef Verschueren, & Eline Versluys (eds), *Handbook of Pragmatics*, 1–21. Amsterdam: John Benjamins.

Weinreich, Uriel. 1968. *Languages in Contact*. The Hague: Mouton.

I
Spoken Language Processing

Chapter 2
Speech Perception and Comprehension
François Grosjean

Even though there are many more bilinguals in the world who listen to two or more languages than read them (recall that many bilinguals may not know how to read and write one of their languages), the studies pertaining to bilingual speech perception and comprehension have been less numerous than those pertaining to reading (see Chapter 4). The situation is changing, however, and it is now possible to give an overview of how bilinguals perceive and comprehend their different languages.

This chapter has several aims. The first is to describe how bilinguals process just one language when there are no elements of the other language(s) in it – we call this "monolingual speech." Bilinguals have to deal with it in their everyday lives when they are in a monolingual mode (see Chapter 1), and it is important that we understand how they do so.

The second aim is to describe how bilinguals process bilingual speech, that is, speech that contains code-switches and/or borrowings. As we saw in Chapter 1, bilinguals in a bilingual mode often bring in the other language, and it is worth asking how listeners process both the base language – the main language being heard – as well as the guest elements of the other language.

A third aim will be to introduce readers to the methodology used to study oral language perception and comprehension in bilinguals. Unlike with speech production, where we can learn a lot about the underlying production mechanisms involved from the speech produced, with speech perception and comprehension this is not possible. We therefore have to resort to experimental paradigms to "open a window" into the mind of the bilingual listener.

This chapter contains three sections. In the first, we offer a rapid overview of how speech perception and comprehension takes place. We will end the section with a short discussion of the ways in which bilinguals are invariably different from monolinguals when doing this type of processing. In the second section, we will examine two aspects related to how bilinguals process monolingual speech. The first relates to the activation of the other language, that is, the language not being heard. In essence, does that other language play a role and, if so, when and how? We will see that the selective/nonselective processing issue already discussed in Chapter 1, Section 1.4 is far more subtle than was thought at first and that the answer is less categorical than many have believed. The second aspect will concern the more permanent influence of the other language on processing. This pertains primarily to how the dominant language may influence the processing of the nondominant (weaker) language. Finally, the third section of this chapter will examine how speech that contains code-switches and/or borrowings is processed by bilinguals. Much less is known about this but what we do know is fascinating and well worth a description.

2.1   From the Speech Wave to the Mental Representation

The processing of spoken language – something that we do every minute of the day without being aware of it – is a highly complex, but also very rapid, process that we now understand reasonably well thanks to the research of psycholinguists over the years. For it to take place smoothly, one needs a number of components to be present, as shown in Figure 2.1. First, we have to have a speech wave (called the "speech input" in the diagram) produced by a speaker. It is referred to as "bottom-up" information, hence the upward arrow above the speech wave in the figure. We also need to know the language in question (we have called this "linguistic knowledge," on the right of the main box) and we have to have available a certain number

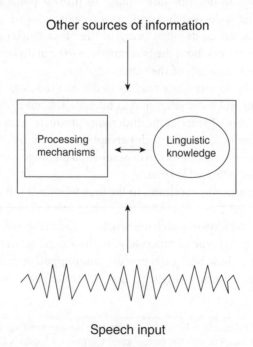

Figure 2.1: The basic components involved in speech perception and comprehension.

of processing mechanisms (see the left area of the box). Finally, speech perception and comprehension is helped greatly if we have other sources of information such as the context in which the speech situation is taking place, knowledge about the world we live in, information about what has been said so far, and so on. Note that these sources of information are often called "top-down" information (see the downward arrow in the figure). The final outcome of the work done by the processing mechanisms, with the contribution of linguistic knowledge and the other sources of information present, is called the mental (or interpretative) representation, that is, the enriched meaning of what has been said.

Although all the components of Figure 2.1 play a vital role during comprehension, we will concentrate on the processing mechanisms. To illustrate how processing takes place, let's follow a very simple spoken utterance, "The window is closed," from the moment it is said to the moment it is fully understood. As soon as the speech wave that corresponds to the beginning of the utterance is heard, phonetic processing starts to take place. That is, the phonetic and prosodic units that comprise it are identified. Thus, we perceive the two phonemes that correspond to the first word "the," the five phonemes that correspond to "window," and so on. We also perceive that the intonation is falling, that the speech rate is normal, and that there is a slight emphasis on the word "closed."

As soon as the first sounds have started to be perceived, lexical processing begins, that is, the recognition of the words "the," "window," "is," and "closed." They are activated in our internal lexicon (also known as our mental dictionary), along with other words that have similar beginnings, and little by little we isolate them and finally "accept" them. By doing so, we gain access to the information about these words that is contained in our lexicon – their meaning or meanings (if there are several), their grammatical categories, the syntactic and semantic structures that they can occur in, and so on. Along with this, we undertake morphological processing on the words that need it, for example computing that "is" refers to the third person singular of the verb "to be." With the information obtained at this processing level, we can undertake syntactic processing, that is, identifying the constituents of the utterance (e.g., "the window" is a noun phrase, "is closed" is a verb phrase) as well as the way in which the constituents are structured together.

While this is taking place, the next levels of processing are already at work, using the information that has been obtained so far. In semantic processing, the literal mental representation is computed, that is, the basic meaning is obtained. Some believe it takes the form of propositions that contain predicates and arguments. In this case, the mental representation of our utterance would look something like "closed (window)," meaning that the window is closed. Finally, pragmatic processing will use the context in which the utterance was said, as well as our knowledge about the world and of the rules of communication, to help reach a conclusion about meaning. The literal meaning may then be modified so as to produce an enriched final representation. Let us assume here that the utterance was said by someone who entered a room that was overheated (this is part of the context of the utterance). Let us also assume that it was cold outside, colder than in the room. We all know through our knowledge of the world that a way of cooling a room is to open a window IF it is colder outside than inside. Finally, we know through our internalized rules of communication that we can ask for something with an indirect speech act such as a statement. The final enriched mental representation will therefore be of the type, "She's asking me to open the window."

Two remarks need to be made at this point. First, we have greatly simplified the working of the processing stages that take place; each one is highly complex and the object of specific research in the cognitive and brain sciences. Second, even though we have talked of the processes taking place one after the other, it has been known since the pioneering work of Marslen-Wilson (1975) that processing is "parallel" in that all processes occur quasi-simultaneously. In addition, they take place "on-line" (as the utterance is being uttered, from its beginning to its end), and many researchers agree that they are also "interactive," that is, information is exchanged between processes to accomplish the task that is theirs.

A few general comments can now be made about processing in bilinguals before we examine specific issues in the rest of this chapter.

Whatever the type of speech being processed (monolingual or bilingual), the basic processing components and levels presented above are found in bilinguals as well as monolinguals. Thus bilinguals analyze the speech input with the same processing mechanisms (phonetic, lexical, syntactic, semantic, and pragmatic), their linguistic knowledge is called upon during processing, and other sources of information such as context, knowledge of the world, and information about what has been said so far play an important role in building the enriched mental representation. In addition, speech processing in bilinguals takes place in parallel, on-line, and most probably in an interactive fashion.

Despite these similarities with monolinguals, however, there are also important differences. First, bilinguals process not just one language but two or more. Thus the central components depicted in Figure 2.1 will be multiplied, at least in part, by the number of languages involved (see Sections 2.2 and 2.3). Second, since bilinguals are rarely equally fluent in all of their languages (recall that they use them for different purposes, in different domains of life, and with different people), the linguistic knowledge they have of their languages will be different, and this will have an impact on speech perception and comprehension. Some languages may be less well processed than others and, within a language, missing linguistic elements such as vocabulary items may affect perception and comprehension. This is clearly exemplified when bilinguals are asked to perceive speech in adverse conditions such as when there is background noise; they practically always do less well than their monolingual counterparts (see Lecumberri, Cooke, & Cutler, 2010, for a review).

Third, depending on the linguistic make-up of each language, the processing mechanisms called upon may function differently, at least in part. For example, at the level of phonetic processing, the perception of tones may be crucial for one language but not for the other; during lexical processing, there may be complex morphological analyses in one language but simpler analyses in the other; and at the level of syntax, specific syntactic processes may occur in one language but not in the other, and so on.

Fourth, as has been mentioned already, the utterance that has to be processed may be "monolingual" in that all the elements in it originate in just one language or be "bilingual" in that the interlocutor is in a bilingual mode and is using code-switches and borrowings. These will be contained in the speech stream and will have to be processed by the bilingual listener.

Finally, even when only one language is being processed (the signal is "monolingual"), the processing mechanisms called upon may be influenced, momentarily or in a more permanent way, by those of the other language(s). This can be due to simple coactivation of the other language(s) or by processing mechanisms and strategies that impose themselves on the language being processed.

In the following sections, we will concentrate primarily on these last two points. By doing so, we have simplified things slightly and so we should keep in mind that the overall picture that will one day emerge concerning speech perception and comprehension in bilinguals will be more complex than what is proposed here.

2.2 Processing Monolingual Speech

Figure 2.2 presents the processing components involved when the listener is bilingual. To simplify things, we represent just two languages, La and Lb, but we should

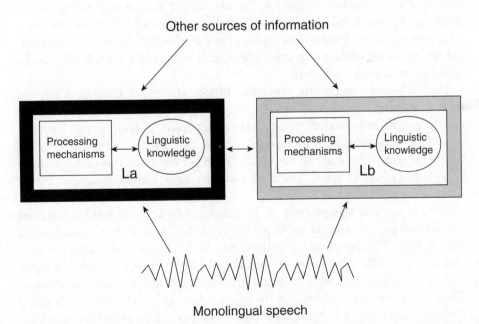

Figure 2.2: The components involved in speech perception and comprehension in bilinguals when the input is monolingual.

keep in mind that more languages may be known. In the figure, the person is listening to speech input that is monolingual (the language being heard is La) and hence only the linguistic knowledge and the processing mechanisms of that language are active (see the black rim around the left-hand box). The other language (Lb) is also present but it is deactivated, hence the grey rim. It should be noted that the monolingual speech input is transmitted to both language systems and that the other sources of information also feed into both systems.

2.2.1   The activation of the other language

The first issue we will discuss relates to the activation of the other language (Lb in our diagram), that is, the language not being heard. Even though we show it deactivated in Figure 2.2, many researchers believe that it is also active and that, in essence, it plays a role when the input is monolingual and in the other language. Hence, to the question of whether processing in bilinguals is selective (when one language is heard, only that language is active and is processed) or nonselective (the bilingual's different languages intervene while processing takes place), many researchers have opted for the latter answer in recent years. However, we will show that things are more complex than that.

Evidence for the simultaneous activation of the two languages, and hence non-selective processing, even in a monolingual mode, has come from studies using written language (see Chapter 4), and in more recent years from speech studies that have used an eye-tracking technique. The first one of its kind with bilinguals was conducted by Spivey and Marian (1999) with Russian-English bilinguals. They used a head-mounted eye tracker which allows the experimenter to see where the participant is looking while speech comprehension is taking place. We will describe the Russian part of their study here.

Their bilingual participants were asked to look at a board situated in front of them containing a number of objects. The example in Figure 2.3 is based on the description the authors give. Note that the target object, a stamp, which has to be moved by the participant, is in the bottom right-hand square. In the top left-hand square there can be one of two objects: a competitor object (in this case, a marker) or a control object (a ruler). There are also filler objects in the other two corner squares.

In the Spivey and Marian study, the participants heard pre-recorded instructions which asked them to displace the target object on the board, such as, "Poloji marku nije krestika" (Put the stamp below the cross). In the interlingual competitor condition, some of the objects on the board had English names that shared initial phonetic characteristics with the onset of the name of the Russian target object. Thus, in the example presented on the board, when the target object was a stamp ("marku" in the above sentence) the interlingual competitor object was a marker, an object whose English name shares the same word beginning as "marku."

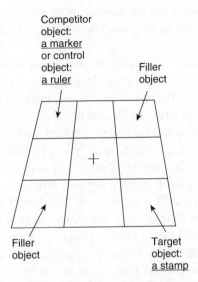

Figure 2.3: A visual representation of the board used by Spivey and Marian (1999) based on the description they give.

The researchers examined the eye movements made to this interlingual competitor object as compared to a control object, in exactly the same position, such as a ruler (see the top left-hand corner of the figure). In this second condition, the object's name bore no phonetic similarity with the name of the target object ("marku"). The results obtained showed that the participants made significantly more eye movements to the interlingual competitor object (32%) than to the control object (7%). Why is that? It would seem that the word onset of the target object (e.g., "marku") not only activated Russian words in the Russian lexicon but also English words in the English lexicon that began in a similar way ("marker" is very similar to "marku"). This happened through bottom-up processing, that is, the processing of the speech input (see the upward arrows leading from the speech wave to both languages in Figure 2.2). Based on this, the authors concluded that processing is nonselective.

Later studies were conducted by other researchers which also used the eye tracking approach but where the board was on a computer screen. Many reported similar findings. Thus, for example, Ju and Luce (2004), using Spanish-English bilinguals, showed that even a subtle phonetic cue in the other language was enough to activate both lexicons. To do this, they changed a critical aspect of the first consonant of Spanish words to its English counterpart by means of sound editing. More precisely, they manipulated the Voice Onset Time (VOT) of the consonant, that is, the brief delay between the release burst and glottal pulsing. Thus, for example, the Spanish /p/ of the word "playa" (beach) was in essence replaced with the English /p/ sound. This was enough to attract eye movements to the interlingual competitor object (a picture of "pliers") when the participants were asked in Spanish to click on the picture that corresponded to the target word ("playa" said with the English /p/ sound).

Bottom-up information can therefore sometimes activate both the language being spoken and the bilingual's other language. But can the activation of the nonused language, at other times, also be reduced and even neutralized? The answer is "yes," as we will see from two studies. In the first, Chambers and Cooke (2009), also using the eye-tracking technique but working with English-French bilinguals this time, preceded the target words (e.g., "poule" (chicken)) with nonrestrictive and restrictive sentences. In the former case, such as in "Marie va décrire la poule" (Marie will describe the chicken), there was very little prior semantic constraint on the target word (here "poule") since the verb "décrire (describe)" can be followed by any number of nouns (one can describe many things in life!). But in the restrictive sentence case (e.g., "Marie va nourrir la poule" (Marie will feed the chicken)), the predicate constrained the noun (in this example, to animate objects that can be fed). The competitor object was the picture of an interlingual homophone (the picture of a "pool" in our example). The participants listened to the French sentences and dragged the target object on the screen to the middle square. What the researchers found was that consideration of the interlingual competitor object was greatly reduced when the context sentence was restrictive: there were on average 0.28 eye movements (saccades) in this context compared to 0.48 saccades in the nonrestrictive context. Why was the number not reduced to zero? Quite simply because homophones were used in the study and they were activating both the French lexicon and the English lexicon in a bottom-up manner.

Finally, Marian and Spivey (2003) conducted a further study that shows that the activation of the other language cannot just be reduced but neutralized in certain situations, resulting in selective processing in essence. They realized that the contextual factors in their first study had pushed their participants toward a bilingual mode of processing, thereby activating both languages, and hence encouraging nonselective processing. Among the factors they mentioned was that participants knew they were taking part in an experiment on bilingualism, they were tested by bilingual experimenters who were fluent in both languages, and the two languages were tested in adjacent experimental sessions. (To these factors we can add several others presented in Chapter 1, Section 1.4). So as to put their participants in as close to a monolingual mode as possible, Marian and Spivey used different experimenters for the Russian and the English sessions who posed as monolingual speakers. (Note that what follows concerns the Russian session once again). During testing, they used only the language of the session, and participants only took part in the one or the other session. The results they obtained were quite convincing. The participants looked only at interlingual English competitor objects in 8% of the trials as opposed to 5% for the control object, a nonsignificant difference. (Recall that in their first study, the percentages had been 32% and 7%, respectively.) Hence, in this case, the other language had been totally "closed out" and processing had now become selective.

What can we conclude, therefore, about bilingual language processing and, more specifically, about whether processing is selective or nonselective? The answer is quite simply that it depends. The bottom-up, phonetic, information that is heard is processed by the language(s) that contain(s) elements of that input and this can lead to nonselective processing, such as when words are used that have similar word beginnings in the other language, or when homophones, homographs, and cognates are involved (as studies have shown repeatedly). Of course, if the input only contains elements of one language, then only one language will process it. The activation of just one language may be reinforced, in a spoken utterance, by aspects that are specific to that language: certain sounds, word forms (see Vitevitch, 2012, who found that English and Spanish share very few phonological neighbors), as well as prosodic information such as intonation, stress, rhythm, and so on.

To this should be added top-down factors ("other sources of information" in Figure 2.2) such as the interlocutor and the context which, in the case of bilinguals, influence the language mode the interlocutors are in (see Chapter 1, Section 1.4). Sometimes this top-down information may even "contradict" the bottom-up information, as when, for example, the listener is "shocked" upon hearing the speaker say something in a language that is not expected. We should add that things are further complicated by the fluency bilinguals have in their different languages, among other things. It would appear that if the stronger language is being processed, the weaker language will not be activated as much (or at all), and hence will not "interfere" with processing. However, if it is the weaker language that is being processed, then the stronger language may be active and may influence the processing that is taking place (see, for example, Weber and Cutler, 2004, who have shown this to be the case). Extreme care must therefore be taken when talking about whether processing of monolingual speech in bilinguals is selective or nonselective, since both outcomes are possible.

2.2.2 More permanent influences of the other language

In addition to the possibility that the language not being processed can be activated from time to time and hence can intervene in the processing of monolingual speech, as we have just seen, there may be more permanent influences of one language on the other (depicted by the horizontal arrows between the two languages in Figure 2.2). This pertains primarily to how the dominant language may influence the processing of the nondominant (weaker) language. We will examine two studies in particular, among many others, that show this. The first will deal with the perception of sounds and the second with the processing of grammatical gender.

It has been known for some time that the sound categories of a stronger (dominant) language can influence the sound categories of a weaker (nondominant) language. Thus, if the stronger language only has one category and the weaker language has two, these two categories may be assimilated to just one category in the weaker language. For example, the two English categories /æ/, as in "sat," and /ɛ/, as in "set," are often assimilated by Dutch-English bilinguals to one Dutch category /ɛ/, and so one often hears Dutch speakers of English not being able to differentiate between the pronunciation of "sat" and "set."

Pallier, Colomé, and Sebastián-Gallés (2001) showed how this phenomenon can play a role in speech perception by examining how Spanish-Catalan bilinguals perceive certain Catalan words. Spanish has only five vowels whereas Catalan has eight, among which we find the vowel /ɛ/, which does not exist in Spanish. Thus, Catalan has minimal pairs such as /netə/, (granddaughter) and /nɛtə/, (clean, feminine) whereas Spanish does not; for a Spanish speaker, these two words are homophones. The experimenters used two groups of highly skilled bilinguals fluent in Spanish and Catalan who had comparable, if not fully equivalent, command of the two languages, at least at levels beyond the phonetic level. All had been born in Barcelona and all had received the same kind of bilingual education. The difference was that the Spanish-dominant bilinguals had been raised in a monolingual Spanish environment before attending kindergarten, whereas the Catalan-dominant bilinguals had been raised in a monolingual Catalan environment before kindergarten.

The experimenters used a repetition priming task in which participants were asked to perform a lexical decision (i.e., decide whether an item is a word or a nonword) on lists of stimuli, some of which appeared twice. They cleverly used the well-known repetition effect to see how their bilinguals perceived certain sounds. The effect is quite simply that the reaction time to make a lexical decision is faster when an identical item is presented a second time in an experiment. Would there be a repetition effect, in this case, when one item of a minimal pair in Catalan was heard (e.g., /netə/ (granddaughter)), and the other item of the pair (/nɛtə/ (clean, feminine)) was heard later? The results they obtained were quite clear. Catalan-dominant bilinguals did not show a repetition effect: they processed these words as being quite distinct and showed no facilitation for the "repetition," that is, the other element of the pair. Spanish-dominant bilinguals, on the other hand, behaved as if the words were real homophones; they showed a repetition effect that was of the same amplitude as that observed for a real repetition. The authors concluded that despite being very fluent bilinguals, their Spanish-dominant bilinguals had not created separate perceptual categories for certain Catalan sounds due to the fact that their first language (Spanish) did not have them.

We have just seen how a language can have a permanent influence on the processing of another language. In the example given, we showed that certain categories are not developed in the weaker language and that processing is affected by this. It can also be the case that, in addition to categories not existing, some processing mechanisms and strategies are not acquired because the first language did not have them and/or the second language was acquired later. Our example comes from the domain of word recognition. Guillelmon and Grosjean (2001) were interested in how gender marking is processed by bilinguals. Depending on the language, words may carry any number of genders, from two in French and Italian all the way to six in Swahili. Other word classes may not have gender but they can reflect, in their morphology, the gender of the words that do. Thus a gender agreement marking can appear before or after a noun on a determiner, adjective, pronoun, and so on. For example, in the French phrase, "la petite voiture" (the small car), both the article (la) and the adjective (petite) agree with the feminine noun (voiture) and carry a feminine ending.

We have known for some time that a congruent gender marking (as in the example just given) on the words preceding the noun will speed up the noun's recognition whereas an incongruent marking (e.g., "*le petit fille") will slow it down. Guillelmon and Grosjean asked whether bilingual listeners were also sensitive to gender marking. They tested early and late English-French bilinguals. The early bilinguals started using their two languages in everyday life as early as 5;4 years on average whereas the late bilinguals had only become regular users of their two languages at 24;8 years. The latter had learned French at school but it was only as adults, mostly because of immigration, that they had become regular users of it.

Both groups of participants heard phrases of the type, "le/la/leur joli(e) + noun" (the $_{masculine}$ / the $_{feminine}$ / their nice + noun) and were asked to repeat the noun. Depending on the determiner, the gender marking was congruent (e.g., "le joli bateau" (the nice boat), incongruent (e.g., "*la jolie bateau") or not present (e.g., "leur joli bateau"). The time needed to repeat the noun was used to understand the underlying processes involved. The early bilinguals demonstrated strong congruency and incongruency effects. They had become sensitive to gender early in life and they appeared to use gender marking in perception the way monolinguals do.

The real surprise came when the results of the late bilinguals were analyzed. They were quite simply insensitive to both gender congruency and gender incongruency. It appeared that they simply couldn't use the masculine "le" cue or the feminine "la" cue during the processing of the phrase even though they themselves made very few gender errors in production. Thus the gender processing mechanism, which can help to speed up word recognition and which is acquired by native French speakers and early bilinguals, was never acquired by late bilinguals. There is probably, therefore, a sensitive period to acquire such a mechanism (see Chapter 7) and the late bilinguals, whose first language (English) does not have gender marking of this type, missed it and could not master it later on. Of course, they still recognize words (the late bilinguals reported having very good French oral comprehension) but their lexical access is not speeded up by a congruent gender marking on the preceding word(s). In sum, one language can definitely have a permanent influence on the language processing of the other.

2.3   Processing Bilingual Speech

As was described in Chapter 1, bilinguals may find themselves in a bilingual mode when they are speaking to people who share their languages and where code-switching and borrowing can take place. Thus, the speech input bilinguals have to process may well be bilingual. In Figure 2.4 we show how the two languages are configured when this happens. One language is the base language and is the most active (La in the figure); the other language is also active but less so as it is only

Spoken Language Processing

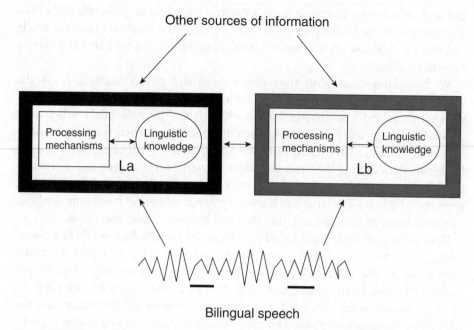

Figure 2.4: The components involved in speech perception and comprehension in bilinguals when the input is bilingual.

called upon from time to time. We have depicted this by making the border around the Lb box slightly less dark than that around La.

In what follows we will first look at the impact that the base language can have when guest words (code-switches and borrowings) are heard. Note that we have depicted them with short horizontal lines below the speech wave in the figure. We will then report on how code-switches and borrowings themselves are processed by bilingual listeners, and we will end with the description of a model which simulates many of the findings that have been obtained by researchers.

2.3.1   The base-language effect

The base-language effect concerns the impact that the base language (La in Figure 2.4) can have on the processing of guest words. Does it, for example, slow down their perception and recognition momentarily? As we will see in this section, there is now good evidence that this is the case. Since in normal bilingual discourse the base language normally makes up some 80–90% of the utterance, it is more strongly activated and hence base-language units (phonemes, syllables, words) are favored over guest-language units, at least for a short period of time.

Grosjean (2008; Chapter 6) describes four studies that all point toward the existence of a base-language effect. We will describe two of them here. Soares and

Grosjean (1984) asked English-Portuguese bilinguals to listen to sentences and to detect words or nonwords within them that began with a pre-specified phoneme. Once they had found the items, they had to make a lexical decision, that is, indicate as quickly as possible whether they were dealing with a word or a nonword. The bilinguals heard three types of sentences – English, Portuguese, and Portuguese with code-switches. Here are examples (the critical words on which a lexical decision had to be made are emboldened and the code-switches are in italics):

English: "After lunch, the children asked for a piece of **cake** for dessert."
Portuguese: "Depois do almoço os miudos pediram uma fatia de **bolo** para sobremesa."
Code-switched: "Depois do *lunch* os miudos pediram uma fatia de ***cake*** para *dessert.*"

The results obtained were interesting. First, in the English condition, the bilinguals were as rapid as the English control participants. Second, there were no differences between their reaction times in the English and the Portuguese condition, indicating thereby that they were equally fluent in their two languages. Third, their mean reaction times to code-switches was significantly slower than to base language words, in the order of about 150 ms. Thus a base-language effect was clearly present in this study.

In another study, conducted by Domenighetti and Caldognetto (1999; described by Grosjean, 2008), the aims were, first, to confirm that the base language delays, however slightly, the recognition of code-switches in a neutral context and, second, to ascertain whether the word following the code-switch is also delayed. This second aim was important for our understanding of the code-switching process. If the delay is carried over to the next word, then the bilingual listener will gradually fall behind the speaker, which seems quite counterintuitive. One possibility is that the delay is momentary and is "caught up" before the code-switched word is finished and, hence, before the next word arrives.

The authors asked French-Italian bilinguals to listen to a short sentence which ended with a short list of words. For example, "J'ai entendu les mots aéroport, grenouille, sapin, collier" (I heard the words airport, frog, fir tree, collar). The participants' task was to repeat the word in the second position of the list, that is, "grenouille" in the example. In the code-switching version, the second word was replaced by an Italian word which took the same amount of time to repeat as the French word in isolation. Thus, in our example, "grenouille" was replaced with "cena" (dinner). The results showed a base-language effect once again; code-switches took on average 50 ms more to repeat than base language words. However, when a second group of participants were asked to repeat "sapin," the word in third position in both types of sentences, the repetition times were similar. Thus, the base-language effect appears to be short lived, and by the time the following word arrives in the sentence, any time that may have been lost will have been caught up. This may explain why certain studies that measure processing later on in sentences containing guest words, or at the end of the sentences, show no base-language effect (see, for example, Cheng & Howard, 2008).

2.3.2   The recognition of code-switches and borrowings

A topic that has been of interest for a number of years pertains to the factors that play a role in how guest words (code-switches and borrowings) are recognized in bilingual speech. Grosjean (2008) presents a list of these factors which he organized into four categories: those that pertain to the listener, such as how fluent the person is in the guest language; those that concern the level of activation of both the base language (La in Figure 2.4) and the guest language (Lb), and which include the base-language effect we have just discussed; those factors that involve various code-switching constraints (it is well known that code-switching is a rule-governed behavior which will probably have an impact on processing); and, finally, the factors that concern the properties of the guest word being heard. We will concentrate on this latter category in what follows since several studies have been conducted on this topic.

A first study   Grosjean (1988) examined the role of a number of guest-word properties during word recognition. He presented French-English bilinguals with English guest words preceded by a French neutral context, "Il faudrait qu'on . . ." (We should) and followed by a final phrase in French. For example, "Il faudrait qu'on *slash* tous les prix" (We should slash all the prices) or "Il faudrait qu'on *lean* contre le mur" (We should lean against the wall). In each example, the guest word is in italics.

Grosjean used the gating task in which a spoken word is presented in segments of increasing duration. Thus, the first gate contained "Il faudrait qu'on" up to, but not including, the onset of the guest word. The second gate contained the same information plus the first 40 ms of the guest word. And from then on, gates were incremented by 40 ms until the end of the word was reached. Once the full word had been presented, three "after offset" gates were added covering the final phrase so that participants could hear the following context in order to resolve any remaining ambiguity concerning the guest word.

After each presentation the participants were asked to: (1) write down the word they thought was being presented after "Il faudrait qu'on"; (2) indicate how confident they were about their guess, and (3) indicate whether they thought the word was French or English.

The three word properties that were examined in the study were the language phonetics of the word, its phonotactics, and the interlanguage neighbor proximity. As concerns language phonetics, the author asked whether guest words which retain a phonetic cue as to which lexicon they belong (by being pronounced clearly in the guest language) are easier to process than words which are integrated phonetically into the base language. In other words, to use the terminology employed in

Chapter 1, would code-switched words, which are pronounced in the guest language and thereby retain phonetic cues as to the lexicon they are a part of, be accessed more easily than borrowings, which are usually integrated into the base language and hence have lost most, if not all, of their phonetic cues.

As concerns phonotactics, the permissible combination of phonemes and syllables in a language, the author asked whether guest words that are marked phonotactically as belonging to the guest language lexicon would be recognized sooner and with more ease than words not marked in this way. Thus, would English "snap" or "slash," where the initial consonant clusters, "sn" and "sl," are more frequent in English than in French, be perceived sooner than words such as "lead" or "pick," which have a consonant-vowel-consonant pattern common to both languages. The reasoning was that the initial consonant cluster would be a strong cue to the lexicon it belonged to.

Finally, as concerns interlanguage neighbor proximity, Grosjean asked whether guest words that have near homophones in the base language would be recognized with more difficulty than other guest language words (for instance, English "pick" is homophonic with French "pique," English "knot" with French "note," etc.).

A combination of these latter two variables – phonotactics and interlanguage neighbor proximity – gave three types of words: Type 1 words which favor English phonotactically and which only exist in English; Type 2 words which favor French phonotactically but which only exist in English; and Type 3 words which also favor French phonotactically but which have a close homophone in the other language.

The results confirmed the importance of the variables under study. First, words that were marked phonotactically as belonging to the guest language only (e.g., "slash," "blot") had a mean identification point that occurred sooner than for words not marked in this way. The identification point was expressed as a percentage of the word needed to identify it correctly. Percentages could range from 0% (no part of the word was needed) to 100% (the whole word was needed). Participants needed 66% of Type 1 words to identify them as opposed to 78% for Type 2 words. Second, words that belonged solely to the guest lexicon (Type 1 and 2 words) were recognized sooner than words that did not belong to just one lexicon (Type 3 words): 97% of Type 1 words and 92% of Type 2 words were identified before their ending whereas only 43% of Type 3 words fell into this category. Third, words in the guest language lexicon that had close homophones in the base language (Type 3 words) were processed with more difficulty than other guest language words: 37% of Type 3 words were isolated after their acoustic offset, but before the end of the sentence, and a full 20% were never identified at all.

As concerns the language phonetics variable, it appeared that the way a guest word was said (i.e., as a code-switch or as a borrowing) affected more the narrowing-in process that led to word identification than the actual point in time at which the word was identified. Grosjean found that during the selection phase which preceded word recognition the proportion of guest language candidates was greater for code-switches than for borrowings. He also noted an interesting interaction between the language phonetics variable and the interlanguage homophone variable. The candidates proposed for Type 3 words were quite different depending on whether they were said as borrowings (i.e., in French) or as code-switches (i.e., in English). In the former case, subjects invariably chose the base language homophone ("pique" for "pick," "note" for "knot") but, in the latter case, only about 20% fell into this category. The majority involved the addition, omission or substitution of one or more phonemes (e.g., "set" proposed for "sit," "fourre" for "fool," "coure" for "cool," etc.). This indicated the very real difficulties subjects had with items in which the language phonetics activated the two lexicons, primarily the English lexicon but also its French counterpart, and where the base-language effect reinforced the French candidates.

In addition to showing the importance of these three variables, the study examined two other variables – sound specificity and interlanguage neighbor frequency. As concerns the former, an analysis of the candidates that were proposed showed that strong language phonetic cues (such as those of a plosive or a lateral) clearly activated either the English or the French lexicon, depending on the phonetics of the guest word, and thus affected the language of the candidates proposed. Concerning interlanguage neighbor frequency, the author noted a great deal of variability in the results of Type 3 words (i.e., those that had close homophones in the other language). This was due to the degree of "frequency pull" of the guest words (i.e., the English items) as compared to their base language counterparts (the French words).

Later studies The Grosjean (1988) study was followed by other studies undertaken by different researchers and with different language pairs. Since each one contributed new information to our understanding of how guest words are processed, they are worth mentioning here. Li (1996) conducted two experiments with Chinese-English bilinguals: the first one was a gating study, similar to Grosjean's study, whereas the second one was a naming (word shadowing) study. Li examined the language phonetics of the English guest words as well as their phonotactics, as had Grosjean, but he also looked at the role of the prior context. He preceded the guest words with a short context (a bit like Grosjean's neutral context) and a long, more constraining, context, in order to see the role it would play in guest word recognition.

The gating results reported by Li were very interesting. First, he showed that guest words pronounced as code-switches provide phonetic cues to the listener and hence are easier to identify than when they are pronounced as borrowings. (It should be noted that this effect was far stronger in his study than in Grosjean's where its impact was situated more in the narrowing-in stage). Second, he found a strong effect for context: if the context was constraining, only 59% of the word was needed for correct identification as compared to 72% of the word if it was not (a result that has been obtained repeatedly with monolingual speech). Finally, he obtained a very interesting result concerning the phonotactics of the words. When the initial syllable was made up of a consonant and a vowel (CV), then code-switches and borrowings were identified at about the same point. However, when the initial syllable was made up of a consonant followed by another consonant (CC), then borrowings required far more information (79% of the word) than code-switches (55%). This comes from the fact that when words are borrowed into Chinese, their configuration is changed quite drastically with certain consonants softened or even dropped. Thus, for words such as "flight" where the code-switch version resembles the English pronunciation, the borrowing version becomes /faɪ/. It makes sense, therefore, that such words need much more information to be identified correctly. It should be noted, finally, that the naming (word shadowing) study provided converging evidence for the results obtained in the gating study concerning all three variables studied.

A few years later, Schulpen, Dijkstra, Schriefers, and Hasper (2003) examined the processing of homophones in Dutch-English bilinguals (the equivalent of Type 3 words in Grosjean's study), for example, Dutch "boel" and English "bull." In a first study, they presented these words in isolation (along with control words) using the gating task and the participants were asked, after each gate, to guess the word being presented, to rate how sure they were, and to rate their confidence that it was either a Dutch or an English word. They found, as could be expected based on prior studies, that homophones were more difficult to isolate than control words (52.8% of the homophones were isolated as compared to 76.1% of the control words). They also found that the language of the target word (Dutch, English) affected the candidates proposed prior to isolation – something both Grosjean (1988) and Li (1996) had previously found. In addition, the bilinguals showed much less confidence in the choices they made when the items were homophones than when they were control words.

In addition, the authors conducted a cross-modal priming study in which the participants heard a word (a prime), then saw a letter string on a computer screen, and then had to decide whether the string was an English word or not. The results again showed that interlingual homophones were more difficult to process than monolingual controls. In addition, participants were sensitive to sublexical cues: they reacted more slowly to the English homophones when they were preceded by spoken primes in the other language. Thus, the Dutch spoken word /liːf/ followed by the visual English LEAF led to longer reaction times than the English spoken word /liːf/ followed by visual English LEAF. The authors concluded that upon the presentation of an auditory input signal, lexical candidates from both languages are activated, depending on the degree of overlap between the input signal of a target word and its internal representation. The selection of the appropriate word in the one or the other lexicon can be facilitated by sublexical cues that are present in the input signal. This view is very similar to the one presented at the end of Section 2.2.1 and originally proposed by Grosjean (1988). We will discuss it in Section 2.3.3, along with the computational model that was developed a few years later.

2.3.3   A model of spoken word recognition in bilinguals

At the end of his 1988 paper, Grosjean proposed the outline of a model of spoken word recognition in bilinguals. Its main characteristics, which have been evoked indirectly at various points of this chapter, are that there are two language networks which are both independent and interconnected. In the monolingual language mode, one language network is strongly activated while the resting activation level of the other language network is very low (as in Figure 2.2). In the bilingual mode, both networks are activated but the base-language network is more strongly activated (see Figure 2.4). The resting level of the language not being used as the base language can be increased or decreased depending on the amount of input from the other language as well as from other, top-down, sources of information. The activation of a unit of one network (e.g., a phoneme) and of its counterpart in the other network depends on their degree of similarity. The activation of units that are specific to one language increases the overall activation of that language network and thus speeds up the processing in that language. Of course, if a unit (i.e., a phoneme or word) in one language has a similar unit in the other language (such as with homophones) then there will be a delay in recognizing it, all other things being equal.

With these general considerations in mind, and after having worked out various specificities, Léwy and Grosjean (in Grosjean, 2008) developed a computational model of bilingual lexical access (BIMOLA). It is similar in certain ways to the Bilingual Interactive Activation (BIA) computational model presented in Chapter 4 in that both deal with word recognition in bilinguals. In addition, both are based on interactive activation models of cognitive processes (see McClelland & Rumelhart, 1981) and both are implemented on computer. However, there are also major differences between the two in that BIA simulates the recognition of visual words whereas BIMOLA is a model of spoken word recognition (it was inspired specifically by McClelland and Elman's [1986] TRACE model). In addition, BIA deals with Dutch and English whereas BIMOLA simulates the recognition of French and English words. Other important differences concern the internal properties of each model (see Thomas & Van Heuven, 2005).

Figure 2.5 presents a simplified visual representation of BIMOLA (the reader may want to compare it to the representation of BIA in Figure 4.4). As can be seen there are three levels of nodes: features, phonemes, and words. The features level nodes are shared by the two languages whereas the two other types of nodes are organized both independently (as subsets) and as one large system. Features activate phonemes that, in turn, activate words. The activation connections between phonemes and words are bidirectional (see the upward and downward arrows between levels) whereas the activation connections between the features level and the phonemes level are simply bottom-up.

Words also receive top-down activation, allowing the language mode to be preset – only one language is active in the monolingual mode at the beginning of word

BIMOLA

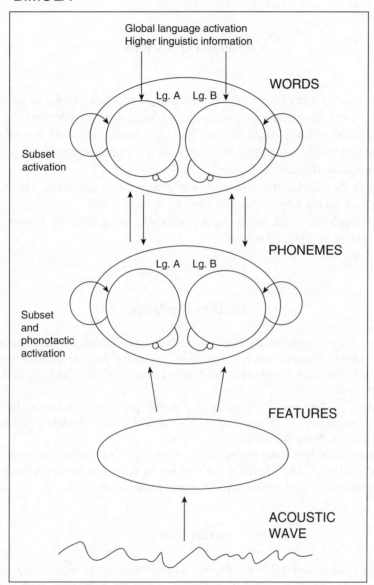

Figure 2.5: A simplified visual representation of BIMOLA – the Léwy and Grosjean bilingual model of lexical access. Adapted from Fig. 11.1, p. 204, in *Studying Bilinguals* by François Grosjean (2008). By permission of Oxford University Press.

recognition whereas the other language can also be active in the bilingual mode. There is also subset activation at the word and phoneme levels as well as phonotactic activation just at the phoneme level. Finally, units within the word and phoneme levels inhibit one another but only within a language. The model has been found to replicate the bilingual effects found in Grosjean (1988): the base-language effect,

the phonotactic effect, the language phonetic effect, and the base-language homophone effect.

Research Questions

1. Why have so many researchers in psycholinguistics believed for so many years
    that monolingual language processing in bilinguals is nonselective?
2. What kind of study could one conduct to show the impact of *two* other lan-
    guages (a second and a third language) when bilinguals are processing just one
    language (as depicted in Figure 2.2)?
3. Specify the role that the prosody of a language (intonation, stress, rhythm, etc.)
    can have on the selective/nonselective processing issue?
4. How would you test whether code-switching rules have an impact on the
    processing of bilingual speech?

Further Readings

Chambers, Craig & Cooke, Hilary. 2009. Lexical competition during second-language listen-
    ing: sentence context, but not proficiency, constrains interference from the native
    lexicon. *Journal of Experimental Psychology: Learning, Memory, and Cognition* 35(4).
    1029–1040.
Cutler, Anne & Broersma, Mirjam. 2005. Phonetic precision in listening. In William
    Hardcastle & Janet Mackenzie Beck (eds), *A Figure of Speech: A Festschrift for John Laver*,
    pp. 63–91. Oxford: Routledge.
Grosjean, François. 2008. *Studying Bilinguals*. Oxford/New York: Oxford University Press.
Lecumberri, Maria, Cooke, Martin, & Cutler, Anne. 2010. Non-native speech perception in
    adverse conditions: A review. *Speech Communication* 52. 864–886.

References

Chambers, Craig & Cooke, Hilary. 2009. Lexical competition during second-language listen-
    ing: Sentence context, but not proficiency, constrains interference from the native
    lexicon. *Journal of Experimental Psychology: Learning, Memory, and Cognition* 35(4).
    1029–1040.
Cheng, Yu-Lin & Howard, David. 2008. The time cost of mixed-language processing: An
    investigation. *International Journal of Bilingualism* 12(3). 209–222.
Domenighetti, Corinna & Caldognetto, Dolorès. 1999. Le rôle de la langue de base dans la
    reconnaissance des alternances codiques chez les bilingues. Unpublished Master's
    Thesis, Language Pathology Program, Neuchâtel University, Switzerland.
Grosjean, François. 1988. Exploring the recognition of guest words in bilingual speech.
    Language and Cognitive Processes 3. 233–274.

Grosjean, François. 2008. *Studying Bilinguals*. Oxford/New York: Oxford University Press.

Guillelmon, Delphine & Grosjean, François. 2001. The gender marking effect in spoken word recognition: The case of bilinguals. *Memory and Cognition* 29. 503–511.

Ju, Min & Luce, Paul. 2004. Falling on sensitive ears: Constraints on bilingual lexical activation. *Psychological Science* 15(5). 314–318.

Lecumberri, Maria, Cooke, Martin, & Cutler, Anne. 2010. Non-native speech perception in adverse conditions: A review. *Speech Communication* 52. 864–886.

Léwy, Nicolas & Grosjean, François. 2008. The Léwy and Grosjean BIMOLA model. Chapter 11 of Grosjean, François. 2008. *Studying Bilinguals*. Oxford/New York: Oxford University Press.

Li, Ping. 1996. Spoken word recognition of code-switched words by Chinese-English bilinguals. *Journal of Memory and Language* 35. 757–774.

Marian, Viorica & Spivey, Michael. 2003. Competing activation in bilingual language processing: Within- and between-language competition. *Bilingualism: Language and Cognition* 6. 97–115.

Marslen-Wilson, William. 1975. Sentence perception as an interactive parallel process. *Science* 189. 226–228.

McClelland, Jay & Elman, Jeff. 1986. The TRACE model of speech perception. *Cognitive Psychology* 18. 1–86.

McClelland, Jay & Rumelhart, David. 1981. An interactive activation model of context effects in letter perception: Part 1. An account of basic findings. *Psychological Review* 88. 375–407.

Pallier, Christophe, Colomé, Angels, & Sebastián-Gallés, Núria. 2001. The influence of native-language phonology on lexical access: Exemplar-based versus abstract lexical entries. *Psychological Science* 12(6). 445–449.

Schulpen, Béryl, Dijkstra, Ton, Schriefers, Herbert, & Hasper, Mark. 2003. Recognition of interlingual homophones in bilingual auditory word recognition. *Journal of Experimental Psychology: Human Perception and Performance* 29(6). 1155–1178.

Soares, Carlos & Grosjean, François. 1984. Bilinguals in a monolingual and a bilingual speech mode: The effect on lexical access. *Memory and Cognition* 12. 380–386.

Spivey, Michael & Marian, Viorica. 1999. Cross talk between native and second languages: Partial activation of an irrelevant lexicon. *Psychological Science* 10. 281–284.

Thomas, Michael & Van Heuven, Walter. 2005. Computational models of bilingual comprehension. In Judith F. Kroll & Annette M.B. de Groot (eds), *Handbook of Bilingualism*, 202–225. Oxford/New York: Oxford University Press.

Vitevitch, Michael. 2012. What do foreign neighbors say about the mental lexicon? *Bilingualism: Language and Cognition* 15. 167–172.

Weber, Andrea & Cutler, Anne. 2004. Lexical competition in non-native spoken-word recognition. *Journal of Memory and Language* 50(1). 1–25.

Chapter 3

Speech Production

François Grosjean

More than two decades ago, Grosjean and Soares (1986) wrote that a psycholinguistic model of language processing in bilinguals would have to account for the production of language in the bilingual's different language modes: the monolingual mode, that is, when the bilingual is communicating with a person who only knows one of the bilingual's languages, and the bilingual mode, that is, when the interlocutors share two or more languages, the languages are active albeit to different degrees, and language mixing can occur between them. Such a model, they argued, has to describe the ways in which bilinguals in the monolingual mode differ from monolinguals in terms of production processes, and it has to explain the actual interaction of the two (or more) languages during processing in the bilingual mode. Some 23 years later, Kootstra, Van Hell, and Dijkstra (2009) expressed a similar viewpoint when they stated that a central question in cognitive research on bilingual language processing is how to account for the ability of bilinguals to keep their languages apart in language production as well as to switch back and forth between their languages. Even though speech production in bilinguals has been studied less extensively than reading (see Chapter 4) or language acquisition (see Chapters 6 and 7), we will attempt, in this chapter, to give an overview of the kind of work that has been done so far.

This chapter has several aims. The first is to examine a central question in bilingual speech production, namely, when bilinguals produce just one language, is their monolingual production language selective or language nonselective; in other words, is the other language involved in the process?

The second aim is to present research that has concentrated on how bilinguals produce bilingual speech, that is, speech where the base language changes or where there are code-switches. One question that has been studied for many years is whether switching languages takes time. More recent studies are concerned with how the production of code-switches is influenced by structural constraints as well as by dialogue partners, and whether code-switches are affected on the phonetic level by the main language being spoken (the base language).

A third aim of this chapter will be to present the approaches used to study speech production in bilinguals. In recent years, interesting experimental methodologies have been used to understand the underlying operations that make up this production process We will attempt to present a few here.

This chapter will contain four sections. In Section 3.1 we will propose a rapid overview of how it is that we go from thought to articulation, that is, how speech production takes place. We will end the section with a short discussion of how bilinguals go about producing speech. In Section 3.2, we will address the question of whether monolingual language production in bilinguals is language selective (only one language is in fact being processed) or nonselective (the other language not being spoken is also involved). We will describe a study that had a large impact on how language production in bilinguals was considered for a number of years. In Section 3.3, we will show that both very recent experimental evidence but also some earlier evidence appear to show that the answer to the selectivity question is much less categorical than was thought at first. We will show that language production in bilinguals is, in fact, a dynamic process – sometimes it is language selective and sometimes nonselective – and we will examine the factors that play a role in this. Finally, Section 3.4 will deal with the production of bilingual speech. We will examine the time course of language switching, how it is constrained by syntactic considerations as well as dialogue issues, and how it takes place at the phonetic and the prosodic levels.

3.1 From Thought to Articulation

Even though several models of speech production have been proposed from different theoretical perspectives over the years, many researchers would probably agree on three broad components of the process – conceptualization, formulation, and articulation (Levelt, 2000; Harley, 2008). During conceptualization, the speaker must choose and organize the information that needs to be expressed based on what the listener already knows. The speaker must also take into account the listener's characteristics (age, level of education, social position, etc.), decide on the register as well as the rhetorical device to use (assertion, request, etc.), and choose whether the speech act will be direct or indirect. The outcome of all this will be a preverbal message which contains, among other things, lexical concepts, that is, concepts for which there exist words in the language being spoken.

Much of what happens during the next stage, formulation, is still hotly debated, as is the process itself: Is it made up of separate levels as proposed by Levelt (1989) or is formulation based on a network of processing units in a spreading activation framework (e.g., Dell, 1986)? What is clear is that words are selected and arranged in the correct syntactic order. (There is no agreement, however, on whether lemmas, i.e., elements that contain the morphosyntactic information of words, exist or not.) The appropriate morphemes are then chosen and are used to build a syllable structure for each word. Larger units are also put together, such as phonological and intonational phrases accompanied by their pitch contour. The speech plan that results is then executed (we are now at the level of articulation) by means of the speaker's articulatory apparatus consisting of a respiratory and laryngeal system, a vocal tract as well as a number of articulators (tongue, velum, lips). Because speakers plan and speak at the same time, and sentences flow one after the other, the whole production process takes place in cascade. This means that levels overlap – information at one level is passed on to the next before its processing is over.

A number of points can be made about the way bilinguals produce speech. First, the three main production components mentioned above, that is, conceptualization, formulation and articulation, are also present in bilinguals. In his well-known model of bilingual production, De Bot (1992) includes these components, and in his more recent multilingual processing model (De Bot, 2004) he again follows the three main stages that have been proposed for monolinguals. A second point is that because bilinguals know and use two or more languages, certain characteristics of language production need to be modified. Thus, for example, De Bot (1992) as well as La Heij (2005) state that the choice of the language to be spoken takes place during conceptualization. As for the lexical items that are called upon in bilingual production, they are stored all together according to De Bot (1992) but the elements of each language are organized into subsets. This is also true for syntactic procedures and sublexical elements, according to his 2004 model. A third point is that since bilinguals use two or more languages when code-switching and borrowing, a mechanism must be introduced to allow for this. De Bot (2004) calls upon a language node to serve as such a mechanism. It controls the various processing components with respect to the language to be used at a particular point in time.

This said, a comprehensive model remains to be developed. Such a model will explain how bilinguals remain in a monolingual mode and speak just one language but nonetheless produce interferences due their other, nonactivated, language(s) (see Chapter 1), and how they go back and forth between their languages when code-switching and borrowing. This is particularly true since models have come and gone over the years. For example, De Bot (personal communication) no longer endorses his 1992 and 2004 models. Since research in bilingual speech production is rapidly evolving, as are the models that integrate the results obtained, we will not attempt in this chapter to present a comprehensive overview of how bilingual speakers produce their languages, separately or together. It is still too early to do so in the development of a field that is young and that has methodological issues to resolve, as we will see. Rather, we will concentrate on a number of questions that have interested researchers in the last 20 years or so.

3.2   Producing Monolingual Speech

A question that has led to considerable research over the years concerns the issue of whether the language production process in bilinguals is language selective or nonselective. In other words, is the other language involved when bilinguals produce just one language? A similar question has been asked concerning oral and written perception and comprehension (see Chapters 2 and 4). One of the studies most cited in defense of language nonselectivity in production was conducted by Hermans, Bongaerts, De Bot, and Schreuder (1998). They asked Dutch-English bilinguals to do a picture-word interference task. The participants had to name pictures presented on a computer screen as quickly as possible while ignoring auditorily presented words (which the authors entitled "interfering stimuli"). We will concentrate on Experiment 2 of their study. Here, the bilingual participants named the pictures (e.g., of a mountain) in English, their second language, and were told to ignore the accompanying Dutch words presented orally. The latter were either phonologically related to the English name (e.g., Dutch "mouw" which means "sleeve" when the name of the picture was "mountain"), semantically related to it (e.g., Dutch "dal" which means "valley"), unrelated to it (e.g., Dutch "kaars" which means "candle") or – and this is important – phonologically related to the Dutch name of the picture (e.g., Dutch "berm" which means "verge," the Dutch name of the picture being "berg"). The authors called this the Phono-Dutch condition.

The time interval between the auditory words and the presentation of the picture (the stimulus onset asynchrony or SOA) was varied, from minus values, meaning that the words were presented before the pictures, to positive values, meaning that the words were presented after the pictures. The crucial result concerns the latency to name the picture (e.g., "mountain") in the Phono-Dutch condition, that is, when the Dutch word ("berm" in our example) was phonologically related to the Dutch name of the picture. It was compared to the latency to name the picture when the unrelated word was heard (i.e., "kaars"). Examples of these two conditions are depicted in Figure 3.1.

The authors found that at negative and zero SOAs, the latency to name "mountain" when "berm" was presented was slowed down significantly. Their explanation was that the auditory word "berm" probably activated the Dutch word "berg" in the participants' internal lexicon and hence made it harder to select the English word "mountain." They concluded that in the initial stages of word selection, bilingual speakers do not appear to be able to prevent their first language from interfering with the production of their second language.

This study, along with others (e.g., Colomé, 2001), convinced researchers for several years that language production in one language involved, at least in the early processing stages, the activation of the bilingual's other language. Thus, Costa (2005) asserted that there is wide agreement in assuming that the conceptual system activates the two languages of a bilingual simultaneously and that this supports the notion that the activation flow from the conceptual system to the lexical system is language nonselective. Several years later, Bialystok, Craik, Green, and Gollan (2009) concurred that it is now well documented that both languages of a bilingual are jointly activated even in contexts that strongly bias toward one of them.

As this research was being done and its results were impacting the field, a few researchers were pointing out that methodological issues had to be taken into account, since it could be that uncontrolled factors might explain these results and

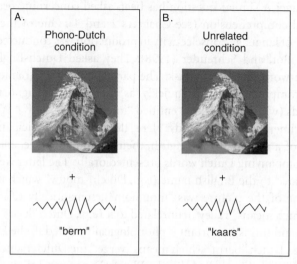

Figure 3.1: Examples of the crucial conditions in Experiment 2 of the Hermans, Bongaerts, De Bot, and Schreuder (1998) study. A) The Phono-Dutch condition where the picture to be named in English (in this example, "mountain") was presented along with an auditory word ("berm") which was phonologically related to the Dutch name of the picture ("berg"). B) The Unrelated condition where the picture was named along with an auditory word ("kaars") unrelated to the name of the picture.

not the actual language nonselectivity of the processing that was taking place. For example, Grosjean (1998) stated that tasks that call on the bilingual's two languages, as in the Hermans *et al.* (1998) study, will activate both languages in the bilingual. This becomes a very real problem when the question being studied pertains to such issues as selective versus nonselective processing. He added that if one is interested in such an issue, one should be careful not to activate the other language by using a task that does just that. When this occurs, it becomes difficult to disentangle what is due to normal bilingual processing from what is due to the bilingual language mode induced by the task. A few years later, Costa, La Heij, and Navarette (2006) stated something very similar: one should assess whether there is activation of the nonresponse language in experimental circumstances in which such a language is not called into play at all. These words of warning started to be heeded by researchers and new studies were undertaken, as we will see in the next section.

3.3 Language Production in Bilinguals Is a Dynamic Process

As we saw in Chapter 1, Section 1.4, bilinguals navigate along a continuum with two endpoints – a monolingual mode and a bilingual mode. Depending on numerous factors, bilinguals will find themselves at various points along the continuum. One consequence of this is that the state of activation of their languages will vary.

This leads to a processing system in bilinguals that is dynamic and that can operate in different language activation states. Hence whether language processing is selective or nonselective will depend on the activation levels of the languages which in turn depend on a number of internal and external factors. In what follows, we will first present experimental evidence for the bilingual's dynamic production process and then evoke the factors that affect the activation of a language that is not being used at a particular point in time.

3.3.1   Experimental evidence

Hermans, Ormel, Besselaar, and Van Hell (2011) undertook a series of phoneme monitoring experiments to show that the bilingual's language production system can operate in different language activation states or modes. They asked Dutch-English bilinguals to look at pictures on a computer screen followed by a letter representing a phoneme and to decide whether the phoneme was part of the English name of the picture presented just before (this task had been used previously by Colomé, 2001). There were three possibilities. First, the phoneme could be part of the English name of the picture. For example, /b/ or /t/ are phonemes of the word "bottle" corresponding to the picture of a bottle presented on the screen. The answer would be "yes" therefore (they called this the affirmative condition). Second, the phoneme could be the first consonant of the Dutch name of the picture being presented (e.g., /f/ is part of "fles," the Dutch translation equivalent of "bottle"). Here the answer would be "no" (they called this the cross-language condition). And finally, the phoneme could be part of neither the English nor the Dutch name (e.g., /p/ is not part of "bottle" or "fles"). They called this the unrelated condition. In the three experiments, the authors were particularly interested in how participants fared in these two latter conditions.

The pictures were divided up into two categories: half the pictures were used in the experimental condition where there was an English name and a noncognate translation equivalent in Dutch. Examples are: "bottle" ("fles" in Dutch); "pillow" ("kussen" in Dutch), and so on. The other half were used in the filler condition. It is in this condition that the three experiments differ from one another. In the first experiment, all the filler pictures had noncognate names in Dutch and English. (The authors define cognates as translation equivalents that have similar orthographic and phonological forms in both languages, e.g., English "apple" and Dutch "appel"). Examples of noncognates would be English "money" and Dutch "geld"; English "present" and Dutch "cadeau," etc. The results the authors obtained showed that there was no difference between the cross-language condition and the unrelated condition, be it in response latencies or in accuracy scores. They concluded from this that the Dutch name of the picture is *not* phonologically activated during phoneme monitoring in the bilinguals' second language.

In the second experiment, all the authors did was to change the filler stimuli. The fillers now contained cognate names in English and Dutch, such as "moon" and

Dutch "maan," "mouse" and "muis," and so on. (The authors noted that this is what occurred in the Colomé [2001] study although it was not overtly reported in the article.) This time the two critical conditions (cross-linguistic and unrelated) did produce different response latencies and accuracy scores. It took the participants more time to do the task in the cross-linguistic condition than in the unrelated condition, and they were also less accurate. In their third experiment, the authors simply replicated the second experiment with 25% of the fillers that were cognate and 75% that were not cognate. They obtained results similar to those of the second experiment.

Based on these findings, the authors concluded that the bilingual language production system is indeed dynamic and that it can operate in different activation states depending on a number of factors, one of which is the composition of the stimulus list (see the list in Section 3.3.2 for additional factors). If the list contains filler pictures that have noncognate names exclusively, then the Dutch names of the pictures are not activated when monitoring takes place in English (see the first experiment in this study). However, when the stimulus list contains filler pictures that do have cognate names in Dutch and English (this was the case in the second and third experiments), then the phonological representations of the Dutch picture names are activated and they slow down the response regarding the presence of a phoneme in the English name.

Additional evidence that the bilingual production system can operate in different activation states comes from language mode studies. Grosjean (2008) describes three such studies that show the reality of the language mode concept and the fact that a bilingual speaker can be in different language activation states. In these studies, bilingual participants retold stories and/or described cartoons to interlocutors. Sometimes these interlocutors were present and at other times they were absent but would be listening to the tapes in a "telephone chain" study. The interlocutors were either monolinguals or very poor speakers of one of the languages being used, or were bilinguals of different types.

In the first study, French-English bilinguals were tested in French and two factors were manipulated – the topic of the stories and cartoons, and the interlocutor. As concerns the topic, the situations were either typically French or typically American. Since the stories were told in French, the ones depicting American situations contained code-switches. As for the three interlocutors being addressed (they were absent in this study), the first person ("French") was a newcomer to the United States and did not speak English well, the second person ("Bilingual A") taught French and worked for a French government agency (he did not code-switch much in his everyday life), and the third person ("Bilingual B") worked for an American firm, used both languages daily, and often intermingled them. The cartoons were described, and the stories retold, to each interlocutor and the amount of English and French syllables were tabulated, as were the hesitation phenomena.

The results showed that the participants changed their production behavior as a function of the variables tested. First, typically American stories and cartoons produced about ten times more English in the form of code-switches and borrowings than their French counterparts (recall that the base language was French). Second, depending on whom they were speaking to, the participants varied the amount of English and French they spoke and they also varied their hesitation phenomena. Thus, the productions for Bilingual B contained the most code-switches and borrowings and the least amount of hesitation phenomena (both languages were possible and so the participants did not have to hesitate very much). The productions aimed at the "French" interlocutor contained the least amount of code-switches and borrowings and the most hesitation phenomena. The latter reflected the participants' search for words and expressions normally said in English but that had to be said in French to the interlocutor in question. As for Bilingual A, who was considered a language purist by the participants, the values were situated in between those of the other two interlocutors. In sum, both the topic and the interlocutor had an impact on the level of activation of the guest language (English in this case) and hence on the amount of code-switching and borrowing that took place.

The second study, conducted by Weil (1990; see Grosjean, 2008, for a full account), replicated the first study but this time Swiss German-French bilinguals addressed three interlocutors whose knowledge of Swiss German ranged from minimal to totally fluent. Since the stories to be retold were in Swiss German, with or without French code-switches, the interesting finding was that the participants changed base language with two of the three interlocutors. In other words, they retold the stories in French, and not Swiss German, so as to resolve the problem of addressing someone in the "wrong language," either because the person could not understand it or because they preferred the other language. As for the third study, conducted by Caixeta (2003) and also summarized in Grosjean (2008), it involved Brazilian Portuguese-French bilinguals whose knowledge of French was either intermediate or advanced. They spoke in French to two interlocutors who were present, a French monolingual and a Portuguese-French bilingual. The results obtained showed not only that there were more code-switches and borrowings (guest elements) in the bilingual mode (i.e., when the bilingual interlocutor was addressed) but also that the participants who had an intermediary level of French produced more guest elements than the participants with an advanced proficiency. This confirmed that dominant bilinguals speaking their weaker language will code-switch and borrow more than bilinguals who have a good knowledge of the language.

This last study can be compared to the one conducted by Fokke, De Ruyter de Wildt, Spanjers, and Van Hell (2007). Two groups of Dutch participants of different English proficiencies (less proficient and proficient) saw cartoons in three different conditions. In the monolingual condition, the cartoon was in Dutch and the experimenter only spoke Dutch to them. In the intermediate condition, the cartoon was also in Dutch but the experimenter switched from time to time to English. Finally, in the bilingual condition, the participants saw the English version of the cartoon and the experimenter also code-switched with them. The participants were asked to retell the cartoon in Dutch. The results were similar to those in the studies already mentioned: No code-switches into English in the monolingual condition, some code-switches in the intermediate condition, and practically a doubling of the amount of code-switching in the bilingual condition. However, the authors did not find any difference in the amount of code-switching produced by the two proficiency groups. This may seem surprising at first when compared with the results obtained in the Brazilian Portuguese-French study. However, in that study the participants were speaking in their second language (French) and if their knowledge of it was not sufficient, then they would code-switch, especially if the interlocutor was bilingual. In the Dutch study, the participants were asked to retell the cartoon in Dutch, their first and dominant language. There was much less need therefore to code-switch into English for a word or an expression. In sum, the language that is spoken, and how well one knows it, is a crucial factor in its level of activation and hence in the amount of code-switching that may occur.

3.3.2   Factors that affect the activation of languages

As we have seen, there is now ample proof that language production in bilinguals is a dynamic process and that the languages known, but not being used, can be at various levels of activation. This, in turn, will have an impact on the internal processes that precede the actual output as well as on the amount of code-switching and borrowing that may take place. There are a number of factors that can affect the activation level of a language that is not being used at a particular point in time, as listed here:

1. *Language involved* – proficiency; dominant or non dominant status (general and in specific domains); similarity with language being used; age and manner of acquisition (e.g., learning context); recency of use; automaticity of processing
2. *General context* – bilingual environment; presence of speakers of the language
3. *Context of the study* – study relating to bilingualism; laboratory doing bilingual research; reports from other participants; use of two languages in the session
4. *Other people present* – bilingual interlocutor; bilingual experimenter
5. *Topic* – of stimuli (sentences, discourse); of discussion
6. *Stimuli* – contain cognates/homographs/homophones; contain code-switches/borrowings
7. *Experimental task* – calls on both languages; bilingual instructions

These factors are quite straightforward and will not be discussed further here (some of them have appeared in the preceding sections of this chapter). Many of them have been mentioned by researchers worried about confounding variables in studies aimed at the question of whether monolingual language production in bilinguals is language selective or not (e.g., De Bot, 2004; Costa, La Heij, & Navarette, 2006; Grosjean, 1998; Hanulová, Davidson, & Indefrey, 2011; Kroll, Bobb, & Wodniecka, 2006; Wu and Thierry, 2010). What is important is that this list is kept in mind in future research and when consulting studies, in various subdomains of bilingual research, in order to ascertain if some of these factors could help explain the results obtained, in addition to, or in lieu of, the variables that were explicitly manipulated.

3.4   Producing Bilingual Speech

Much research in bilingual language production has concentrated on how bilinguals produce bilingual speech, in particular speech that involves a change of the base language and/or speech that contains code-switches. In this section we will first examine whether switching languages takes time, then we will look at how the production of code-switches is influenced by structural constraints as well as by dialogue partners, and finally we will examine whether the phonetics of code-switches is affected by the main language being spoken.

3.4.1   Does language switching take time?

One of the longest studied topics in bilingual speech production concerns the time it takes to switch from one language to the other. Close to half a century ago, Kolers (1966) asked bilingual participants to read passages aloud that contained a mixture of English and French and he determined that each switch took them between 0.3 and 0.5 seconds. A few years later, Macnamara, Krauthammer, and Bolgar (1968) examined just the production side of things by asking participants to read numerals in one language or the other. They found that when bilinguals were forced to switch languages, it took them about half the time found by Kolers. The authors concluded that language switching takes an observable amount of time but that this is not usually reflected in natural discourse because bilinguals anticipate a switch before actually changing languages.

Despite this important conclusion (spontaneous bilingual speech containing code-switches takes no extra time than monolingual speech), the topic of language switching in the laboratory has retained the interest of cognitive psychologists over the years. Thus, Meuter and Allport (1999) asked bilingual participants to read aloud, as fast and as accurately as possible, lists of numerals in either their first or their second language. The numerals appeared in the center of either a blue or yellow rectangle, the color telling them in which language to name the numerals. The authors showed once again that switching takes time (as compared to no switching) but, more interestingly, they found that the switching cost was larger when switching to the dominant L1 from the weaker L2 than the other way around. The reason they gave for this "paradoxical asymmetry" is that the L1 is more strongly inhibited in such tasks and overcoming it takes time. Meuter (2001) found similar results in bilingual discourse. Spanish-English bilinguals took part in 1-to-1 conversations and had to change topic and language every 3 minutes. She found that the time to initiate speech was significantly increased for L1 but this asymmetry

disappeared about 10 seconds into the exchange, re-establishing the normal dominance pattern.

Language switching was then taken up by Costa and his colleagues in two studies.
Costa and Santesban (2004) first replicated the switching cost in L2 speakers using
a slightly different approach. They asked Spanish speakers who had been learning
Catalan for about 1.5 years as well as native speakers of Korean who had been learning Spanish for an average of 4 years to name pictures (and not numbers) and to
respond in the language that was cued by the color in which the picture appeared.
They too found a greater L1 switching cost. They then studied whether the same
switching cost would be found in highly proficient bilinguals (recall that the preceding studies had used bilinguals who were dominant in one language). They tested
native speakers of Spanish who were also highly proficient speakers of Catalan and
they found, this time, equal switching costs in L1 and L2. The authors suggested
that highly proficient bilinguals may have developed a different sort of selection
mechanism that does not require inhibition of the nonresponse language for the
successful selection of words in the intended language, whatever the language in
question. To test this, they examined whether these bilinguals would show an asymmetrical cost or not when asked to perform a switching task in their L1 and in their
much weaker L3 (English). They found that here, too, there was no asymmetrical
cost, leading them to believe that these bilinguals had indeed developed a different
selection mechanism.

Costa, Santesban, and Ivanova (2006) pursued this research and kept obtaining
the same result even though they manipulated the similarity between languages
(e.g., Spanish and Basque vs. Spanish and Catalan), age of acquisition of the L2
(early or late), the absence of L1 in the study (they examined switching between an
L2 and an L3), etc. The only asymmetry they found was when they examined
switching between L3 (English studied for 8 years in school) and L4 (French studied
for just 1 year). They concluded that this result might be revealing certain limits in
the cognitive flexibility of the highly proficient bilinguals' selection mechanism. It
might not be available when the switching task does not involve one of the bilinguals' stronger languages.

High proficiency in at least two languages may thus alter the switching-cost
pattern but a far more prosaic variable may also be a factor – the preparation time
participants are given before making their response. Verhoef, Roelofs, and Chwilla
(2009) asked Dutch-English dominant bilinguals to name the pictures they showed
them. To indicate which language they should make their response in, they used a
symbolic cue (a Dutch or an English flag). They varied the interval time between
the presentation of the cue and the presentation of the picture, either 500 ms or
1250 ms. What they found was that for the short interval, the switch costs were
asymmetrical (larger for L1 than for L2) but for the long interval, the switch costs
were symmetrical. They therefore proposed that the switch-cost pattern is not proficiency dependent, as suggested by Costa and his collaborators, since they obtained
both asymmetrical and symmetrical switch-cost patterns with the same group of
language-dominant bilinguals. Rather, they suggested that the larger switch cost for

L1 in dominant bilinguals compared to L2 rests on the fact that L1 repeat trials (i.e., successive trials where participants are naming pictures in L1 only) are disproportionately fast, since the nontarget L2 is not competing for selection (they call this the L1-repeat-benefit hypothesis). In balanced bilinguals, on the other hand, both languages are well established and they compete for selection, even on repeat trials. Therefore, balanced bilinguals do not show the L1-repeat-benefit.

We should end this section with some words of caution expressed by various researchers. For example, Hanulová, Davidson, and Indefrey (2011) write that mixing two languages within a short time span, on an external cue given by the experimenter, is a somewhat nonstandard situation, even for bilinguals. And Gollan and Ferreira (2009) state that because bilinguals named pictures out of context, it remains possible that naturally occurring language switches are not costly because grammatical constraints could lessen the cost of switching.

3.4.2   Code-switching is rule governed

As we saw in Chapter 1, Section 1.5, code-switching has been widely studied by linguists over the years (for an overview, see Gardner-Chloros, 2009) but much less so by psycholinguists (the discussion in 3.4.1 concerned language switching and not code-switching as such). In this section, as well as in Section 3.4.3, we will report on studies that have examined the process of code-switching using the methodologies employed by psycholinguists.

In a study that augurs well for the future of experimental work in this domain, Kootstra, Van Hell, and Dijkstra (2010) investigated how the constraints that govern code-switching play a role in its production. They also showed how code-switching can be influenced by a dialogue partner. The constraint they focused on is known as the "equivalence constraint" (Poplack, 1980) and it states that code-switches will tend to occur at points in discourse where the juxtaposition of L1 and L2 elements does not violate a syntactic rule in either language, i.e., at points around which the surface structures of the two languages map onto each other. In other words, the word order immediately before and immediately after a switch point must be possible in both languages; if this is not so, a switch cannot occur. An example taken from Poplack will clarify this constraint. We first present the same sentence in each of the two languages, English and Spanish, and then the actual code-switched sentence that was produced by a bilingual:

English: I/told him/that/so that/he/would bring it/fast.
Spanish: (Yo)/le dije/eso/pa'que/(él)/la trajera/ligero.
Code-switch: I told him that *pa'que la trajera ligero.*

The boundaries indicated by slashes in the monolingual sentences are permissible switch points and, as we see below them, a switch did take place at one of these boundaries. Switching could also have occurred after "I," after "him," or after "that."

However, because the English segment "told him" is different from the Spanish segment "le dije," a code-switch cannot occur after "told." This is also the case for "would bring it," where the equivalence constraint rules out a switch after "would" and after "bring."

Kootstra, Van Hell, and Dijkstra studied the impact of the equivalence constraint on Dutch-English code-switching in transitive sentences. English has only one possible word order (SVO: Subject–Verb–Object), whereas Dutch has three (SVO, SOV, and VSO), depending on the sentence context. Thus, in the following three examples, the English sentence keeps to the SVO order whereas in Dutch three different orders are used (they are in italics):

(1) English SVO: Everyone is happy, because John kisses Mary
    Dutch SVO: Ledereen is blij, want *Jan kust Marie*
(2) English SVO: Peter points at a picture, on which John kisses Mary
    Dutch SOV: Peter wijst naar een plaatje, waarop *Jan Marie kust*
(3) English SVO: Yesterday John kissed Mary
    Dutch VSO: Gisteren *kuste Jan Marie*

The equivalence constraint predicts that Dutch–English bilinguals will avoid code-switching when producing a sentence with SOV or VSO structures; code-switching should be largely restricted to sentences with the (shared) SVO structure. In Experiment 2 of their study, Kootstra, Van Hell, and Dijkstra told their Dutch-English bilingual participants, who reported that they code-switched in their daily lives, that they had to read aloud Dutch sentence fragments on a computer screen (like the examples given above, but not including the words in italic) and to complete them by describing the picture depicted below each fragment. When doing so, they had to use at least one English word when the picture's background color was green (switching required condition) and at least one Dutch word when the background was red (no switching required condition). As in natural code-switching, they could switch at any sentence position they wanted, as often as they wanted, and use whatever word order they wanted. Note, however, that the sentence fragments cued the SVO, SOV, or VSO word orders in Dutch, and thus sometimes created word order conflicts between Dutch and English, namely when the fragments cued SOV or VSO.

The results showed that the participants generally followed the word order cue when no code-switching was required. Thus when SVO was cued in the lead-in fragment, the proportion of SVO in the description was 82%. When SOV was cued, SOV was produced 84% of the time, and when VSO was cued, VSO was used 80% of the time. However, when the participants had to switch from Dutch to English in their description, they invariably preferred to use the SVO structure in their output, whether they had read aloud the SVO fragment (SVO response 100% of the time) or the SOV fragment (SVO response 85% of the time) or the VSO fragment (SVO response 86% of the time). This is a clear indication that code-switching is governed by constraints and that speakers adhere to them when producing code-switches.

The second part of the Kootstra, Van Hell, and Dijkstra study examined the role of a dialogue partner (whom they called a "confederate") during the code-switching task. Their theoretical base was Pickering and Garrod's (2004) Interactive Alignment Model, which states that dialogue is a cooperative process in which dialogue partners build on each other's language and copy elements of each other's expressions. Basically, the linguistic representations of the partners are coupled at all levels of linguistic processing, all the way from the pragmatic level (which they call the situation level) to the phonological level. The question asked was whether, when code-switching, bilinguals adapt their syntactic choices to those of their dialogue partner.

The same materials were used but this time the task was embedded in a dialogue game where the confederate and the participant took turns describing a picture and selecting the matching picture. The confederate was scripted to use word orders that are either shared between Dutch and English (SVO) or specific to Dutch (SOV and VSO) and to code-switch at prescribed syntactic positions. The confederate thus primed both word order and the syntactic position of the switch. The results showed that when participants did not have to switch, and only used Dutch, they always used the word order cued by the lead-in fragment. However, when they had to switch, and use English in their picture description, the SVO order was still always used in the SVO condition but it was now used only half the time in the SOV and VSO conditions (recall that in the preceding experiment the SVO order was used 80% of the time or more in all conditions). The alignment might have been even greater had the confederate's lead-in sentences with code-switches always been grammatical. Unfortunately, many of the lead-ins were of the type, "Op dit plaatje…kicks the girl the horse," where the English part is definitely not grammatical, something the researchers recognize. That said, the general finding shows that the syntactic choice in code-switched dialogue is influenced by an interaction between the need for alignment and the need to respect code-switching constraints.

3.4.3   The phonetics of code-switching

Very few studies have examined how code-switches are actually produced at the phonetic level. We will describe two of them here. In the first, Grosjean and Miller (1994) asked whether there is a base-language effect in the production of code-switches. As we saw in Chapter 2, Section 2.3.1, there appears to be a momentary dominance of base-language units (phonemes, syllables, words) at code-switching boundaries in perception. This in turn can delay slightly the perception of units in the guest language. The authors asked themselves whether in speaking, the phonetic momentum of the base language carries over into the guest language and hence affects at least the beginning of code-switches. On the one hand, there might be some base-language influence at code-switch onsets (during the first phoneme or the first syllable) but on the other, given the flexibility of the production mechanism, a switch between languages might involve a total phonetic change, not only at the lexical level but also at the phonetic level.

In a first experiment, French-English bilinguals were asked to retell stories in English, in French with English code-switches, and then in French with no code-switches. Sprinkled throughout the stories were proper and common nouns that began with an unvoiced stop consonant and that were close homophones in the two languages, e.g., Tom, Carl, Paul, taxi, telephone (téléphone), etc. The researchers measured the voice onset time (VOT, i.e., the interval of time between the release of the stop and the onset of voicing) of the initial consonant of the monosyllabic proper nouns produced in the three conditions.

The results showed that the participants made a clear difference between English and French VOT values, as has been reported over the years. As for the English code-switch values, they were quite different from the French values and similar to the English values. Thus, it would appear that switching from one language to another involves a total change at the phonetic level.

In a second experiment, the authors asked themselves how immediate the change-over was in a code-switch. Could it be that bilinguals plan their code-switches ahead of time and start changing over to the phonetics of the guest language before reaching the onset of the code-switch? The shift could take place one or two words before, for example. As for going back to the base language, might it be done after the code-switch, during the word or words that follow? In order to examine the time course of code-switching, the authors tracked the phonetic shift from one language to another by means of a reading task. The bilingual participants were asked to read aloud sentences such as, "During the first few days, we'll tell him to copy Tom constantly," as well as the French version, "Pendant les premiers jours, il faudra qu'il copie Tom constamment." For the latter sentence, "Tom" was pronounced as a code-switch (in English therefore) or in French.

The authors examined the VOT values at three locations: the /k/ of "copy/copie," the onset of the stimulus word ("Tom" in the above sentence), and the /k/ at the beginning of "constantly/constamment." The results showed once again that for the stimulus words (Tom, Carl, Paul) the English and French values were very different and that the code-switching values were different from the French values and similar to the English values. As for the values of the initial consonant of "copy" and "constantly" in the sentences with code-switches, they showed absolutely no trace of the code-switch that was present in the sentence. The authors concluded that bilinguals do not start switching one or two words before the guest word and do not switch back to the base language during the words that follow.

In sum, the base language does not seem to have an impact on the production of code-switches, at least at the segmental level (but see a study by Grosjean and Soares, 1986, for the suprasegmental level). This is fortunate for bilingual listeners, as a clearly marked code-switch onset undoubtedly counterbalances, at least to some extent, the perceptual base-language effect (see Chapter 2, Section 2.3.1) and hence reduces the duration of the perceptual ambiguity.

What is interesting is that there might be some variability in how "clean" code-switches are depending on the bilingual speakers and the language they are switching into. This was shown by Bullock and Toribio (2009) who examined the VOT productions of three groups of English-Spanish bilingual participants when reading monolingual sentences in English and in Spanish as well as sentences that contained code-switches, either into Spanish (the beginning was in English) or into English (the beginning was in Spanish). The group that most closely resembled the one used by Grosjean and Miller (1994) were L1 Spanish bilinguals who had acquired English in their adolescence. In the sentences with code-switches where the base language was Spanish (in Grosjean and Miller it was French), the authors found very stable Spanish VOT values, with no difference with the monolingual Spanish values. This replicated Grosjean and Miller's results with a different language pair and different types of stimuli. However, when these same bilinguals switched into Spanish from an English base, there appeared to be a convergence toward Spanish several syllables before the switch, thereby showing some anticipation of the switch. The authors account for this by a possible lack of control of the English VOT in this condition.

As for the other two groups, the early bilingual group that had acquired both languages before the age of 5 performed the closest to monolingual-like norms in both languages, but the L1 English bilinguals who had acquired Spanish in their adolescence may have over-controlled their Spanish VOT and hence produced what seemed to be slightly Spanish-accented English before and at the switch site. In sum, the results revealed that bilinguals do maintain separate phonological categories in their two languages but that at times there may be a phonetic anticipation of a switch or a phonetic perseveration from a switch. Additional research is definitely needed in this area.

The phonetics of a language concerns not only its segmental elements but also the suprasegmental aspects known also as prosody. There is even less research on this aspect of code-switching but there does exist an intriguing pilot study that was conducted by Grosjean and Soares (1986; see also Grosjean, 2008). The authors examined the fundamental frequency (F0) of different-sized English switches – a clause, a coordinated clause, and a word – in French sentences. What they found is that when a code-switch occurs at an independent clause break, the prosody changes along with the segmental aspects and takes on the prosody of the guest language. For coordinated clauses, however, especially if they are short, the intonation contour remains characteristically that of the base language. As for switches involving individual words, they too have a base language contour.

Thus, unlike what is found, with some variation, at the segmental level, the prosody of code-switches does not always follow the pattern of the guest language. If the code-switch is short and is a minor syntactic unit, then it might well be integrated into the prosody of the base language. If, on the contrary, it is longer and is a more important syntactic unit, then it will carry the prosodic pattern of the guest language. This raises an interesting issue regarding the perception of code-switches (see Chapter 2, Section 2.3.2). Even though a speaker may have no accent in either language and the code-switches are clearly marked phonetically as belonging to the guest language, the listener may receive ambiguous information from the prosody. Thus, the segmental information heard by the listener may point one way, i.e., to the guest language, but the suprasegmental information may point the other way, i.e., toward the base language. This ambiguity, added to the basic base-language effect, may delay the processing of code-switches. To compound things, we should remember that many bilinguals may have an accent in their second language (and in their other languages, if they are multilingual). Thus, when they bring guest words or phrases from their second language into their first language, they will be code-switching "with an accent," and this can make the task of the listener even more difficult.

Finally, this whole research raises the question of how one wants to define a code-switch (see Chapter 1, Section 1.5.1). So far, researchers have talked of a complete shift to the other language for a word, a phrase, or a sentence. This appears to be true at the segmental level (at least for someone with no accent in either language) but, as we have just seen, it may not always be true at the prosodic level. One may therefore want to change the definition of a code-switch to "a complete *segmental* shift to the other language . . ." so as to take into account the lack of a shift in prosody in certain contexts.

Research Questions

1. Why is it that general models of speech production in bilinguals are so difficult to elaborate?
2. Take a factor or two from the list in Section 3.3.2 and think of a study that would show, in one experiment, selective language production in bilinguals and, in a second experiment, nonselective production. Use the Hermans, Ormel, Besselaar, and Van Hell (2011) study to help you.
3. What do the studies on delay in language switching in bilinguals tell us about everyday bilingual language activities such as changing base language and/or code-switching? How could this issue be studied in spontaneous language production?
4. Think of a study that would investigate prosodic features such as fundamental frequency in the production of code-switches and borrowing.

Further Readings

Costa, Albert & Santesteban, Mikel (eds). 2006. Lexical access in bilingual speech production. Special Issue of *Bilingualism: Language and Cognition* 9.

Grosjean, François. 2008. *Studying Bilinguals*. Oxford/New York: Oxford University Press.

Hermans, Daan, Ormel, Ellen, Besselaar, Ria, & Van Hell, Janet. 2011. Lexical activation in bilinguals' speech production is dynamic: How language ambiguous words can affect cross-language activation. *Language and Cognitive Processes* 26(10). 1687–1709.

Kootstra, Gerrit, Van Hell, Janet, & Dijkstra, Ton. 2010. Syntactic alignment and shared word order in code-switched sentence production: Evidence from bilingual monologue and dialogue. *Journal of Memory and Language* 63(2). 210–231.

References

Bialystok, Ellen, Craik, Fergus, Green, David, & Gollan, Tamar. 2009. Bilingual minds. *Psychological Science in the Public Interest* 10(3). 89–129.

Bullock, Barbara E. & Toribio, Almeida Jacqueline. 2009. How to hit a moving target: On the sociophonetics of code-switching. In Ludmilla Isurin, Donald Winford, & Kees de Bot (eds), *Interdisciplinary Approaches to Code-switching*, pp. 189–206. Amsterdam: John Benjamins.

Caixeta, Paulo. 2003. L'impact de la compétence linguistique du bilingue en L2 sur le mode langagier: une étude de production. Neuchâtel, Switzerland: Master's Thesis, Institute of Linguistics, Neuchâtel University.

Colomé, Angels. 2001. Lexical activation in bilinguals' speech production: Language-specific or language-independent? *Journal of Memory and Language* 45. 721–736.

Costa, Albert. 2005. Lexical access in bilingual production. In Judith Kroll & Annette de Groot (eds), *Handbook of Bilingualism: Psycholinguistic Approaches*, pp. 308–325. Oxford/New York: Oxford University Press.

Costa, Albert, La Heij, Wido, & Navarette, Eduardo. 2006. The dynamics of bilingual lexical access. *Bilingual: Language and Cognition* 9(2). 137–151.

Costa, Albert & Santesban, Mikel. 2004. Lexical access in bilingual speech production: Evidence from language switching in highly proficient bilinguals and L2 learners. *Journal of Memory and Language* 50. 491–511.

Costa, Albert, Santesban, Mikel & Ivanova, Iva. 2006. How do highly proficient bilinguals control their lexicalization process? Inhibitory and language-specific selection mechanisms are both functional. *Journal of Experimental Psychology: Learning, Memory and Cognition* 32(5). 1057–1074

De Bot, Kees. 1992. A bilingual production model: Levelt's "Speaking" model adapted. *Applied Linguistics* 13(1). 1–24.

De Bot, Kees. 2004. The multilingual lexicon: Modeling selection and control. *The International Journal of Multilingualism* 1(1). 17–32.

Dell, Gary. 1986. A spreading-activation theory of retrieval in sentence production. *Psychological Review* 93. 283–321.

Fokke, Joke, De Ruyter de Wildt, Imie, Spanjers, Ingrid, & Van Hell, Janet. 2007. Eliciting code-switches in Dutch classroom learners of English: The language mode continuum and the role of language proficiency. Poster presented at the 6th International Symposium of Bilingualism, Hamburg, Germany.

Gardner-Chloros, Penelope. 2009. *Code-switching*. Cambridge: Cambridge University Press.

Gollan, Tamar & Ferreira, Victor. 2009. Should I stay or should I switch? A cost-benefit analysis of voluntary language switching in young and aging bilinguals. *Journal of Experimental Psychology: Learning, Memory and Cognition* 35(3). 640–665.

Grosjean, François. 1998. Studying bilinguals: Methodological and conceptual issues. *Bilingualism: Language and Cognition* 1(2). 131–149.

Grosjean, François. 2008. *Studying Bilinguals.* Oxford/New York: Oxford University Press.

Grosjean, François & Miller, Joanne. 1994. Going in and out of languages: An example of bilingual flexibility. *Psychological Science* 5(4). 201–206.

Grosjean, Francois & Soares, Carlos. 1986. Processing mixed language: Some preliminary findings. In Joytsna Vaid (ed.), *Language Processing in Bilinguals: Psycholinguistic and Neuropsychological Perspectives*, pp. 145–179. Hillsdale, NJ: Lawrence Erlbaum.

Hanulová, Jana, Davidson, Douglas, & Indefrey, Peter. 2011. Where does the delay in L2 picture naming come from? Psycholinguistic and neurocognitive evidence on second language word production. *Language and Cognitive Processes* 26 (7). 902–934.

Harley, Trevor. 2008. *The Psychology of Language: From Data to Theory.* Hove/New York: Psychology Press.

Hermans, Daan, Bongaerts, Theo, De Bot, Kees, & Schreuder, Robert. 1998. Producing words in a foreign language: Can speakers prevent interference from their first language? *Bilingual: Language and Cognition* 1(1). 213–229.

Hermans, Daan, Ormel, Ellen, Besselaar, Ria, & Van Hell, Janet. 2011. Lexical activation in bilinguals' speech production is dynamic: How language ambiguous words can affect cross-language activation. *Language and Cognitive Processes* 26(10). 1687–1709.

Kolers, Paul. 1966. Reading and talking bilingually. *American Journal of Psychology* 3. 357–376.

Kootstra, Gerrit, Van Hell, Janet, & Dijkstra, Ton. 2009. Two speakers, one dialogue: An interactive alignment perspective on code-switching in bilingual speakers. In Ludmila Isurin, Donald Winford, & Kees de Bot (eds). *Multidisciplinary Approaches to Code-switching*, pp. 129–159. Amsterdam/Philadelphia: John Benjamins.

Kootstra, Gerrit, Van Hell, Janet, & Dijkstra, Ton. 2010. Syntactic alignment and shared word order in code-switched sentence production: Evidence from bilingual monologue and dialogue. *Journal of Memory and Language* 63(2). 210–231.

Kroll, Judith, Bobb, Susan, & Wodniecka, Zofia. 2006. Language selectivity is the exception, not the rule: Arguments against a fixed locus of language selection in bilingual speech. *Bilingualism: Language and Cognition* 9(2). 119–135.

La Heij, Wido. 2005. Selection processes in monolingual and bilingual lexical access. In Judith Kroll & Annette de Groot (eds), *Handbook of Bilingualism: Psycholinguistic Approaches*, pp. 289–307. Oxford/New York: Oxford University Press.

Levelt, Willem. 1989. *Speaking: From Intention to Articulation.* Cambridge, MA: MIT Press.

Levelt, Willem. 2000. Speech production. In Alan E. Kazdin (ed.), *Encyclopedia of Psychology*, pp. 432–433. Washington: APA and Oxford University Press.

Macnamara, John, Krauthammer, Marcel, & Bolgar, Marianne. 1968. Language switching in bilinguals as a function of stimulus and response uncertainty. *Journal of Experimental Psychology* 78. 208–215.

Meuter, Renata. 2001. Switch costs in bilingual discourse: An exploration of relativity in language proficiency. Poster presented at the Third International Symposium on Bilingualism, University of the West of England, April 2001.

Meuter, Renata & Allport, Alan. 1999. Bilingual language switching in naming: Asymmetrical costs of language selection. *Journal of Memory and Language* 40. 25–40.

Pickering, Martin & Garrod, Simon. 2004. Toward a mechanistic psychology of dialogue. *Behavioral and Brain Sciences* 27. 169–190.

Poplack, Shana. 1980. Sometimes I'll start a sentence in Spanish y termino en Español: Toward a typology of code-switching. *Linguistics* 18. 581–618.

Verhoef, Kim, Roelofs, Ardi, & Chwilla, Dorothee. 2009. Role of inhibition in language switching: Evidence from event-related brain potentials in overt picture naming. *Cognition* 110. 84–99.

Weil, Sonja. 1990. Choix de langue et alternance codique chez le bilingue en situations de communication diverses: une étude expérimentale. Basle, Switzerland: Master's Thesis, Institute of Romance Studies, Basle University.

Wu, Yan Jing & Thierry, Guillaume. 2010. Investigating bilingual processing: The neglected role of language processing contexts. *Frontiers in Psychology*, http://www.frontiersin.org/Language_Sciences/10.3389/fpsyg.2010.00178/abstract [accessed on-line July 4, 2012].

II
Written Language Processing

Chapter 4

Reading

Annette M.B. de Groot

Although the speed with which a reader absorbed in an engrossing book turns page after page suggests otherwise, reading (like listening; see Chapter 2) is a complex skill that involves many different constituent processes that together operate on an extensive and multifaceted knowledge base. The knowledge base that enables reading consists of memory units that represent the written and spoken forms of complete words and their constituent parts. In addition, it consists of memory units that represent the meanings of words, grammatical and general world knowledge, and knowledge regarding reading strategies. The processes operating on this knowledge base include letter and word recognition, grammatical analysis, and text integration. Fluent readers perform these processes in a highly effective, fine-tuned orchestration that enables them to process around four words per second. Considering the fact that their vocabularies consist of tens of thousands of words, this is an amazing feat. Apparently, on average each quarter of a second they manage to make the proper connection between a printed word form and its representation in this vast memory store, meanwhile retrieving each word's meaning and performing the higher-level operations of grammatical analysis and text integration. This feat is all the more impressive in the case of bilinguals and multilinguals literate in more than one language. Knowing and using more than one language implies double (or triple, or quadruple etc.) sets of the knowledge units of the types distinguished above. Having multiple sets of knowledge units in memory plausibly implies noisier processing because not only units belonging to the currently targeted language but also those of the contextually inappropriate one(s) may respond to the input.

The aim of this chapter is to introduce the reader to psycholinguistic studies on bilingual reading and the insights that have emerged from them. Following Section 4.1, which presents a general outline of the reading process, Sections 4.2 and 4.3 discuss visual word recognition in bilinguals. Because reading is about reconstructing the message contained by the text and much of this message is communicated by the text's words, word recognition is arguably reading's most central constituent

The Psycholinguistics of Bilingualism, First Edition. François Grosjean and Ping Li.
© 2013 Blackwell Publishing Ltd with the exceptions of Chapter 1, Chapter 2, Chapter 3, Chapter 7, Chapter 10 © 2013 François Grosjean and Ping Li. Published 2013 by Blackwell Publishing Ltd.

process. A basic idea in Sections 4.1 through 4.3 is the conception of mental process-ing during reading as the activation of memory units that store information relevant to reading. The main question addressed in Sections 4.2 and 4.3 are the following: If bilinguals encounter a written word, is the ensuing activation in the memory system – which contains two linguistic subsystems – restricted to the contextually appropriate subsystem or does coactivation occur in the contextually inappropriate subsystem, even when the input is monolingual? In agreement with common con-vention, the contextually appropriate and inappropriate language subsystems will be referred to as the "target language" and the "nontarget language," respectively. Section 4.2 presents the results of various types of studies that examined this question, while Section 4.3 presents a couple of models of bilingual visual word recognition that have been developed to account for the results obtained in these studies. Finally, Section 4.4 discusses sentence processing in bilinguals. Specifically, it poses the question of how bilingual readers resolve a particular type of syntactic ambiguity and how they process semantic and syntactic anomalies in sentences.

4.1   An Outline of the Reading Process

As mentioned, a core component of the reading process is word recognition. Word recognition is the outcome of activation dynamics in "sublexical" and "lexical" memory units in the mental lexicon, the component of long-term memory that stores word knowledge. Sublexical memory units represent units smaller than the word, such as visual features and letters, while lexical memory units represent whole words. When the reader sees a word, the memory representations of its con-stituent parts are activated first and then send their activation on to higher-level representations in the word-recognition system. The activation is transmitted along connections formed between these various types of memory representations during past reading practice. This transmission of activation along memory connections is usually called "spreading activation." Plausibly, common "subsyllabic" clusters of letters (i.e., letter clusters smaller than a syllable) and whole syllables are also rep-resented as such in the recognition system and activated when the reader encounters them in print, through spreading activation from lower representation levels. In their turn, all of these activated sublexical "orthographical" memory representations ("orthographical" because we are dealing with units that represent script or "orthog-raphy" here, not speech) activate the corresponding sublexical phonological memory representations, which represent their sounds (e.g., Frost, 1998). The moment the activation in a lexical memory unit (usually called a "lexical representation" or "word representation") surpasses some critical level, called the "recognition thresh-old," the encountered word is recognized. At this moment, the further information associated with this word, among which are its meaning and syntactic specifications, becomes available for further processing.

The meaning of a sentence is not simply the aggregate of the meanings of all the words it contains and sentence comprehension therefore entails more than just assembling the meanings rendered available by the process of word recognition expounded above. The vast majority of all words have more than one meaning and writers (and speakers) have only one of these in mind when using a particular word in a specific linguistic expression. Therefore, in reconstructing the meaning of a written sentence, for every word that it contains the reader must select the contextually appropriate meaning and suppress the contextually inappropriate ones (assuming that multiple meanings automatically become available upon word recognition; this in itself is a debatable issue; see Simpson, 1994). The selected meanings then have to be integrated during sentence comprehension. The grammar of a sentence also contributes to its meaning ("The rat attacked the weasel" means something different from "The weasel attacked the rat.") So in assigning meaning to a sentence, grammatical analysis, or "parsing," must also take place. During parsing the grammatical structure of the sentence is uncovered and the constituent parts are identified as subject, object, verb, and so on. Grammatical analysis is driven by the syntactic information that is stored in word representations and becomes available upon word recognition.

While all these constituent processes take place, a mental representation of the prior text must be kept in memory and an understanding of the text part that is currently focused on must be integrated with this text representation, thus extending it. Among various operations that take place during this integration process, anaphora – words that refer to persons and things expressed before, such as "he" and "they" – must be resolved, that is, the reader must locate their antecedents in the text representation stored in memory. A consultation of the mental text representation is also required to connect noun phrases that start with a definite article with their antecedent. This is because the use of the definite (instead of the indefinite) article signals that the person or entity mentioned next has been introduced in an earlier text portion and must therefore already be represented in the stored text representation.

To conclude this brief outline of the types of mental operations a reader is involved in while enjoying the engrossing book mentioned in the introduction, a final process to mention is the retrieval of "world knowledge," or "background knowledge," from memory. It is a well-known fact that a text is like an iceberg, with only a portion of the message it aims to convey explicitly contained by the text, the rest of its meaning only implied. The authors of a good text have anticipated their audience, making an assessment about what they are likely to know already and then deciding what information to provide explicitly and what to take for granted. Text comprehension therefore requires that the information that *is* there triggers the readers to access their general knowledge store and retrieve the information that fills in the textual gaps.

To summarize, reading involves: (1) the activation of different types of sublexical memory units, both orthographic ones and, via these, the corresponding phonological units; (2) the activation of word (or "lexical") representations beyond some critical level, at which point the word's meaning and syntactic information become available; (3) sentence comprehension processes during which the meaning of the sentence is assembled from (parts of) the meanings of the words it contains, the outcome of parsing procedures, and background knowledge; (4) the construction of a mental text representation that must be updated continuously and that enables the reader to resolve anaphora, among other things.

This outline of the reading process, complex as it already is, is still a simplification of the full process because it ignores the fact that many people master more than one language. As mentioned, knowing and using more than one language plausibly implies noisier processing operations due to parallel activation in the two or more language subsystems. Section 4.2 reviews studies that examine the occurrence of such parallel activation during word recognition in bilinguals. The occurrence of coactivation of elements of the nontarget language during word recognition is known as "language-nonselective word recognition." Selective activation of knowledge units belonging to the target language during word recognition is known as "language-selective word recognition."

4.2   Word Recognition in Bilinguals

In trying to find out whether bilingual visual word recognition is language selective or language nonselective, many researchers have examined the effects of form and meaning similarity between words in a bilingual's two languages on word recognition. This approach has led to the frequent use of three types of word stimuli in the pertinent studies: "interlexical homographs," "interlexical neighbors," and "cognates." Interlexical homographs (henceforth also simply called "homographs") are words that exist in two languages but have totally different meanings in these languages. In other words, they share form but not meaning between a pair of languages. They are like ambiguous words within a language, where one and the same form has two completely distinct meanings (e.g., "bank" in English, which means a financial institution or an embankment). Interlexical neighbors (henceforth also: "neighbors") are like interlexical homographs, except that the forms of interlexical neighbors overlap largely but not completely between the languages (e.g., Dutch "mand," *basket*, is an interlexical neighbor of English "sand"). Finally, cognates are words that share both (orthographic and/or phonological) form and meaning between a pair of languages (although not necessarily completely). Phrased differently, a pair of cognate words is a translation pair with similar forms (e.g., the Dutch-English pair "appel-apple"). In this section evidence of language-(non)selective bilingual word recognition as obtained in experiments using these three types of stimuli will be presented. In addition, some evidence of language-nonselective phonological activation during bilingual word recognition will be presented.

4.2.1   Interlexical homograph studies

Beauvillain and Grainger (1987) were among the first to study the processing of interlexical homographs in bilinguals. They used a version of the "lexical-decision" task that is often used in word-recognition research. In a lexical-decision task the participants are presented with letter strings on a screen, one string at a time, and have to decide for each of these whether or not it is a word. The participants notify their decision by pressing a "yes" or a "no" button. The nonword stimuli are typically "pseudowords," that is, letter strings that obey the orthography of the target language and thus only differ from words in that they lack meaning (e.g., "plenk" or "flup" are English-like pseudowords). In a version of this task called "primed lexical decision," prior to the presentation of the target (the word to which the participant must respond) a "prime" word is presented and the effect of the prime on target processing is measured. A common finding is that a target that is semantically related to the preceding prime (e.g., prime: "flower"; target: "tree") is responded to faster than a target that follows an unrelated prime (prime: "power"; target: "tree"). This "priming effect" is often attributed to a process of activation spreading along a connection between the representations of prime and target in the mental lexicon that speeds up the recognition of the target word as a result of pre-activation: The moment the target is presented, less activation still has to be accumulated in its representation for the recognition threshold to be exceeded.

Beauvillain and Grainger (1987) used a cross-language version of this primed lexical-decision task. They presented English-French bilinguals with stimulus pairs, each consisting of a French prime word and an English target word (or an English-like pseudoword), prime and target appearing successively on a screen. The participants were instructed to read the prime and to perform a lexical decision on the target. Most of the primes were exclusively French words, but some were words in both French and English; that is, they were French-English interlexical homographs (such as "coin," meaning *corner* in French). The question of interest was whether the homograph's English meaning would be activated in addition to its French meaning, despite the fact that the participants were told that all primes were words in French. Such would prove to be the case if a target semantically related to the prime's English meaning (e.g., the target "money" following the prime "coin") was responded to faster than when the same target followed a non-homographic control prime (say French "chien," *dog*). Such a priming effect indeed occurred, but only when the interval between prime and target was short (150 ms), not when it was longer (750 ms). These findings suggest that, even though the majority of the primes were only words in French, both meanings of the homographic primes were initially activated and only later was the contextually inappropriate English meaning suppressed. In other words, under the specific circumstances of this experiment, bilingual word recognition was language nonselective.

The data pattern obtained by Beauvillain and Grainger (1987) does not suffice, however, to reject a language-selective account of bilingual word recognition. As mentioned, while the target language in this experiment was English, all the primes were French words. With the experimental materials thus containing words from both of the participants' languages, it is hardly surprising that both language sub-systems were activated. In terms of Grosjean's "language-mode theory" (Grosjean 1997, 2001; see also Chapter 1), which assumes differential activation states of a bilingual's language system depending upon specific characteristics of the communicative setting, the dual-language nature of the stimulus materials in Beauvillain and Grainger's experiment likely put the participants in a "bilingual mode," where both language subsystems are activated.

A stronger test of language-selective vs. language-nonselective bilingual word recognition would involve the presentation of stimulus materials from only one of the bilinguals' two languages (in contextual circumstances that are as unilingual as possible; Grosjean, 1998; Wu & Thierry, 2010). In many of the more recent interlexical-homograph studies this research strategy was adopted, the question being whether, with all the stimulus materials in one language, the other language might nevertheless be activated. In most of these studies the lexical-decision task was used, while a couple of them used the "word-naming" task. In a word-naming task the participants simply read printed words aloud and response times and accuracy are registered.

In a subset of these unilingual studies the priming methodology was used, but with primes and targets now in one and the same language (although it should be kept in mind that homographs belong to two languages). In some of these priming studies (e.g., Kerkhofs, Dijkstra, Chwilla, & De Bruijn, 2006) the prime word preceding a target was always an isolated word, as in Beauvillain and Grainger (1987). In other priming studies the prime word was embedded in a sentence context (e.g., Elston-Güttler, Gunter, & Kotz, 2005). Because words are not normally encountered in isolation but as part of larger linguistic structures such as sentences and paragraphs, this latter procedure resembles natural language processing more closely than the former.

However, the majority of the unilingual studies did not use the priming methodology. Instead, on each trial the participants were presented with an unprimed single word (or pseudoword) as the target (e.g., De Groot, Delmaar, & Lupker, 2000, Experiments 2 and 3; Dijkstra, Van Jaarsveld, & Ten Brinke, 1998). The critical targets were either interlexical homographs or non-homographic control words and the response times and error rates in these two conditions were compared. A large number of non-homographic filler targets are typically added to the critical targets. If an interlexical homograph only gives rise to activation in the contextually appropriate language subsystem, homographs and non-homographic controls should be processed equally fast (and produce equally as many errors). On the other hand, if a homograph gives rise to activation in both language subsystems, a difference in response times (and possibly also in error rates) between homographs and non-homographic controls should show up. In other words, the occurrence of a "homograph effect" (i.e., a difference in response times and/or error rates between homographs and control words) would suggest that bilingual word recognition is language nonselective whereas the non-occurrence of such an effect would suggest that it can also be language selective.

In some of these unprimed lexical-decision experiments, the participants were instructed to give a "yes" response if the presented letter string was a word, irrespective of the language to which the word belonged, and to give a "no" response if the letter string was not a word in either of their two languages. This task version is known as "language-neutral" (or "generalized") lexical decision. In other experiments the participants were instructed to give a "yes" response if the presented stimulus was a word in one of their languages (specified beforehand) and to give a "no" response if not. This version of the task is known as "language-specific" lexical decision. In some of the latter type of experiments, language-specific performance was forced upon the subjects by the inclusion of a relatively small number of non-homographic words from the nontarget language that had to be treated as nonwords (i.e., they required a "no" response). Without the inclusion of such "nonwords," the participants may be tempted to reconfigure the task as if it concerned its language-neutral version instead, which would impact on the way interlexical homographs are processed: In language-neutral lexical decision the correct response to homographs ("yes") may be based on the homograph making contact with either one of its lexical representations, ignoring language membership, while in language-specific lexical decision the response must be based on the homograph making contact with its lexical representation in the target language. The inclusion of non-homographic words that belong to the nontarget language probably prevents the use of the language-neutral processing strategy because this strategy would lead to errors on these words (a "yes" response where a "no" response is required). But, of course, an unfortunate consequence of the inclusion of some words from the nontarget language as nonwords is that the experiment is not completely unilingual after all.

In the majority of the lexical-decision studies in which the homographs were presented in isolation a homograph effect was obtained. The task version that was used determined the *direction* of this effect, with language-neutral lexical decision typically resulting in faster response times to homographs than to controls and language-specific lexical decision resulting in slower processing of the homographs. The *size* of the effect depended upon the relative frequency of the homograph in the two languages in combination with the task version used: The effect was especially large when the participants performed language-specific lexical decision and the homograph was more frequent in the nontarget language than in the target language. Figure 4.1 illustrates this pattern of results with data from De Groot *et al.* (2000). These data were obtained in an experiment in which one group of Dutch-English bilinguals (with native Dutch slightly stronger than L2 English) performed language-specific lexical decision with Dutch as the target language and a second group performed this task with English as the target language. The inclusion of a small number of "nonwords" that were in fact words from the nontarget language forced the participants to use the requested language-specific processing strategy. As shown, in both language conditions the (inhibitory) homograph effect was substantially larger when the homograph's less frequent meaning was targeted (Condition LF) than when its more frequent meaning was targeted (Condition HF).

These homograph effects are thought to indicate that bilingual word recognition is language nonselective. In a few of these studies, however, no homograph effect

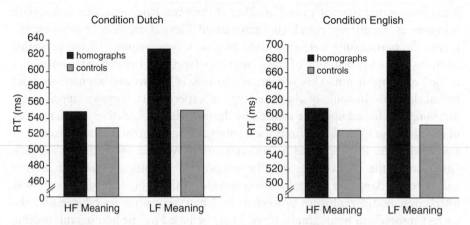

Figure 4.1: Mean lexical decision response time (RT) as a function of language (Dutch, English), stimulus type (homograph, control), and the frequency (high, low) of homographs in the participants' two languages. Based on De Groot, Delmaar, and Lupker, 2000.

was obtained, especially when the participants performed language-specific lexical decision and none of the nonwords was a word in the other language (e.g., De Groot *et al.*, 2000, Experiment 2; Dijkstra *et al.*, 1998, Experiment 1). Instead of concluding that bilingual word recognition can be language selective under at least specific sets of circumstances, the authors of these publications preferred various explanations of this null-effect in terms of language nonselective word recognition. One of these was that, contrary to the instructions to perform language-specific lexical decision, on a subset of trials the participants may have adopted a language-neutral process-ing mode. As a consequence, an inhibitory homograph effect resulting from language-specific task performance and a facilitation effect resulting from language-neutral task performance (both resulting from language-nonselective processing) cancelled one another out. In conclusion, the results of the lexical-decision experi-ments in which homographs were presented in isolation may all be compatible with the view that bilingual word recognition is language nonselective.

Still, further interlexical-homograph studies have revealed a number of factors that moderate the influence of the nontarget language in bilingual visual word recognition. A study in which the word-naming task was used provided evidence to suggest that the occurrence of a homograph effect depends on (1) whether or not the activation level of the nontarget language is boosted prior to naming the critical words and (2) whether the target language is the stronger or weaker of the participants' two languages. In the study in question (Jared & Szucs, 2002), English-French bilinguals named blocks of English words in two conditions: A block of English words was preceded by a block of French words, to be named in French, or it was not preceded by a French naming block. A subgroup of participants for whom English, the target language, was weaker than nontarget French named the interlexical homographs more slowly than the non-homographic control words, irrespective of whether or not a block of French trials preceded the English block. In other words, for both conditions a response pattern suggesting language-nonselective word recognition was observed. In contrast, a subgroup of participants for whom target English was the stronger language, a homograph effect only materialized when the block of English target words was preceded by a French naming block. These findings suggest that in unbalanced bilinguals the stronger language can be immune to an influence of the weaker language, unless the activation level of the weaker language is boosted somehow, here, by a prior session of naming words in this language.

A final study to be presented here goes one step further by suggesting that under specific circumstances the weaker language of unbalanced bilinguals can also be immune to an influence of the other language. It concerns a semantic-priming study by Elston-Güttler *et al.*, (2005). On each trial, German-English bilinguals read an English sentence – English being their second and weaker language – and performed a lexical decision to an English target word (or pseudoword) that was shown after the sentence. In a related condition, the last word of the sentence was a German-English homograph and the target word was the English translation of this homograph's German meaning. An example is the sentence "The woman gave her friend a pretty GIFT" followed by the target word POISON (the German word for poison is "Gift"). In an unrelated condition, the same sentences and target words were used except that now the last word of the sentence was a non-homographic control and its meaning was completely unrelated to the target's meaning (e.g, "The woman gave her friend a pretty SHELL" followed by the target word POISON).

Prior to this (data-collection) part of the experiment, the researchers presented the participants with what they called a "global language context": The participants watched an originally silent movie, supplied with either a German narrative spoken by a native speaker of German or an English narrative spoken by an English native speaker. This manipulation was intended to boost the level of activation in either target English or nontarget German prior to data collection.

In this study, in addition to behavioral measures (response times and errors), "event-related potentials" (ERPs) were measured (see Chapter 10 for a description of this methodology). The ERP component that Elston-Güttler *et al.* (2005) were specifically interested in was the N400, which reflects semantic integration. Previous studies have shown that the N400 component is typically less negative to targets preceded by related primes than to targets preceded by unrelated primes. The likely cause of this effect is that semantic integration is relatively easy in the former case. The critical question addressed by the authors was whether the N400 to a target (POISON) following a homographic prime (e.g., GIFT) is less negative than the N400 following a non-homographic control word (SHELL). If so, it could be concluded that the homograph's meaning in nontarget German was also activated during target processing, a finding that would indicate that bilingual word recognition is language nonselective even when the word's surroundings promote the use of one language only. The researchers measured the N400s separately for the first and second halves of the data-collection session, on the assumption that a prior bias to German evoked by an earlier film fragment with German voices might disappear over the course of the, all English, data-collection session. It turned out that, with one exception, similar N400s were obtained in the related and unrelated conditions, thereby suggesting language-selective processing. The exception concerned the first half of the data-collection session following the German film fragment. In other words, only when the activation in the German language subsystem had been boosted prior to data collection, nontarget German influenced the processing of target English, and this only temporarily. The behavioral measures converged with this data pattern. In conclusion, then, in the condition that most resembled natural language processing, the all-English condition, word recognition was not influenced by the nontarget language (despite the fact that English was the participants' weaker language).

To summarize, the joint studies discussed in this section produce a mixed pattern of results, showing that the occurrence of a homograph effect depends on the exact composition of the stimulus set, the experimental task, the relative strength of the target language and nontarget language, prior activation of the nontarget language, and linguistic context. Therefore, the interlexical-homograph data do not clearly rule out either one of the two theoretical positions regarding bilingual word recognition.

4.2.2   Interlexical neighbor studies

A visually presented word not only activates "its own" lexical representation in memory but also those of orthographically similar words. This insight emerged from monolingual studies in which the effect of a word's "intralexical neighborhood" on visual word recognition was examined (e.g, Andrews, 1989). A word's intralexical neighborhood is the set of words that all share a substantial part of their form (say three letters out of four) with the target word, target and neighbors all belonging to the same language. Monolingual neighborhood studies have shown that the time it takes to recognize a word (e.g., "sand") depends on the number and frequency of its "neighbors," words orthographically similar to the target word (e.g., "hand," "land," "sane").

This finding provided bilingual researchers with a further way to study the degree to which bilingual word recognition may be language nonselective, namely, by examining whether a word's neighbors in the nontarget language influence this word's processing. If so, the likely explanation is that elements of the nontarget language are also activated while the target word is being processed, thus suggesting that bilingual word recognition can be language nonselective.

The first study to suggest that neighbors in the nontarget language indeed influence word recognition was performed by Grainger and Dijkstra (1992). These researchers instructed French-English bilinguals to make lexical decisions on three types of English target words (and nonwords) presented visually. Words of the

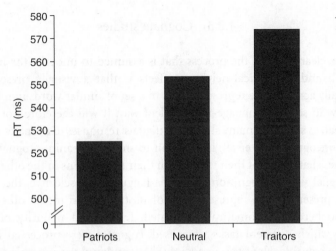

Figure 4.2: Mean lexical decision response time (RT) to English words as a function of their neighbors in English and French. Based on Grainger and Dijkstra, 1992.

first type, called "patriots," had more neighbors in target English than in nontarget French. Words of the second type, called "traitors," had more neighbors in nontarget French than in target English. Finally, words of the third type, called "neutral," had an equal number of neighbors in both languages. The results of this experiment are shown in Figure 4.2. They clearly indicate an influence of neighbors in the nontarget language on performance: Lexical-decision times were longer for traitors than for neutral words, and longer for the latter than for patriots. (The beginning of an explanation is given in Section 4.3.)

This specific type of evidence that bilingual word recognition can involve the activation of word representations in both of a bilingual's language subsystems has since also been obtained in studies that exploited other tasks and paradigms. In one of these, again testing French-English bilinguals, the word-priming methodology was used but with the primes presented so briefly that they could not be identified by the participants (Bijeljac-Babic, Biardeau, & Grainger, 1997). Primes that were orthographic neighbors of the targets slowed down the responses to the targets as compared with orthographically dissimilar primes. This was found both when primes and targets belonged to the same language (e.g., French "soin" as prime followed by French "soif" as target) as when they were from different languages (English "soil" followed by French "soif"). This study thus demonstrated that, even when a word cannot be consciously perceived, it triggers the word-recognition system into activity and that the set of word representations in a bilingual's mental lexicon triggered this way includes word representations of both languages. The fact that the primes do not have to be perceived consciously for these effects to occur in turn suggests that the activation arising in the word-recognition system upon the presentation of a word comes about automatically.

4.2.3   Cognate studies

As must be clear by now, the process that is assumed to underlie the interlexical-homograph and interlexical-neighbor effects is that a visually presented word automatically activates the representations of a set of similar words in memory and that it may do so in a language-independent way. It will therefore not come as a surprise that, as shown in many studies, bilinguals' responses to cognates differ from those to noncognates. After all, in addition to sharing meaning, cognates but not noncognates share (part of their) form with their translations in the other language. So if bilingual word recognition would be language nonselective, the moment a cognate is presented, the representation of its translation in the other language should also become automatically activated. In the vast majority of pertinent studies, in which different tasks were used, cognates were processed faster than noncognate controls. However, in a study that employed word naming (Schwartz, Kroll, & Diaz, 2007), cognates were responded to more slowly than noncognates. This difference in the direction of the cognate effect can presumably once again be accounted for in terms of differences in the processing requirements posed by different tasks (cf. the interpretation in 4.2.1 of the different directions of the interlexical-homograph effects across two versions of the lexical-decision task; see Dijkstra and Van Heuven, 2002, for details).

In most of the "cognate studies," the cognates and noncognates were presented as isolated words, but in a few of them (Duyck, Van Assche, Drieghe & Hartsuiker, 2007; Schwartz & Kroll, 2006; Van Assche, Duyck, Hartsuiker & Diependaele, 2009; Van Hell & De Groot, 2008) they were presented in a sentence context. As we have seen, the homograph effect disappears when the homographs are presented in a same-language sentence context (Elston-Güttler *et al.*, 2005). In contrast, in some of the cognate studies the cognate effect also showed up when the cognates were embedded in a same-language sentence context. This was especially the case in a "low-constraint" condition, where the cognate or the noncognate control stimulus could not be predicted on the basis of the prior sentence context. In a condition where it could be, the cognate effect disappeared. Figure 4.3 presents the cognate effects obtained in one of the pertinent experiments (Duyck *et al.*, 2007). In this experiment Dutch-English bilinguals performed lexical decisions to L2 English target words, cognates or noncognate controls (or to pseudowords) that appeared as the final words of low-constraint English sentences (e.g., "Lucia went to the market and returned with a beautiful cat [cognate]/ bag [control]." A subset of the cognates had identical forms in Dutch and English (e.g., "plan"; left part of Figure 4.3), whereas for the remaining cognates the Dutch and English forms did not overlap completely (e.g., "cat – kat"; right part of Figure 4.3). The cognate effect was significantly larger for identical cognates than for non-identical cognates, but also for the latter the effect was significant. On the assumption that especially the low-constraint condition resembles natural language processing, these findings suggest that bilingual word recognition is

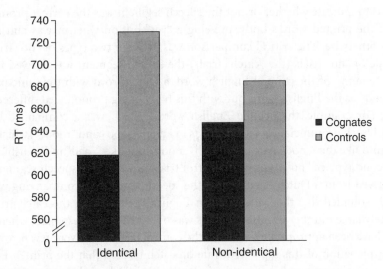

Figure 4.3: Mean lexical decision response time (RT) to English-Dutch cognates and non-cognate controls presented in low-constraint sentences in two conditions: identical and non-identical. Based on Duyck *et al.*, 2007.

language nonselective. But when drawing this conclusion, it remains to be explained why the cognate effect is more resistant to sentence context than the homograph effect.

4.2.4 Language-nonselective phonological activation in bilingual visual word recognition

Monolingual studies have shown that during visual word recognition the printed word's phonology is automatically activated. This not only holds for sound-based scripts (alphabets and syllabic scripts), where the basic units of print map onto units of speech (albeit not consistently so), but even for logographic scripts such as Chinese, where the written characters are not directly mapped to phonemic units. Apparently, phonological activation plays a central role in the processing of written language in general (Frost, 1998). This raises the question of whether in bilinguals a visually presented word automatically leads to phonological activation in *both* language subsystems.

Van Leerdam, Bosman, and De Groot (2009) used a new task, the "bimodal matching task," to examine this question. Dutch-English bilinguals, with English being the participants' L2, were shown monosyllabic printed English words (e.g., "mood"), one word per trial, while at the same time a speech segment was presented. This speech segment was either the correct pronunciation of the printed word's "body" – the vowel and final consonant(s); e.g., the spoken "-ood" part of "mood" – or it sounded differently (e.g., the spoken "-oad" part of "road"). The participants' task was to indicate whether or not the speech segment was the correct pronunciation of the printed word's body, pressing a "yes" button when it was and a "no" button otherwise. The critical comparison was between two types of "no" trials. In one type of "no" trials (the "catch" trials) the speech segment was derived from a Dutch "enemy" of the printed English word: a Dutch word with the same printed word body as the English word but with this body being pronounced differently in Dutch. For example, the printed English word "mood" was accompanied by the correct Dutch pronunciation of "-ood" (as in Dutch "lood" and "rood"), which does not sound like the "-ood" part of English "mood" but like "-oad" in English "road." The second type of "no" trials were control trials in which the speech segment was not derived from a Dutch enemy (e.g., the speech segment accompanying printed "mood" sounded like the "-ide" part in English "bride"). On the catch trials an extremely large number of false positives was obtained ("yes" responses where "no" would have been appropriate), whereas the control trials led to very few errors. The likely explanation of this high error rate on catch trials is that the printed English words gave rise to parallel phonological activation in both language subsystems (e.g., printed "mood" activated both English and Dutch words containing "ood" and, subsequently, the corresponding pronunciations). The match between the Dutch words activated this way and the speech fragment on the catch trials subsequently led to an error. In other words, phonological activation in bilingual visual word recognition appears to be language nonselective.

English and Dutch, the languages tested by Van Leerdam *et al.* (2009), both exploit the Roman alphabet. Evidence of phonological activation in the contextually inappropriate language subsystem has also been obtained in forms of bilingualism involving two languages that use different alphabets. In one of these studies, Gollan, Forster, and Frost (1997) tested Hebrew-English bilinguals, Hebrew and English using completely different alphabets. The researchers used a masked-priming paradigm in which on each trial a clearly visible target was preceded by a masked prime, which the participants did not perceive consciously. The participants performed lexical decisions to the targets. In a between-language condition all primes were in one language and all targets were in the other language. The primes and word targets in this condition were either translations of one another or they were completely unrelated words. Primes and targets within the translation pairs were either phonologically similar in Hebrew and English or they were phonologically totally dissimilar. When the primes were from the participants' (stronger) L1 and the targets from their (weaker) L2, a "translation-priming" effect occurred: Responses to targets that were translations of the preceding primes were faster than those to unrelated targets. Importantly, this priming effect was larger for translation targets that were phonologically similar to the preceding primes than for phonologically dissimilar translation targets. This finding suggests that the primes, although not consciously perceived, activated the corresponding representations in the nontarget language subsystem, including the memory units storing the primes' phonology. This phonological pre-activation subsequently shortened the response to the phonologically similar translation targets.

In conclusion, evidence from both same-alphabet and different-alphabet bilingualism suggests that visually presented words may give rise to automatic phonological activation in the nontarget language subsystem.

4.3   Models of Bilingual Visual Word Recognition

A number of models have been developed to account for the findings presented in Section 4.2. The earliest one of these is a computational model that was specifically developed to account for the interlexical-homograph and interlexical-neighbor effects, especially those obtained when the critical words were presented in isolation. This model, called the Bilingual Interactive Activation model (BIA; Dijkstra & Van Heuven, 1998; Van Heuven, Dijkstra, & Grainger, 1998), implements the idea that word recognition in bilinguals is initially language nonselective. The model, illustrated in Figure 4.4, concerns an extended version of the Interactive Activation

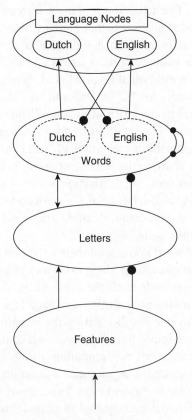

Figure 4.4: The Bilingual Interactive Activation (BIA) model of bilingual visual word recognition. Based on Dijkstra and Van Heuven, 1998.

model of monolingual visual word recognition pioneered by McClelland and Rumelhart (1981).

BIA contains four levels of representation units (or "nodes"), which represent visual features, letters, the orthographic forms of complete words, and language information, respectively. The levels of feature and letter nodes are shared between a bilingual's two languages and the level of word nodes consists of two integrated lexicons. The level of language nodes contains two nodes only, one for each language. The model is called "interactive" because representations at one particular level can activate and inhibit representations at adjacent higher and lower levels. Activation and inhibition between levels come about via spreading activation along excitatory and inhibitory connections (visualized by means of arrowheads and bullet heads, respectively). In addition, the existence of inhibitory connections between all word nodes is assumed, both between the word nodes of one and the same language as well as between those of different languages. (Because of this feature of the model its lexicon is said to be "integrated.") As a consequence of these inhibitory connections, the word nodes mutually suppress each other's activation. This process is called "lateral inhibition."

When a reader sees a printed word, this word first activates the feature nodes that correspond to the input. The activation in these feature nodes is then transmitted upward, exciting the nodes for letters that contain these features and inhibiting those for letters not containing them. Similarly, activated letter nodes transmit activation to word nodes containing these letters and inhibit word nodes that do not contain them. For instance, when English "sand" is seen, it will activate, via the feature level, the letter nodes for "s," "a," "n," and "d," which in turn will activate the word node that represents the target word "sand." The word nodes of the orthographic neighbors of "sand" (e.g., the word nodes for "hand," "sank," and "sane") will also be activated upon the presentation of "sand," via the activation of the features and letters they share with "sand." Importantly, the model assumes that activated letter nodes transmit their activation to word nodes in both language subsets. So, given a Dutch-English bilingual, the word nodes of the Dutch neighbors of English "sand" (for instance, "zand," "mand," and "tand") will also be activated to some extent by the input "sand."

In their turn, activated word nodes send their activation upward to the language node of the corresponding language along excitatory connections. Via inhibitory links between this language node to all the word nodes of the other language, the activation in the word nodes of the other language is suppressed. All activated word nodes compete with one another during the recognition process, inhibiting one another through lateral inhibition. These processes continue until the activation in one of the word nodes exceeds the recognition threshold (see Section 4.1) and the stimulus word is recognized. This moment is generally reached earlier for frequently used words than for infrequent ones. This follows from a further assumption implemented in the model, namely, that word nodes which represent frequent words have a higher baseline level of activation (they are more strongly pre-activated) than those representing infrequent words. Consequently, when the word recognition system is fed with a frequent word, the recognition threshold will be reached relatively rapidly. Similarly, because (unbalanced) bilinguals typically do not use their two languages equally often, the word nodes from the language used most often (the stronger language) have, on average, a higher baseline level of activation in the model than the word nodes from the language used less often (the weaker language).

In terms of BIA, the fact that interlexical neighbors affect bilingual word recognition directly follows from the language-nonselective, bottom-up activation process assumed by the model: Interlexical neighbors lead to more competition in the bilingual word-recognition system than control words that are orthographically similar to words in the target language only. To account for the interlexical-homograph effects, Dijkstra and Van Heuven (1998) assumed that interlexical homographs are represented in two word nodes in the bilingual language system, one node for each language. Due to the perfect match of a stimulus with both word nodes, the presentation of a homograph to the system will lead to a high level of activation in both these nodes and, consequently, a strong competition between the two. In the authors' words: ". . . the two readings . . . 'strangle' each other via mutual inhibition" (Dijkstra & Van Heuven, 1998, p. 209).

As mentioned in Section 4.2.1, interlexical-homograph effects are especially large when the homograph is more frequent in the nontarget language than in the target language (see Figure 4.1). This effect is explained in terms of the relation between word frequency and baseline levels of activation of word nodes mentioned above: Because of its higher baseline level of activation, the word node associated with the homograph's higher-frequency reading has a head start in the recognition process and will therefore start suppressing the node representing its lower-frequency reading earlier than vice versa. Similarly, the different levels of activation of the word nodes representing words of the stronger and weaker language in unbalanced bilinguals can account for the finding reported above that the stronger language (with a higher average baseline level of activation of the word nodes) can be immune to an influence of the weaker language.

A final point to mention regarding BIA – and plausibly the most important one in the present context – is that it has not only successfully simulated the interlexical homograph and neighbor effects as obtained in a number of the studies that presented the critical stimuli in isolation (which suggest that bilingual word recognition can be language nonselective), but also the apparent null effects that have emerged with specific combinations of task demands and stimulus sets (which, at face value, suggest that bilingual word recognition can also be language selective). In other words, this specific computational model of bilingual visual word recognition, which assumes that under *all* circumstances bilingual word recognition is initially language nonselective, not only accounts for obvious evidence of language-nonselective bilingual word recognition but also for apparent counterevidence.

As we have seen in Section 4.2.4, activated nodes that represent orthographic knowledge in their turn activate the corresponding phonological nodes. BIA cannot account for this phonological activation because it only includes orthographic representations. Furthermore, it may have struck the reader that BIA is able to account for interlexical-homograph effects despite the fact that it does not represent semantic information. After all, the most salient distinction between an interlexical homograph and a non-homographic control word is the fact that the former but not the latter is semantically ambiguous between a bilingual's two languages. Plausibly, the way this semantic ambiguity is resolved contributes to the homograph effect as well. Irrespective of whether or not this is the case, any model of word recognition will ultimately have to take meaning into account, because the ultimate goal of word recognition is to retrieve the word's meaning. For these reasons, the lack of phonological and semantic representations clearly indicates two lacunae in BIA.

In two successors of BIA, SOPHIA (short for the Semantic, Orthographic, and PHonological Interactive Activation model) and BIA+, these lacunae were remedied: They contain phonological and semantic representations in addition to orthographic representations. SOPHIA (Van Heuven & Dijkstra, 2001; see also Thomas & Van Heuven, 2005) is illustrated in Figure 4.5.

As can be seen, SOPHIA represents orthography at a more detailed level than does BIA: Two additional layers of nodes are installed in between the original levels of letter and word nodes (the latter now called "O-words"). These intermediate levels represent letter clusters and syllables. Phonology is represented in four analo-

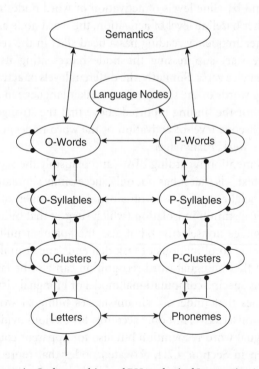

Figure 4.5: The Semantic, Orthographic, and PHonological Interactive Activation (SOPHIA) model of word recognition. Based on Van Heuven and Dijkstra, 2001.

gous levels of nodes that represent phonological units of different sizes. Orthographic units activate the corresponding phonological units and vice versa. Activated orthographic and phonological word nodes activate the corresponding meanings (in the subpart of the system called "semantics"). A further difference between BIA and SOPHIA is that the inhibitory connections from a language node to the word nodes of the other language as included in the original model have been removed. The consequence is that language nodes no longer inhibit words from the other language.

SOPHIA has successfully simulated a number of phonological effects obtained in studies of monolingual visual word recognition (Van Heuven & Dijkstra, 2001) but the model still has to be applied to bilingual word recognition data.

Dijkstra and Van Heuven (2002) developed a further, theoretical, model called BIA+, in which a word-recognition system containing orthographic, phonological, and semantic representations is augmented with a language-external control system. In terms of this model, linguistic-context effects (such as Elston-Güttler *et al.*'s 2005, finding that a linguistic context can nullify the interlexical-homograph effects; see Section 4.2.1) arise from activation processes within the word-recognition system, whereas effects of non-linguistic context (such as the specific requirements of the experimental task) emerge from the workings of the language-external control system. The fact that the direction of the homograph effects varies with the task to be performed by the participants and the exact composition of the stimulus set can also be attributed to the workings of this control system.

In their current forms, neither BIA, nor SOPHIA, nor BIA+ have much to say about the origin of the cognate effects, except that "The available studies suggest that cognates have a special representation" (Dijkstra & Van Heuven, 2002; p. 185). Various suggestions have been advanced regarding the exact nature of this special representation for cognates, for instance, that cognate translations share a morphological representation between a bilingual's two languages (Sánchez-Casas & García-Albea, 2005) or that their semantic representations are more integrated between the two languages than the semantic representations of noncognate translations (Van Hell & De Groot, 1998). Future implementation of the various possibilities in the models and simulations of these extended computational models should reveal which one best accounts for the behavioral data.

4.4   Sentence Processing in Bilinguals

In addition to examining the way bilinguals recognize visually presented words and what the underlying representation system looks like, researchers have investigated how bilinguals process sentences. Within this research area, two types of studies can be distinguished. One of these tries to discover how bilinguals parse syntactically ambiguous sentences for which the preferred solution differs between their two languages. Do they parse these structures the same way in both languages, perhaps applying the solution favored by one of their languages to the other one as well, or perhaps using each of the strategies in both languages some of the time? Alternatively, do they use the strategy that is most appropriate for the language they are currently processing, thus processing syntactically ambiguous structures the way monolingual language users do? The second type of studies examines how bilinguals process syntactically and/or semantically anomalous sentences, the main question addressed being whether or not bilinguals are equally sensitive to these anomalies as monolinguals. This section reviews some of the pertinent studies.

4.4.1   The resolution of syntactically ambiguous sentences

Several researchers have exploited one specific relative clause ambiguity in examining the question of how bilinguals process syntactically ambiguous sentences (e.g., Dussias & Sagarra, 2007; Frenck-Mestre, 2002). The sentences in question contain a complex noun phrase and either the head of this complex phrase or a second noun in this phrase can temporarily be assigned the subject of a subsequent relative clause. An example is the sentence "An eloquent student addressed the colleague of the secretary who stood in the hallway," in which "the colleague of the secretary" is the critical complex noun phrase. In this sentence either "the colleague" or "the secretary" can be the subject of the relative clause (the sentence part starting with "who"). Different languages are known to prefer different solutions of this ambiguity. For instance, Spanish and French favor "N1 attachment," assigning the first noun in the complex noun phrase ("the colleague") the role of subject of the relative clause. In contrast, English favors "N2 attachment," assigning this role to the second noun ("the secretary"). The question now is how people who master two languages that differ from one another in this respect process sentences of this type.

Dussias and Sagarra (2007) examined this question, specifically looking at the effect of amount of current exposure to the L2 on processing this type of sentences in L1. The participants in this study were Spanish monolinguals, Spanish-English bilinguals living and tested in the United States, and Spanish-English bilinguals living and tested in Spain. Both groups of bilinguals were highly proficient in L2 English but their L1 Spanish was still slightly stronger. The degree of L2 proficiency did not differ significantly between the two bilingual groups.

The participants in all three groups had to read L1 Spanish sentences of the above type. The sentences were presented one by one on a computer screen and the participants were instructed to read each sentence at their own pace. Meanwhile, the duration of their eye fixations to the separate words in the sentences was measured by means of eye-tracking equipment. In studies that use this methodology, the length of time a word is fixated on is thought to reflect the reading time for that word.

Unlike in English, in Spanish there is gender agreement between nouns and their modifiers. Therefore, sentences can be created in which the exact form of the words in the relative clause disambiguates the ambiguity toward either the preferred L1 solution or the preferred L2 solution. Consider, for instance, the following sentences from Dussias and Sagarra's study:

1. "El policía arrestó a la hermana del criado que estaba enferma desde hacía tiempo" ("The police arrested the sister of the servant who had been ill for a while")
2. "El policía arrestó al hermano de la niñera que estaba enferma desde hacía tiempo" ("The police arrested the brother of the babysitter who had been ill for a while")

In Sentence 1 the modifier "enferma" in the relative clause agrees in gender with "hermana," the first noun in the complex noun phrase, but not with "criado," the second noun in this phrase (the "a" signals femininity, the "o" masculinity). In contrast, in Sentence 2 the modifier "enferma" agrees in gender with the second noun of the complex phrase ("niñera") but not with the first ("hermano"). In other words, the proper solution of the ambiguity in Sentence 1 is the favored N1-attachment solution in Spanish whereas the proper analysis of Sentence 2 requires the non-preferred N2-attachment solution. In Spanish monolinguals, this difference should be reflected in a reading time difference between these two conditions for "enferma," the disambiguating word. Specifically, the authors predicted a longer reading time for this word in the N2-attachment condition (Sentence 2) than in the N1-attachment condition (Sentence 1). If such a difference were to materialize, it would subsequently be of interest to see what the response pattern would look like for the bilinguals, of whom L1 Spanish and L2 English favor different solutions, and whether current exposure to L2 English biases the ambiguity resolution process toward the N2-attachment strategy favored in English.

The results were clear-cut: Both the monolinguals and the bilinguals living in an L1 Spanish environment spent more time looking at "enferma" when it agreed in form with the second noun of the complex noun phrase (in other words, when N2 attachment was required) than when it agreed in form with the first noun of the complex noun phrase. The pattern reversed for bilinguals living in an L2 English environment: They spent more time looking at "enferma" when its form agreed with the first noun in the complex noun phrase (and, thus, N1 attachment was required). The authors concluded that, while parsing L1 sentences, "sources of information guiding L2 parsing decisions seep into the L1 comprehension system" (Dussias & Sagarra, 2007, p. 114).

In addition to current exposure to the L2, level of proficiency in this language has been shown to play a role in how bilinguals resolve the above type of syntactically ambiguous sentences. This was shown by Frenck-Mestre (2002), who reported the results of two experiments in which the performance of a group of English-French bilinguals on such sentences was compared with that of a monolingual French control group. As in Spanish, N1 attachment is preferred in French. In one of these experiments the bilinguals were relatively nonproficient in French;

in the other they were highly proficient in it. The bilinguals were tested on L2 French sentences and in an L2 French environment. In other words, any performance difference between the two bilingual groups to emerge could not be attributed to a difference in current L2 French language exposure. In both experiments the French monolinguals showed a clear preference for N1 attachment. Interestingly, an equally strong N1-attachment preference was observed for the proficient bilinguals, whereas the nonproficient bilinguals showed a clear preference for N2 attachment, that is, for the attachment strategy preferred in their L1 English. This pattern of results suggests that, with increasing L2 proficiency, L2 parsing strategies change from those consistent with the bilinguals' L1 to those consistent with their L2. In other words, with increasing L2 proficiency L2 speakers' parsing procedures may come to resemble those of native speakers.

4.4.2   The processing of syntactic and semantic anomalies

A persistent question in the study of bilingualism is whether the age at which bilinguals first started to acquire the L2 influences the way this language is ultimately processed, such that bilinguals who acquired it in early childhood ("early bilinguals") process it in a quantitatively and/or qualitatively different way from those who acquired it after childhood ("late bilinguals"). An important reason for posing this question is the idea that during a limited number of years in childhood humans are especially sensitive to linguistic input, perhaps because neural tissue dedicated to language learning is only temporarily available (Pinker, 1994). Language learning during this "critical period" is thought to be relatively effortless and automatic (see Chapter 7 for a discussion of the critical period hypothesis). Once this period of heightened sensitivity to language input is passed, language learning becomes a cumbersome enterprise which requires the exploitation of conscious learning strategies and the end state of these efforts is thought never to equal the level of proficiency reached by early learners.

   A couple of ERP studies have examined the question of whether early and late bilinguals differ from one another, and from native speakers, in the way they process visually presented sentences that are syntactically and/or semantically anomalous (e.g., Ardal, Donald, Meuter, Muldrew, & Luce, 1990; Weber-Fox & Neville, 1996). The authors of a further study (Ojima, Nakata, & Kakigi, 2005) wondered whether the processing of such sentences might be affected by L2 proficiency. Accordingly, instead of manipulating L2 acquisition age, Ojima *et al.* manipulated L2 proficiency. Whereas Ardal and collaborators only manipulated semantic anomaly, Ojima *et al.*, and Weber-Fox and Neville, manipulated both semantic and syntactic anomaly. The type of materials used in the three studies is exemplified in Sentences 3 through 6, taken from the (Japanese-English) study of Ojima and colleagues:

3.   "The house has ten rooms in total"
4.   "The house has ten cities in total"

5.   "Turtles move slowly"
6.   "Turtles moves slowly"

ERPs were measured from the critical words ("rooms," "cities," "move," "moves"). In Section 4.2.1 it was mentioned that a particular ERP, the N400, reflects the ease with which a word can be semantically integrated with its context. Accordingly, the authors of the present studies predicted the N400 to differ between sentence types 3 and 4 in monolingual native speakers. If so, the next question is what the N400 to the critical words looks like in early and late bilinguals.

Syntactic processing is known to be indexed by two other ERPs, an early negative one that is thought to emerge from neural activity in anterior regions of the left hemisphere and that is sometimes called ELAN (for early left anterior negativity) and the P600, a positive one that is maximally strong 600 ms after presentation of the critical word (Hahne & Friederici, 1999). (See Chapter 10 for further discussion of ERP components for language processing.) The critical words in sentence types 5 and 6 – Type 6 but not Type 5 containing a syntactic anomaly – were therefore expected to show different ELAN and P600 responses in monolingual speakers and the question of special interest was whether this would also be the case for bilinguals.

The results of the studies by Ardal and colleagues (English-French) and Weber-Fox and Neville (Chinese-English) suggested that semantic processing is *qualitatively* the same in monolinguals, early bilinguals, and late bilinguals, because all these participant groups showed an N400 to the critical words and a difference between the amplitude of the N400 to semantically correct critical words ("rooms") and to semantically anomalous critical words ("cities"). The only group difference to emerge in Ardal *et al.*'s study concerned the time course of the N400 to anomalous words: The N400 was delayed in bilinguals as compared with monolinguals, and it was delayed in the bilinguals' L2 as compared with their L1. In other words, semantic integration appears to come about faster in monolinguals than in bilinguals, and faster in bilinguals' L1 than in their L2. L2 acquisition age did not modulate these effects. However, in the study by Weber-Fox and Neville, only the late bilinguals showed a delayed N400 in L2 English as compared with English monolinguals (they did not test the bilinguals in their L1).

Weber-Fox and Neville (1996) showed that, in contrast to semantic processing, syntactic processing *does* qualitatively differ between native monolingual and L2 speakers: Whereas in native speakers syntactic violations modulated the ELAN and the P600 as compared with correct sentences, these effects were not evident in L2 speakers. These results have been taken to mean that first-pass parsing and second-pass re-analysis may differ between native and L2 speakers of a language. The important contribution of Ojima *et al.* (2005) is that they showed that these differences between native and L2 speakers in syntactic processing do not occur when the L2 speakers in question are highly proficient L2 users.

In conclusion, L2 proficiency appears to be a more important determinant of L2 sentence processing than age of acquisition. This conclusion is in agreement with Frenck-Mestre's (2002) results that completed Section 4.4.1. Those findings and the present ones of Ojima *et al.* (2005) converge on the conclusion that with increasing L2 proficiency syntactic processing of the L2 comes to resemble the syntactic processing of native speakers of that language.

Research Questions

1. Consider how interlexical homographs are processed and explain why the direction of the homograph effect in lexical decision varies with the exact version of the lexical-decision task used.
2. Try to think of reasons why the cognate effect is more resistant to sentence context than the homograph effect.
3. Design and draw a theoretical model of visual word recognition for bilinguals with languages that use different alphabets. Include phonological representations in the models.
4. If one of a bilingual's languages favors N1 attachment whereas the other favors N2 attachment, both amount of current exposure to L2 and level of proficiency in L2 will influence the way the syntactic ambiguity illustrated in Sentences 1 and 2 is processed (see Section 4.4.1). This has been shown in studies that manipulated either the one or the other of these two variables. Design an eye-tracking experiment with four groups of bilinguals that together vary on *both* these variables and predict the pattern of looking times to the critical region for each of the four groups.

Further Readings

De Groot, Annette. 2011. *Language and Cognition in Bilinguals and Multilinguals: An Introduction*. Hove/New York: Psychology Press.

Desmet, Timothy & Duyck, Wouter. 2007. Bilingual language processing. *Language and Linguistics Compass* 1. 168–194.

Scheutz, Matthias & Eberhard, Kathleen. 2004. Effects of morphosyntactic gender features in bilingual language processing. *Cognitive Science* 28. 559–588.

Van Hell, Janet & Tokowicz, Natasha. 2010. Event-related brain potentials and second language learning: Syntactic processing in late L2 learners at different L2 proficiency levels. *Second Language Research* 26. 43–74.

References

Andrews, Sally. 1989. Frequency and neighborhood effects on lexical access: Activation or search? *Journal of Experimental Psychology: Learning, Memory, and Cognition* 15. 802–814.

Ardal, Sten, Donald, Merlin, Meuter, Renata, Muldrew, Shannon, & Luce, Moira. 1990. Brain responses to semantic incongruity in bilinguals. *Brain and Language* 39. 187–205.

Beauvillain, Cécile & Grainger, Jonathan. 1987. Accessing interlexical homographs: Some limitations of a language-selective access. *Journal of Memory and Language* 26. 658–672.

Bijeljac-Babic, Ranka, Biardeau, Agnès, & Grainger, Jonathan. 1997. Masked orthographic priming in bilingual word recognition. *Memory & Cognition* 25. 447–457.

De Groot, Annette, Delmaar, Philip, & Lupker, Stephen. 2000. The processing of interlexical homographs in translation recognition and lexical decision: Support for non-selective access to bilingual memory. *The Quarterly Journal of Experimental Psychology* 53A. 397–428.

Dijkstra, Ton & Van Heuven, Walter. 1998. The BIA model and bilingual word recognition. In Jonathan Grainger & Arthur Jacobs (eds), *Localist Connectionist Approaches to Human Cognition*, pp. 189–225. Mahwah, NJ: Lawrence Erlbaum.

Dijkstra, Ton & Van Heuven, Walter. 2002. The architecture of the bilingual word recognition system: From identification to decision. *Bilingualism: Language and Cognition* 5. 175–197.

Dijkstra, Ton, Van Jaarsveld, Henk, & Ten Brinke, Sjoerd. 1998. Interlingual homograph recognition: Effects of task demands and language intermixing. *Bilingualism: Language and Cognition* 1. 51–66.

Dussias, Paola & Sagarra, Nuria. 2007. The effect of exposure on syntactic parsing in Spanish-English bilinguals. *Bilingualism: Language and Cognition* 10. 101–116.

Duyck, Wouter, Van Assche, Eva, Drieghe, Denis, & Hartsuiker, Robert. 2007. Visual word recognition by bilinguals in a sentence context: Evidence for nonselective lexical access. *Journal of Experimental Psychology: Learning, Memory, and Cognition* 33. 663–679.

Elston-Güttler, Kerrie, Gunter, Thomas & Kotz, Sonja. 2005. Zooming into L2: Global language context and adjustment affect processing of interlingual homographs in sentences. *Cognitive Brain Research* 25. 57–70.

Frenck-Mestre, Cheryl. 2002. An on-line look at sentence processing in the second language. In Roberto Heredia & Jeanette Altarriba (eds), *Bilingual Sentence Processing*, pp. 217–236. Amsterdam: Elsevier.

Frost, Ram. 1998. Toward a strong phonological theory of visual word recognition: True issues and false trails. *Psychological Bulletin* 123. 71–99.

Gollan, Tamar, Forster, Kenneth, & Frost, Ram. 1997. Translation priming with different scripts: Masked priming with cognates and noncognates in Hebrew-English bilinguals. *Journal of Experimental Psychology: Learning, Memory, and Cognition* 23. 1122–1139.

Grainger, Jonathan & Dijkstra, Ton. 1992. On the representation and use of language information in bilinguals. In Richard Harris (ed.), *Cognitive Processing in Bilinguals*, pp. 207–220. Amsterdam: Elsevier.

Grosjean, François. 1997. Processing mixed language: Issues, findings, and models. In Annette de Groot & Judith Kroll (eds), *Tutorials in Bilingualism: Psycholinguistic Perspectives*, pp. 225–254. Mahwah, NJ: Lawrence Erlbaum.

Grosjean, François. 1998. Studying bilinguals: Methodological and conceptual issues. *Bilingualism: Language and Cognition* 1(2). 131–149.

Grosjean, François. 2001. The bilingual's language modes. In Janet Nicol (ed.), *One Mind, Two Languages: Bilingual Language Processing*, pp. 1–22. Oxford: Blackwell.

Hahne, Anja & Friederici, Angela. 1999. Electrophysiological evidence for two steps in syntactic analysis: Early automatic and late controlled processes. *Journal of Cognitive Neuroscience* 11. 194–205.

Jared, Debra & Szucs, Carrie. 2002. Phonological activation in bilinguals: Evidence from interlingual homograph naming. *Bilingualism: Language and Cognition* 5. 225–239.

Kerkhofs, Roel, Dijkstra, Ton, Chwilla, Dorothee, & De Bruijn, Ellen. 2006. Testing a model for bilingual semantic priming with interlingual homographs: RT and N400 effects. *Brain Research* 1068. 170–183.

McClelland, James & Rumelhart, David. 1981. An interactive activation model of context effects in letter perception. Part 1: An account of basic findings. *Psychological Review* 88. 375–407.

Ojima, Shiro, Nakata, Hiroki, & Kakigi, Ryusuke. 2005. An ERP study of second language learning after childhood: Effects of proficiency. *Journal of Cognitive Neuroscience* 17. 1212–1228.

Pinker, Steven. 1994. *The Language Instinct: How the Mind Creates Language*. New York: William Morrow and Company.

Sánchez-Casas, Rosa & García-Albea, José. 2005. The representation of cognate and noncognate words in bilingual memory: Can cognate status be characterized as a special kind of morphological relation? In Judith Kroll & Annette de Groot (eds), *Handbook of Bilingualism: Psycholinguistic Approaches*, pp. 226–250. New York: Oxford University Press.

Schwartz, Ana & Kroll, Judith. 2006. Bilingual lexical activation in sentence context. *Journal of Memory and Language* 55. 197–212.

Schwartz, Ana, Kroll, Judith &, Diaz, Michele. 2007. Reading words in Spanish and English: Mapping orthography to phonology in two languages. *Language and Cognitive Processes* 22. 106–129.

Simpson, Greg. 1994. Context and the processing of ambiguous words. In Morton Ann Gernsbacher (ed.), *Handbook of Psycholinguistics*, pp. 359–374. San Diego, CA: Academic Press.

Thomas, Michael & Van Heuven, Walter. 2005. Computational models of bilingual comprehension. In Judith Kroll & Annette de Groot (eds), *Handbook of Bilingualism: Psycholinguistic Approaches*, pp. 202–225. New York: Oxford University Press.

Van Assche, Eva, Duyck, Wouter, Hartsuiker, Robert, & Diependaele, Kevin. 2009. Does bilingualism change native-language reading? Cognate effects in a sentence context. *Psychological Science* 20. 923–927.

Van Hell, Janet & De Groot, Annette. 1998. Conceptual representation in bilingual memory: Effects of concreteness and cognate status in word association. *Bilingualism: Language and Cognition* 1. 193–211.

Van Hell, Janet & De Groot, Annette. 2008. Sentence context modulates visual word recognition and translation in bilinguals. *Acta Psychologica* 128. 431–451.

Van Heuven, Walter & Dijkstra, Ton. 2001. The Semantic, Orthographic, and PHonological Interactive Activation model. Poster presented at the 12th Conference of the European Society for Cognitive Psychology. Edinburgh, Scotland.

Van Heuven, Walter, Dijkstra, Ton, & Grainger, Jonathan. 1998. Orthographic neighborhood effects in bilingual word recognition. *Journal of Memory and Language* 39. 458–483.

Van Leerdam, Martin, Bosman, Anna, & De Groot, Annette. 2009. When MOOD rhymes with ROAD: Dynamics of phonological coding in bilingual visual word perception. *The Mental Lexicon* 4. 303–335.

Weber-Fox, Christine & Neville, Helen. 1996. Maturational constraints on functional specializations for language processing: ERP and behavioral evidence in bilingual speakers. *Journal of Cognitive Neuroscience* 8. 231–256.

Wu, Yan & Thierry, Guillaume. 2010. Investigating bilingual processing: the neglected role of language processing contexts. *Frontiers in Psychology* 1. 1–6.

Chapter 5

Writing

Rosa M. Manchón

The ability to express oneself in writing is crucial in everyone's life regardless of variations in one's own linguistic repertoire and language configuration. As noted by Ken Hyland, writing "is central to our personal experience and social identities, and we are often evaluated by our control of it" (Hyland, 2002, p. 1). Bilinguals are no exception to this rule. In fact, multiliteracy development (the development of literacy skills – reading and writing – in more than one language) is a very common phenomenon in our world as a result of globalization, mobility, and the implementation of various educational programs.

The globalization of scholarship justifies the abundant research on professionals, notably academics, of various language backgrounds writing in English, the *lingua franca* of scientific publishing. Due to mobility, various groups of bilinguals need to develop literacy skills in one or more of their languages for their professional activities, a situation rather common across Europe with the free movement of workers within the European Union, although the phenomenon is not exclusive of Europe. In fact, during the last 50 years the workforce worldwide has gradually become more multilingual (Roberts, 2009), with the result that bilingual professionals are considered the "backbone of the global and virtual economy" (Day & Wagner, 2009, p. 392). Multiliteracy can also be the outcome of numerous and varied educational initiatives, including bilingual programs, immersion programs in monolingual and bilingual societies, adult literacy courses, or university language for specific purposes programs (especially for academic purposes).

The main aim of this chapter is to explore the defining characteristics of bilingual text production processes as a way of contributing to a fuller understanding of the psycholinguistics of bilingualism. We shall focus on those studies that have looked into complex, reader-oriented writing (i.e., complex and demanding texts written to be read by others) by bilingual adults (including young adults) who need to write in one or more of their languages for academic, educational, or work-related purposes. We will therefore look into the psycholinguistic processes behind, for instance,

The Psycholinguistics of Bilingualism, First Edition. François Grosjean and Ping Li.
© 2013 Blackwell Publishing Ltd with the exceptions of Chapter 1, Chapter 2, Chapter 3, Chapter 7, Chapter 10 © 2013 François Grosjean and Ping Li. Published 2013 by Blackwell Publishing Ltd.

the research output of academics, the theses, terms papers, and reports written by students in study abroad or international programs, or the reports written by doctors or engineers residing and working in a foreign country.

Our review will cover two main strands of research. The first corresponds to "intra-subject" studies, that is, those that have compared bilinguals' writing in their various languages. This research is scarce in comparison to the second group of studies we shall account for: those that have looked into bilingual writing processes in an additional language (L2), that is, a language added to bilinguals' linguistic repertoire once language (not necessarily, literacy) skills had already been developed in a previously acquired language (L1). Some of the studies in this second group have described bilinguals' L2 writing processes, whereas others have compared bilinguals' L2 writing with monolinguals' L1 writing. The latter are referred to as "inter-subject" or "between-subject" studies.

It is important to mention at this point that these various strands of research focus on bilinguals as defined in Chapter 1, that is, on individuals who use two or more languages in their everyday life, regardless of the degree of language dominance or of writing expertise in each of the languages in their repertoire. It should also be clarified that there is very scarce research on balanced bilinguals' writing. These various issues will be further elaborated upon as we progress through the chapter.

The research to be reviewed here has made use of various approaches, although we are mainly concerned with laboratory controlled studies, and survey studies. The latter have accounted for bilingual writing by asking participants to reflect on their own composing processes via questionnaires, usually triangulated with interview data. The former have looked into the psycholinguistics of bilingual writing by asking participants to engage in actual writing (usually in experimental conditions) and by using various elicitation procedures to gain access to what otherwise is invisible, that is, writing processes. The use of multiple-data collection procedures has been the norm, including direct observation, text analysis, and introspection techniques such as interviews, questionnaires, think-aloud protocols, and retrospective verbal reports. Think-aloud (or concurrent) protocols represent a technique used in many psychological studies and which consists of asking participants to verbalize their thoughts concurrently while performing a task (studies using this procedure will be presented in Section 5.2.1), whereas in the case of retrospective data elicitation procedures, participants are asked/guided to reflect on their performance just after having completed a given task.

The chapter is organized as follows. Section 5.1 elaborates on the psycholinguistic dimension of writing in general, and of bilingual writing in particular. Against this background, Section 5.2 offers a more detailed analysis of the most defining features of bilingual text production processes, including an analysis of the strategic role that the use of L1 in L2 writing may have in bilingual writing. Finally, our focus in Section 5.3 will be the analysis of the empirical evidence on the interplay between writing expertise and linguistic ability in bilingual writing, together with what is known about the transfer of writing knowledge and skills across languages.

5.1 The Psycholinguistics of Bilingual Writing: Mapping the Terrain

In order to understand the psycholinguistic mechanisms that underlie bilinguals' text production processes, we must first reflect on the process of writing in general, that is, on what research has uncovered about which processes take place from the moment ideas are generated to the time they are transformed into linguistic units (Section 5.1.1). This will help us understand the multidimensional and cognitively demanding nature of writing (Section 5.1.2) as well as the distinctiveness of bilingual writing and hence the questions and issues addressed in the specialized research (Section 5.1.3).

5.1.1 The writing process

The study of the psycholinguistic dimension of bilingual writing has been approached with the aid of models elaborated to describe L1 writing. This application rested on the assumption that the processes writers activate while composing are independent of the specific linguistic problems involved. These L1-based models (see Flower & Hayes, 1980, 1981; Hayes, 1996; Kellogg, 1996) assume that composing is a dynamic process that consists of several subprocesses – basically planning, formulation, and revision – that interact with one another in a cyclical fashion, that is, they are not implemented in a linear fashion but rather recursively throughout the composing process.

Planning is a conceptual activity, the content of which may be self-elaborated by the writer, prescribed by the writing assignment, or both. In addition to knowledge of the content of the message to be conveyed, two crucial dimensions in the planning process are the writer's degree of familiarity with (or metacognitive knowledge of) similar texts, and his/her knowledge of the writing context. These knowledge sources together help the writer plan at various levels, including the content of the text, or its structure and function. Writers also plan their procedures, that is, how they are going to go about producing their texts. It is important to mention that not all planning takes place at the pre-writing stage (which is called "advanced planning" in the relevant literature) as writers may continue planning throughout the writing process (referred to as "on-line planning").

The second macro-writing process is *formulation*. During this process, writers transform the content of their intended message into language. This transformation involves the construction of sentences through the selection of appropriate forms/items from the writer's mental lexicon. This selection process is dependent on the availability and accessibility of linguistic forms, their corresponding syntactic restrictions, and the stylistic concerns and rhetorical considerations involved in the production of the text at hand. Addressing these various concerns may give rise to a variety of problems (called "problem spaces" in the problem-solving literature in cognitive psychology) that, if properly solved (through the use of writing strategies, as we will see in Section 5.1.2), may allow the writer to end up with a text on the page, or the screen.

Revision, a further component of the writing process, involves the solution of various types of mismatches between the writer's intentions and their linguistic expression, ranging from whether the text in effect conveys the intended message and whether the ideas in the text have been successfully structured, to whether the linguistic choices made are accurate and/or appropriate in consideration of the function of the text or its intended audience.

We mentioned at the start of this section that the process of writing is cyclical: this means that writers do not usually engage in the three processes mentioned above one after the other in linear fashion, but rather cyclically, or recursively. Hence, in the course of the composition, some processes are activated (generating content, for example) while others are deactivated (e.g., searching for appropriate words or structures) as a function of the problems that each individual writer poses him/herself at each specific moment in the composing process. This control or monitoring function, which is taken to be a further component of the L1-based models we have referred to, enables the writer to take decisions, such as the precise moment at which a certain subprocess can be brought to a halt, or when some revision of the text produced so far is required.

5.1.2   The multidimensional and cognitively demanding nature of writing

The description of the writing process presented in 5.1.1 shows that becoming a skilled writer entails acquiring various types of knowledge, as well as learning how to integrate different elements at various levels concurrently. As Flower and Hayes (1981, p. 371) once put it, writers need to "juggle and integrate the multiple constraints of their knowledge, their plans, and their text into the production of each new sentence."

At a *product level*, skilled writers must be able to produce texts that are appropriate for given social purposes and contexts of use. Therefore, developing writing expertise means learning the conventions that guide the production of such texts as well as the language needed to convey their intended meaning when writing in different genres (Gentil, 2011), understood as "complex oral or written responses by speakers or writers to the demands of a social context" (Johns, 2002, p. 3). It follows that skilled writers must acquire both "genre" knowledge (i.e., the conventions guiding the use of language to achieve specific purposes, in particular texts, produced in particular situations, and for particular readers) and "language" knowledge.

At a *process level*, writing is best characterized as a cognitively demanding, problem-solving task in which various demands (ideational, textual, linguistic, procedural, etc.) compete for attention. Given that attentional resources are limited, and in order to avoid cognitive overload, writing entails continuous decision making regarding which aspect of writing to prioritize at each point in the composing process. This is done through the monitoring function mentioned in Section 5.1.1.

The cognitively demanding nature of writing should also be linked to the writer's continuous problem-solving activity during composing. Problem solving in this context means that writers frequently cannot move ("cross gaps" in the problem-solving literature) between two points (known as "initial state" and "end state," respectively) automatically, that is, they need to engage in a search process. To put it in a different way, writers cannot always achieve their goals and address their self-imposed or other-imposed concerns without a search process. The goals pursued may be related to any possible dimension of text production, ranging from macro-problems, such as how to structure the text or what information to include, to more local problems, such as how to link two paragraphs or how to access and/or improve lexical options. The writer's problem-solving behavior is the thinking process engaged in to get from the initial to the end state, which is done through a sequence of cognitive operations known as problem-solving strategies.

It follows that, seen from a psycholinguistic perspective, becoming a skilled writer entails (i) having (automatic) access to the relevant linguistic knowledge needed to express one's intended meaning in different genres, (ii) possessing genre-specific knowledge that can be accessed and used when required, and (iii) developing the ability to juggle with the various constraints that need to be addressed concurrently while composing challenging and demanding texts.

5.1.3   The linguistic and cognitive demands of bilingual writing

Bearing in mind the linguistic and cognitive demands of writing mentioned in Section 5.1.2, in the following four paragraphs we describe some of the characteristic features of bilingual writing, with an indication of the way in which they have been addressed in the specialized research.

1.   We have mentioned that skilled writers need to develop both genre knowledge and language knowledge. Bilingual writers may need to develop these in more than one language, or only in one of their languages, which in many instances is their L2, as is the case of immigrants who are illiterate in their L1 (see Leki, Cumming, & Silva, 2008), academics from various language backgrounds who need to publish in English (their L2), various professionals working in a foreign country, or graduate and postgraduate students completing their studies abroad. In addition, genre knowledge and language knowledge (both can be regrouped under "language sources") and their accessibility may vary across the bilingual's languages. Therefore, even accepting that bilinguals may not need to develop the same writing skills in all of the languages that form their linguistic repertoire, bilingual writers nevertheless have to cope with the processing demands of writing in their various languages. This is one question that has attracted considerable scholarly attention with regard

to the similarities and differences that may exist in the way in which bilinguals deal with these demands. This research is reviewed in Section 5.2.

2. Bilingual writing also shows its own characteristics with respect to the constraints on the allocation of attention that derive from the cognitively demanding and problem-solving nature of writing mentioned in Section 5.1.1. As compared to their monolingual counterparts, when bilingual writers write in their weaker language, there might be additional linguistic constraints that compete for attention, with the result that attentional resources may need to be divided between higher-level concerns (such as idea generation, content planning, or revision and evaluation of content or text structure) and lower-level linguistic concerns derived from limited (access to) knowledge of, for instance, relevant lexis and/or grammar. As we shall see below, this explains why different studies have found that when L1-dominant bilingual writers write in their L2, most of their attentional resources and writing time are devoted to formulating their texts.

3. In contrast to monolinguals, bilinguals possess linguistic resources in more than one language and upon which they can draw when engaged in the various macro-writing processes. Following a general interest in studies of bilingualism in the phenomenon of language switching, the specialized literature on the psycholinguistics of bilingual writing has looked into the strategic use bilinguals can make of their various languages during their writing problem-solving behavior. As we shall see in Section 5.2.1, some bilingual writers change languages while generating, formulating, and revising their texts, in addition to resorting to their various languages for monitoring the writing process. The research in this area has certainly contributed to shedding further light on the phenomenon of "language mode" reported in Chapter 1, Section 1.4, in addition to expanding our understanding of the variables mediating the amount and purposes of use of more than one language in bilingual performance.

4. Given the interplay between general writing skills and language abilities in any form of writing, and given also that bilinguals may not achieve the same level of development of such skills and abilities in their various languages, the study of bilingual writing has looked into (i) the transfer of knowledge and skills among languages, and (ii) the potential interplay between language expertise, on the one hand, and linguistic ability, on the other. In this respect, plenty of research efforts have gone into elucidating whether or not the development of linguistic abilities in bilinguals constrains the development of their writing skills, particularly in the case of L2 literacy acquisition. We will discuss these issues in Section 5.3.

5.2 Bilingual Text Production Activity: Processes and Strategies

In what follows we account for some of the characteristic features of the problem-solving nature of bilingual text production processes, including the strategic use bilinguals can make of language switching in writing. It should be recalled that, first, most of the available empirical findings derive from studies of bilinguals writing just in their L2 and, second, there are very few studies of highly proficient, balanced bilinguals.

5.2.1   Bilingual text production processes within and across languages

As is the case in the oral modality, *fluency* in writing has been found to vary across a bilingual's languages. Making use of the introspection techniques mentioned in the introduction to this chapter, research has consistently shown that writing fluency (operationalized as the total number of words written, or as the number and length of pauses) varies across languages. As compared to their monolingual counterparts or to their own performance in their L1, bilinguals, especially L1-dominant bilinguals, produce shorter texts in the L2 condition, pause more often, and produce a lower number of words between pauses (see Leki, Cumming, & Silva, 2008 for a review of studies).

Regarding the *allocation of attentional resources*, some studies have found that, similar to monolingual writing, bilingual writers make a priority of text generation, that is, the process of transforming ideas into language. However, important quantitative differences exist: while in L1 writing writers devote around 50% of their composing time to generating their texts, this can go up to 80% in the L2 condition. For instance, Wang and Wen (2002), in a study of Chinese speakers writing in English, found that their participants devoted over 60% of their time to sentence construction. Similar results were obtained in a series of "intra-subject" studies on the L1 and L2 writing of three groups of Spanish speakers with various degrees of L2 (English) proficiency (pre-intermediate, intermediate, and advanced) and writing expertise (see Manchón, Murphy, & Roca de Larios, 2005 for a full account of the methodological aspects of this research). This program of research used two main data sources: think-aloud protocols while writing argumentative and narrative tasks in the participants' L1 and L2; and retrospective questionnaires. In preparation for the think-aloud sessions, the participants were asked to verbalize all thinking while composing, and to practice thinking aloud with a mock composition. They were then given an hour to complete each task (4 in total, 2 in their L1 and 2 in their L2). No example of the think-aloud approach was provided, to avoid influencing the participant's use of language (L1 or L2) for their composing process. The retrospective questionnaires asked the participants to reflect, *inter alia*, on their attitudes about the topics of the compositions, their writing under think-aloud conditions, and their perceptions of their own composing processes. The researchers operationalized attention in terms of amount of time spent on a given cognitive activity and found that, depending on L2 proficiency, the time devoted by their participants to text generation ranged from 62% (in the case of the advanced group) to 80% (the pre-intermediate group) of their total composition time. The rest of their composition time was devoted to other composing processes, such as planning or revision. The amount of time allocated to these other processes was also proficiency dependent; for example, planning increased with proficiency.

This greater allocation of attentional resources to L2 text generation processes may be taken as an indication of the more labor-intense nature of this composing process in L2 in the case of L1-dominant bilinguals, something that appears to apply even in cases of bilinguals with advanced competencies in their L2. For instance, Mu and Carrington (2007) report that their participants (three Chinese postgraduate students in an Australian higher education institution) did not have to think about words and expression while writing in Chinese, whereas lexical retrieval constrained their thinking processes while writing in English. Similarly, in a series of survey studies on Chinese scholars writing in English, Flowerdew and Li (2009) found that, as compared to native English writers, Chinese scholars experienced greater difficulties in their English (their L2) writing – they took longer to write, they had access to more limited lexical resources, and they found it more difficult to "make claims about their research with the appropriate amount of force" (p. 171). Similarly, talking about his own experience while writing his dissertation in English, Gentil reports that "lexicogrammatical choices did not and still do not come to me as intuitively in English as in French" (Gentil, 2011, p. 18).

In addition to shedding light on differences in the quantity of problem-solving activity across a bilingual's languages, research findings also point to the existence of variation in the nature of the *problems tackled by bilinguals* when producing texts in their various languages. Thus, some studies have empirically confirmed a reduction in the number of higher-level goals (for instance, those of an ideational, pragmatic, or textual nature) in L2 composing and an increase in morphosyntactic and lexical problems. Nevertheless, individual differences have been observed as a function of what writers value in their writing. A telling example is reported in Crosby's (2009) study of two bilinguals in the United Stated attending a composition class, a Vietnamese-English bilingual and a multilingual speaker who had developed literacy skills in Taiwanese, Mandarin, English, and Japanese. They differed in what they valued as good writing and, accordingly, in their approach to writing. The former identified good writing with knowledge of grammar and lexis and hence linguistic problems were his main preoccupation while writing in English. The latter, in contrast, believed that becoming a skilled academic writer consisted of acquiring the language of a discourse community and, accordingly, her main preoccupations were whether her text was interesting and whether it included the right kind of evidence to support her arguments rather than whether it was grammatically correct.

In short, bilingual L2 text production processes show their own characteristics in terms of fluency and amount and type of problem-solving behavior engaged in. Two variables that have been found to mediate these processes are the degree of competence in the language of writing, on the one hand, and the writer's own beliefs and assumptions about what constitutes good writing, on the other.

5.2.2   Bilinguals' problem-solving strategies

The available empirical research has greatly contributed to uncovering bilinguals' writing strategic behavior. In the next two sections we will account first for intra-subject studies, that is, those that have compared bilinguals' strategic behavior in their various languages, and then we shall report on what is known about language switching as a strategic resource in bilingual writing.

Writing strategies in L1 and L2 writing. Beare and Bourdages (2007) is one of the few studies that have compared the strategies of fully bilingual writers who were skilled writers in their L1 and L2. The researchers investigated the text-generation strategies employed by 8 postgraduate students or professors (4 native speakers of Spanish and 4 native speakers of English) who were skilled writers in their L1 and L2 and who all used both of their languages in their work/studies and at home as they wrote and published in English and Spanish. The participants were asked to write a composition in their L1 and L2 under time-constrained conditions while thinking aloud. The researchers found that each language group of participants showed similar strategy use preferences across languages and, most interestingly, the preferences of the two groups (i.e., Spanish L1 and English L1 bilinguals) differed. Thus, native speakers of Spanish generated their L1 and L2 texts using idea genera-tion strategies (through, for instance, translation or reading the assignment), whereas English L1 speakers opted for rereading their already written text as a springboard for further text generation while writing in either English or Spanish. However, the researchers also stressed the presence of individual differences in strategy deployment, a finding also reported in other studies of proficient, experi-enced writers (see Mu & Carrington, 2007).

In contrast to these similarities in strategy use across languages, differences in strategy deployment in L1 and L2 writing have been reported in the case of less balanced bilinguals. For instance, with the intention of shedding light on the trans-fer of processes and strategies across languages, Wolfersberger (2003) asked three lower proficiency Japanese students of English in an intensive language program in the United States to write an essay in their L1 and L2. The analysis of the partici-pants' think-aloud verbalizations showed that, first, the language problems these writers had to face in the L2 condition drew their attentional resources away from the composing processes they implemented while writing in Japanese (their L1) and, second, the strategies used also differed across languages. For instance, one of the participants frequently used rereading as a strategy to generate her Japanese text, whereas in English she mainly used rehearsing, with the result that the composing process implemented while writing in Japanese (which consisted of thinking, writing, and rereading) was disrupted when writing in English. The author con-cludes by arguing that the transfer of L1 strategies to L2 writing is inhibited when L2 writers do not possess the necessary proficiency level to perform a given writing task. We shall come back to the phenomenon of transfer in Section 5.3.

The use of L1 in bilingual writing. As is the case in bilingual language use in general, using the L1 is a very characteristic feature of bilingual writing performance, to the point that, as we shall see here, some bilingual writers (especially L1-dominant bilinguals) appear to function in a continuous "bilingual mode" (see Chapter 1, Section 1.4) while producing their L2 texts. What is more, writing, in contrast to other linguistic modalities of bilingual performance, shows its own idiosyncrasy regarding the purposes of and variables mediating the use of the L1. This research, however, has only investigated the use of L1 in L2 writing, thereby highlighting the lack of research on fully balanced or highly proficient bilinguals.

In terms of *purposes* of use, we mentioned in Section 5.2.2 that bilinguals have been reported to resort to their L1 for a wide range of functions, such as planning the content of their texts, solving the various linguistic problems to be tackled while generating and revising their texts, and even monitoring the composing process by changing languages. For instance, bilingual writers have been found to deploy a range of L1-based lexical *retrieval* strategies such as the following (Manchón, Roca de Larios, & Murphy, 2007b): (a) reformulating the intended meaning in the L1 as a way of finding the L2 equivalent; (b) retrieving the L1 term that expresses one's intended meaning and concentrating on/repeating it, hoping that the L2 term will finally come to mind; (c) thinking of the L1 term that expresses the intended meaning, paraphrasing it, and then translating the paraphrase into the L2; or (d) starting a search in the L1, evaluating the option found and, if acceptable, finally translating it into the L2.

In addition to uncovering the purposes of L1 use in L2 writing, research has also provided evidence of the *variables* that govern the quantitative and qualitative use of this strategy in bilingual writing. The general consensus is that L1 use is inversely related to *L2 proficiency*: the more competence in the L2, the less use of the L1, and vice versa. However, this research finding has to be taken with caution, for two reasons. A first reason is that there exist notable individual differences among L2 writers of the same proficiency level. A second reason is that few studies have investigated highly proficient bilinguals and hence whether or not the trend observed with less proficient writers would apply to highly proficient or balanced bilinguals is still largely an empirical question.

Regarding the individual variation observed, a number of studies also support the lack of the use of L1 in L2 writing by proficient bilinguals, in contradiction to what was stated earlier in this section. This was the case with the highly proficient writers in Beare and Bourdages' (2007) study, and with the four Japanese university professors studied by Matsumoto (1995). By contrast, some highly proficient writers report generating their texts entirely in their L1. Whether this variation is the result of the language in which one has received literacy training and instruction remains an open question. In addition, it is also worth mentioning in passing that the same individual variation has been reported in the case of less experienced writers. For instance, in his study of a group of Japanese novice researchers reporting their writing of their first scientific research articles for publication in English, Gosden (1996) found four different patterns in their writing of the first draft. Some participants wrote the full draft in Japanese and then translated it into English. Others opted for writing an outline in Japanese and subsequently translated into English. Still others wrote notes in English, transformed them into full sentences, and then completed their first draft. As could be expected, some writers did write their first draft completely in English.

Despite the existence of individual differences in L1 use among writers of the same proficiency level, Manchón, Roca de Larios, and Murphy (2007a) interpret the available research findings as pointing to an L1 use continuum. When L2 proficiency is low, L2 writing heavily relies on the L1 as a compensatory strategy for a wide variety of purposes, such as generating ideas, accessing language, or evaluating the appropriateness of linguistic choices through backtranslation. As proficiency develops, fluency increases, although writers still find help in solving many types of problems through the use of their L1, particularly lexical problems (as we have seen). With still more proficiency, and a reduction in the amount of text generation problems to be tackled, more attentional capacity is available for higher levels of processing (such as planning, monitoring or evaluation processes). This additional attentional capacity also allows writers to pose themselves more sophisticated linguistic, stylistic, and textual problems. Writers can find it helpful to resort to their native language for these higher-level processes as a way of overcoming task demands and also to facilitate the engagement in deeper levels of processing, as attested in some recent studies (see Manchón, Roca de Larios, & Murphy, 2009; Van Weijen, Van den Bergh, Rijlaarsdam, & Sanders, 2009).

This use of the stronger language for higher-order processes in writing confirms previous tenets in studies of bilingualism regarding the different social roles that the languages in a bilingual's repertoire may play (see, for example, Grosjean, 1982). In the case of writing, these roles would be those of the "writer" (i.e., the one struggling to plan and get a text on the page), on the one hand, and the "controller" of the process, on the other (Manchón *et al.*, 2009). Some bilinguals appear to perform the role of the "writer" in the language of the text (L2), whereas the L1 is used to perform the role of the controller, for instance, to plan procedures and monitor the entire writing process.

Proficiency is not, however, the only variable mediating the strategic use of L1 in L2 writing. Other cognitive and social variables (in isolation or in combination with each other) have also been found to play a role. For instance, Hu's (2003) study of the writing processes and perceptions of 15 Chinese students completing graduate studies in science and engineering at a Canadian university found that their use of the L2 was the result of the interplay of a constellation of factors, including "the language of knowledge input, the language of knowledge acquisition, the development of L2 proficiency, the level of knowledge demands, and specific task conditions" (p. 39). Similarly, Ferenz (2005) analyzed the language of planning used by advanced MA and PhD English students of Russian and Hebrew origin residing in Israel. The researcher concluded that in addition to a set of cognitive-affective factors (including motivation, the need to overcome cognitive load, or the language in which knowledge is stored), the use of the L1 is socially mediated given that L2 writers are influenced by what is valued and promoted in their social writing networks. This observation once again may point to the role that education may play in the phenomenon of L1 use in bilingual writing.

In short, bilingual writers resort to their L1 for a whole set of purposes. The qualitative and quantitative use of the L1 has been found to be mediated by a range of linguistic, cognitive, and social factors.

5.3   The Transfer of Knowledge and Skills in Bilingual Writing

As discussed in Chapter 1, a bilingual's language history is a complex and dynamic process that results in changes in a person's language configuration throughout his/her lifespan. When it comes to writing, and given that the development of writing skills is dependent on education, bilinguals' trajectories are partly motivated by the various literacy learning experiences they may undergo throughout their life. A central concern in studies of bilingual writing is the potential transfer of writing skills across languages.

It was also mentioned in Chapter 1, Section 1.4 that the rule is for bilinguals to use his/her various languages for different purposes and in different domains of life. In this respect, and in contrast to what is the case for speaking, bilinguals seldom (need to) write in their various languages. A case in point would be that of children of Chinese origin living in Spain and being educated through the means of Spanish: Their literacy learning would be entirely in Spanish unless they participated in "heritage language programs," that is, those aimed at helping them develop language abilities in the language of their ancestors. There are, however, other groups of bilinguals who do develop writing expertise in more than one language throughout their lifespan, although notable individual differences exist. Thus, some bilinguals acquire literacy skills in more than one language concurrently, such as students in bilingual educational programs (see Van Gelderen, Oostdam, & Van Schooten, 2011, for such a program in Dutch and English). Others may develop literacy skills in their L1 and then in an L2 later on in life (for the same or for different purposes), as would be the case, for instance, of professionals who move to a new country or location (see Parks & Maguire, 1999, for a study of francophone nurses moving to an English medium hospital in Montreal, or Cho, 2010, for a study of Korean academics in the US).

Despite these variations in what literacy skills are acquired in which language and when, most of the available research on the transfer of writing skills across languages has focused on bilinguals who have developed literacy skills in their L1 and subsequently acquired writing abilities in an L2. Accordingly, the issue that has attracted most attention is whether or not writing skills acquired in one's L1 can be transferred to the L2 condition, as well as the potential inhibiting role that L2 proficiency may have in this process.

Originally, the scholarly debate in the field centered around the interaction or separation of language abilities and writing skills in bilinguals' L2 writing. Most of the available empirical evidence points to the *independence* of the constructs of L2 proficiency and L2 writing ability, hence considering that L2 proficiency is simply an additive factor in bilingual writing. Therefore, the writing ability already acquired in one language can be transferred to writing in another language if proficiency allows (see Cumming, 1989).

More recent research (Manchón, Roca de Larios, & Murphy, 2009) has added a further piece to the puzzle. As mentioned in Section 5.2.1, this is a program of research in which the L2 composing processes of writers at three levels of L2 proficiency were analyzed. These researchers found a more consistent correspondence between L1 and L2 performance at lower and advanced proficiency levels than at intermediate levels of L2 proficiency. They reported that lower proficiency writers showed similarities in the way in which they approached their writing in their L1 and L2: they engaged in very superficial processing in their L1 writing, which they transferred to their L2 writing, for which their low level of L2 proficiency was sufficient. The advanced participants could also maintain their level of "expert-like" L1 writing performance in the L2 condition because their L2 proficiency allowed them to do so. In contrast, the intermediate participants, also expert writers in their L1, had not reached the necessary level of linguistic competence in their L2 that would have allowed the transfer of their L1 writing skills to the L2 condition. On account of these findings, Manchón *et al.* (2009) concluded that a full understanding of the complexity of multilingual writers' writing performance requires the combined analysis of several variables: language proficiency, writing expertise and, once again, educational experience.

These arguments echo recent attempts to theorize the transfer issue under the tenets of multicompetence (see Gentil, 2011; Ortega & Carson, 2010; Rinnert & Kobayashi, 2012), a theoretical orientation according to which multilingual language users are not the sum of the separate competencies developed in each of their languages. Instead, they are thought to possess a distinct competence in which their various languages interact in intricate ways (see Ortega & Carson, 2010). Accordingly, the central concern is not so much a question of what bilingual writers can or cannot do in their L2 as a function of their L2 proficiency but, rather, how multicompetent language users (i.e., those that have developed language and literacy skills in more than one language) make use of their various knowledge resources and skills when approaching the writing of texts in the various languages that form their linguistic repertoire. In this respect, Gentil (2011) has recently put forward a socially situated view of the transfer of genre knowledge across languages, genre knowledge being, as we mentioned in Section 5.1.2, part of writing expertise and hence part of the knowledge sources potentially transferable across languages. Gentil contends that a crucial factor to be considered in the analysis of the transfer of genre knowledge is the bilingual writer's perception of what is valued in diverse contexts of use. Accordingly, he suggests that "Bilingual writers are more likely to transfer genre knowledge from Language A to Language B if the enactment in Language B of the written genres [. . .] acquired in Language A is socially authorized and valued" (p. 20). This tenet has received empirical validation in Rinnert and Kobayashi's program of research on bilingual Japanese-English writers, which is also informed by theories of multicompetence (Rinnert & Kobayashi, 2009; 2012). They put forward a developmental view of the transfer of writing features across languages, which is a dynamic process that changes with the gradual development of the writer's L1/L2 writing knowledge. They also contend that, rather than transferring writing features across languages, multicompetent writers acquire the ability to produce their texts by controlling and purposefully choosing what they consider to be the most appropriate elements from their knowledge sources, so that their texts are appropriate for particular writing contexts and purposes.

Research Questions

1. Name three features that make bilingual writing distinct from monolingual writing. Discuss their implications for our understanding of the psycholinguistics of bilingualism.
2. Which knowledge sources and skills form a skilled bilingual writer's competence? What kind of study could shed light on the developmental path that bilinguals may follow in the acquisition of such knowledge and skills in their various languages?
3. In what ways is the quantitative and qualitative use of the L1 in L2 writing influenced by the bilingual's degree of language dominance? What kind of study could be designed to look into the purposes and the variables of L1 use in bilingual writing?
4. What kind of study could be designed to provide empirical evidence for the multicompetence nature of bilingual writers (see Section 5.3)?

Further Readings

Belcher, Diane & Connor, Ulla (eds). 2001. *Reflections on Multiliterate Lives*. Clevedon, UK: Multilingual Matters.

Gentil, Guillaume. 2011. A biliteracy agenda for genre research. *Journal of Second Language Writing* 20(1). 6–23.

Leki, Ilona, Cumming, Alister, & Silva, Tony. 2008. *A Synthesis of Research on Second Language Writing in English*. New York: Routledge/Taylor & Francis.

Ortega, Lourdes & Carson, Joan. 2010. Multicompetence, social context, and L2 writing research praxis. In Tony Silva & Paul Matsuda (eds), *Practicing Theory in Second Language Writing*, pp. 48–71. West Lafayette, IN: Parlor Press.

References

Beare, Sophie & Bourdages, Johanne S. 2007. Skilled writers' generating strategies in L1 and L2: An exploratory study. In Mark Torrance, Luuk Van Waes, & David Galbraith (eds), *Writing and Cognition. Research and Applications*, pp. 151–161. Amsterdam: Elsevier.

Cho, Sookyung. 2010. Academic biliteracy challenges: Korean scholars in the United States. *Journal of Second Language Writing* 19. 82–94.

Crosby, Cathryn. 2009. Academic reading and writing difficulties and strategic knowledge of Generation 1.5 learners. In Mark Roberge, Meryl Diegal, & Linda Harklau (eds), *Generation 1.5. in College Composition. Teaching Academic Writing to U.S.-Educated Learners of ESL*, pp. 105–119. New York: Routledge/Taylor & Francis.

Cumming, Alister. 1989. Writing expertise and second language proficiency. *Language Learning* 39. 81–141.

Day, Dennis & Wagner, Johanes. 2009. Bilingual professionals. In Peter Auer & Li Wei (eds), *Handbook of Multilingualism and Multilingual Communication*, pp. 391–404. Berlin: Mouton de Gruyter.

Ferenz, Orna. 2005. First and second language use during planning processes. In Triantafillia Kostouli (ed.), *Writing in Context(s): Textual Practices and Learning Processes in Sociocultural Settings*, pp. 185–205. New York: Springer.

Flower, Linda & Hayes, John. 1980. The dynamics of composing: making plans and juggling constraints. In Lee W. Gregg & Erwin R. Steinberg (eds), *Cognitive Processes in Writing: An Interdisciplinary Approach*, pp. 31–49. Hillsdale, NJ: Lawrence Erlbaum.

Flower, Linda & Hayes, John. 1981. A cognitive process theory of writing. *College Composition and Communication* 32. 365–387.

Flowerdew, John & Li, Yongian. 2009. The globalization of scholarship: Studying Chinese scholars writing for international publication. In Rosa M. Manchón (ed.), *Writing in Foreign Language Contexts: Learning, Teaching and Research*, pp. 156–182. Bristol, UK: Multilingual Matters.

Gentil, Guillaume. 2011. A biliteracy agenda for genre research. *Journal of Second Language Writing* 20(1). 6–23.

Gosden, Hugh. 1996. Verbal reports of Japanese novices' research writing practices in English. *Journal of Second Language Writing* 5. 109–128.

Grosjean, François. 1982. *Life with Two Languages*. Cambridge, MA: Harvard University Press.

Hayes, John. 1996. A framework for understanding cognition and affect in writing. In Michael Levy & Sarah Ransdell (eds), *The Science of Writing*, pp. 1–27. Mahwah, NJ: Lawrence Erlbaum.

Hu, Jim (2003). Thinking languages in L2 writing: Research findings and pedagogical implications. *TESL Canada Journal*, 21(1), 39–63.

Hyland, Ken. 2002. *Teaching and Researching Writing*. London: Pearson.

Kellogg, Ronald. 1996. A model of working memory in writing. In C. Michael Levy & Sarah Ransdell (eds), *The Science of Writing*, pp. 57–71. Mahwah, NJ: Lawrence Erlbaum.

Johns, Ann. 2002. Introduction: Genre in the classroom. In Ann Johns (ed.), *Genre in the Classroom: Multiple Perspectives*, pp. 3–13. Mahwah, NJ: Lawrence Erlbaum.

Leki, Ilona, Cumming, Alister, & Silva, Tony. 2008. *A Synthesis of Research on Second Language Writing in English*. New York: Routledge/Taylor & Francis.

Manchón, Rosa M., Murphy, Liz, & Roca de Larios, Julio. 2005. Using concurrent protocols to explore L2 writing processes: Methodological issues in the collection and analysis of data. In Paul K. Matsuda & Tony Silva (eds), *Second Language Writing Research. Perspectives on the Process of Knowledge Construction*, pp. 191–205. Mahwah, NJ: Lawrence Erlbaum.

Manchón, Rosa M., Roca de Larios, Julio, & Murphy, Liz. 2007a. A review of writing strategies: Focus on conceptualizations and impact of first language. In Andrew Cohen & Ernesto Macaro (eds), *Language Learner Strategies: 30 Years of Research and Practice*, pp. 229–250. Oxford: Oxford University Press.

Manchón, Rosa M., Roca de Larios, Julio, & Murphy, Liz. 2007b. Lexical retrieval processes and strategies in second language writing: A synthesis of empirical research. *International Journal of English Studies* 7. 147–172.

Manchón, Rosa M., Roca de Larios, Julio, & Murphy, Liz. 2009. The temporal dimension and problem-solving nature of foreign language composing. Implications for theory. In Rosa M. Manchón (ed.), *Writing in Foreign Language Contexts: Learning, Teaching and Research*, pp. 102–129. Bristol, UK: Multilingual Matters.

Matsumoto, Kazuko. 1995. Research paper writing strategies of professional Japanese EFL writers. *TESL Canada Journal* 13(1). 17–27.

Mu, Congjun & Carrington, Suzanne. 2007. An investigation into three Chinese students' English writing strategies. *Teaching of English as a Second or Foreign Language (Electronic Journal)*, 11(1). Available at http://www.tesl-ej.org/ [accessed on-line June 2011].

Ortega, Lourdes & Carson, Joan. 2010. Multicompetence, social context, and L2 writing research praxis. In Tony Silva & Paul Matsuda (eds), *Practicing Theory in Second Language Writing*, pp. 48–71. West Lafayette, IN: Parlor Press.

Parks, Susan & Maguire, Mary H. 1999. Coping with on-the-job writing in ESL: A constructivist-semiotic perspective. *Language Learning* 49. 143–175.

Rinnert, Carol & Kobayashi, Hiroe. 2009. Situated writing practices in foreign language settings: The role of previous experience and instruction. In Rosa M. Manchón (ed.) *Writing in Foreign Language Contexts: Learning, Teaching, and Research*, pp. 23–48. Bristol, UK: Multilingual Matters.

Rinnert, Carol & Kobayashi, Hiroe. (2012). Understanding L2 writing development from a multicompetent perspective: Dynamic repertoires of knowledge and text construction. In Rosa M. Manchón (ed.), *L2 Writing Development: Multiple Perspectives*, pp. 101–134. New York: De Gruyter.

Roberts, Celia. 2009. Multilingualism in the workplace. In Peter Auer & Li Wei (eds), *Handbook of Multilingualism and Multilingual Communication*, pp. 405–422. New York: De Gruyter.

Van Gelderen, Amos, Oostdam, Ron, & Van Schooten, Erik. 2011. Does foreign language writing benefit from increased lexical fluency? Evidence from a classroom experiment. *Language Learning* 61. 281–321.

Van Weijen, Daphne, Van den Bergh, Huub, Rijlaarsdam, Gert, & Sanders, Ted. 2009. L1 use during L2 writing: An empirical study of a complex phenomenon. *Journal of Second Language Writing* 18. 235–250.

Wang, Wenyu & Wen, Qiufang. 2002. L1 use in the L2 composing process: An exploratory study of 16 Chinese EFL writers. *Journal of Second Language Writing* 11. 225–246.

Wolfersberger, Mark. 2003. L1 to L2 writing process and strategy transfer: A look at lower proficiency writers. *TESL-EJ* 7(2). Available at http://tesl-ej.org/ej26/a6.html [accessed on-line June 2011].

III
Language Acquisition

Chapter 6

Simultaneous Language Acquisition

Virginia Yip

A foundational aspect of the psycholinguistics of bilingualism is the study of bilingual development in early childhood. In our increasingly globalized world, many children are exposed to two or more languages from birth. The circumstances under which they develop bilingualism are diverse, ranging from one parent–one language families to immigrant communities where the home language differs from that of the wider community.

The study of how children acquire two languages is of both theoretical and practical significance. From a theoretical point of view, bilingual acquisition provides a unique window into how the bilingual child's mind works and develops over time. Studying bilingual acquisition also provides important insights into a general theory of language acquisition. What is it that enables humans to acquire language (as a generic system) and languages (in the plural)? We may assume that the same capacity which serves monolingual acquisition, whether it is innate or otherwise, underlies bilingual acquisition. Indeed, it can be argued that in monolingual contexts, this capacity is not yet put to full use; it is only in bilingual contexts that the potential is realized.

The general pattern of language development is similar in bilingual and monolingual children, that is, bilingual children also pass through the babbling, one-word, and two-word stages. These stages are reached at approximately the same age as in monolingual children, although the child may not reach the same stage in each language at exactly the same time. Childhood bilingualism is traditionally divided into simultaneous and successive modes (see Chapter 7). The line between them is necessarily arbitrary: for example, how are we to classify a child whose exposure to a second language begins at age 1 or 2? McLaughlin (1978) set age 3 as the threshold for successive bilingualism, but this is widely regarded as too broad: there will necessarily be developmental differences between a child whose exposure to both languages begins at birth and one whose exposure to one of those languages begins between ages 2 and 3. Any such threshold is also arbitrary, since there is necessarily a continuum from simultaneous to successive bilingualism to child second language acquisition.

In view of the lack of a clear definition for "simultaneous" acquisition, scholars have adopted a more restrictive notion of *Bilingual First Language Acquisition* (BFLA). Various definitions have been proposed. BFLA is defined by De Houwer (2009, p. 2) as "the development of language in young children who hear two languages spoken to them from birth." This definition is relatively inclusive in that it would include passive bilinguals who do not necessarily use one of the languages, but relatively stringent in requiring exposure from birth. A more relaxed definition is adopted by Deuchar and Quay (2000) who use the term "bilingual acquisition" for children whose exposure to both languages begins within the first year of life. Based on Grosjean's (2008, p. 10) definition of bilingualism as "the regular use of two or more languages," BFLA may be defined as the concurrent acquisition of two languages in a child who is exposed to them from birth and uses both regularly in early childhood. This will exclude passive bilinguals who are exposed to two languages but produce only one. By "early childhood," we mean the preschool years up to around age 5, beyond which the impact of schooling complicates the picture.

Such a definition does not entail that the two first languages develop like those in the monolingual counterparts, nor does it suggest that two monolinguals reside within the bilingual child. On the contrary, as we shall see, bilingual children differ from monolinguals in several areas, including cross-linguistic influence and code-mixing.

In the case of simultaneous acquisition of two languages, neither language can be said to come first, and in principle neither need be privileged over the other, although in practice a dominant or stronger language can often be identified. Thus the notions "first" and "second" language are not generally used in reference to bilingual children, although some studies have discussed the extent to which a child's weaker language does or does not resemble a second language (Schlyter, 1993; Bonnesen, 2007). Many studies have adopted the terms Language A and Language B, typically in explaining how Language A comes to influence Language B (Hulk & Müller, 2000). A bilingual child's languages influence each other in both directions, however (Pavlenko & Jarvis, 2002, pp. 209–210; Yip & Matthews, 2007, p. 223; Mok, 2011). To avoid the implication that Language A comes first or is privileged in any way, we adopt the terms Language A and Language α following Wölck (1987/1988) and De Houwer (2009).

Having delimited the scope of this chapter by defining BFLA strictly for the purpose of research, it must be recognized that this is only a subset of a larger field of investigation, namely childhood bilingualism. There are many other forms of childhood bilingualism which deserve and require research, including

- passive bilingualism, whereby a child understands more than one language but produces only one;
- replacive bilingualism, whereby a child begins to acquire a language A but subsequently acquires language α which replaces language A as the native language

(Francis, 2011). This often happens in the case of adopted children: Gauthier and Genesee (2011) refer to language α as a second first language in the case of Chinese adopted children acquiring French.

In this chapter we will begin in Section 6.1 with a discussion of the theoretical issues. These include balanced vs. unbalanced development, separate development vs. cross-linguistic influence, and the role of input. Section 6.2 discusses methodological issues specific to bilingual development while Section 6.3 considers language differentiation in the early stages. Section 6.4 addresses cross-linguistic influence and Section 6.5 code-mixing in bilingual children. Section 6.6 discusses extensions to trilingual acquisition and to clinical settings.

6.1 Theoretical Issues

The field of bilingual acquisition is gradually coming into its own with a unique research agenda that distinguishes it from other fields. It is interdisciplinary, standing at the intersection of child language acquisition and bilingualism. As with the growth of any field, a solid grounding in theorization and empirical coverage is essential: theoretical issues in language acquisition, linguistic theory, and processing theory have motivated a surge of studies in simultaneous bilingual acquisition. Parallel to monolingual first language acquisition, a range of theoretical approaches including nativist and usage-based theories have framed studies of bilingual acquisition.

The nomenclature of the study of simultaneous acquisition of two languages raises a question of epistemology: "What is the nature of the knowledge of each language being acquired and represented by the learner?" (Yip & Matthews, 2007, p. 23). The two languages of the bilingual child must have the same epistemological status, whatever the acquisition mechanisms responsible for acquiring a first language. This is necessarily so, if only because the acquisition of two languages occurs in parallel.

6.1.1 The logical problem of bilingual acquisition

One starting point for the discussion of theoretical issues in first language acquisition is the logical problem of language acquisition: how does the child develop a grammar on the basis of limited input which underdetermines the target grammar? Although originally discussed under the assumptions of generative grammar (Chomsky, 1980), most aspects of the problem arise regardless of theoretical persuasions. From an emergentist perspective, for example, O'Grady (2005, p. 184) acknowledges that even in monolingual acquisition, "The facts are too complex, the input too sparse, mastery too rapid, and errors too infrequent. Induction from experience is not the answer." Given this characterization of the problem, it is greatly compounded in the case of BFLA where it can be argued that the facts are at least twice as complex, and the input twice as sparse. The "Logical Problem of Bilingual Acquisition" (Yip & Matthews, 2007, p. 30) recognizes that the problem posed by the input is more severe for the bilingual child both quantitatively and qualitatively:

(a) In terms of quantity, assuming an idealized case in which the input available to the child is balanced, the child will hear on average half as much input in each language as the corresponding monolingual child. Under more realistic assumptions, the input will be unbalanced, leaving the child with perhaps 30–40% of her input in one of the two languages. This is the basis for the development of a weaker language.
(b) Qualitatively, the indeterminacy of input – the fact that a given sample of input is compatible with numerous underlying grammars – is compounded in the case of the bilingual child to the extent that the two target grammars may suggest different analyses for a given utterance. This problem forms the basis for the input ambiguity account for cross-linguistic influence (Müller, 1998; Yip & Matthews, 2007).

In the context of bilingual development, the Poverty of the Stimulus (Chomsky, 1980) can be reformulated as the Poverty of the Dual Stimulus (Yip & Matthews, 2007, p. 30). There is also an important difference in the logic of the argument in the case of bilingual acquisition. In addition to accounting for successful acquisition of two languages, an adequate theory has to account for incomplete or divergent outcomes. Failure to develop bilingualism in response to dual input is a common outcome: in her sample of 198 families in Flanders, De Houwer (2009, p. 108) found that only 74% of children exposed to two languages developed the ability to speak both. The development of nontarget grammars in one or both languages is also attested, at least at certain developmental stages, especially in the child's weaker language (see Section 6.4).

6.1.2   Balanced vs. unbalanced development

In the ideal case, the input is split on a 50–50 basis and the child develops two first languages in tandem, with neither noticeably ahead of the other. Although some individuals may approximate this ideal, it is rarely attained in practice. Typically there is functional differentiation such that the child uses language A predominantly for certain purposes (such as play) and language α for another purpose (such as learning). In addition, the overall rate of development of the two languages may differ, resulting in unbalanced development.

In discussing imbalances in bilingual development, Francis (2011) identifies the "Paradox of Bilingual Acquisition": on the one hand, to account for the successful development of grammatical competence in two languages, one must assume that the language faculty is entirely capable of dealing with the challenges of dual input;

on the other hand, unlike the case of first language acquisition, the development of bilingual competence is far from guaranteed, and many children who do develop bilingualism show unbalanced development in their two languages.

6.1.3   Separate development vs. cross-linguistic influence

Assuming that a child is indeed becoming bilingual, what is the relationship between her two developing linguistic systems? One theoretical possibility is that a child initially develops a single system underlying both languages (Volterra & Taeschner, 1978). Much evidence has been adduced to show that this is not the case. In phonology, for example, Bosch and Sebastián-Gallés (2001, 2003) showed that bilingual children can distinguish even closely related languages such as Spanish and Catalan before age 1. A second theoretical possibility is that a child develops entirely separate systems. The Separate Development Hypothesis (De Houwer, 1990, 2009) posits not only that the child has separate systems from the outset, but that these systems develop independently of one another. A third possibility is that a child's linguistic systems are separate but may influence each other (Döpke, 2000; Yip & Matthews, 2007). This view implies that there are constraints on cross-linguistic influence: for example, a child's stronger language may influence the weaker language, and/or the two systems may influence each other when there is actual or perceived overlap between them (Hulk & Müller, 2000; see Section 6.4).

6.1.4   Input effects

Gathercole and Hoff (2007) discuss the role of input from different theoretical perspectives and evaluate the predictions based on these theories. As pointed out by Montrul (2008), input appears to play an even more decisive role in bilingual acquisition than in monolingual acquisition. It is therefore important to have an estimate of the proportion of input in each language. This can be done directly through systematic analysis of the adult utterances in the transcripts, or indirectly through questionnaires administered to parents (Unsworth & Blom, 2010). Qualitative aspects of input are also important. For example, children's English in Singapore shows obvious influence from Chinese, but careful analysis of the input is necessary in order to determine whether these properties derive from cross-linguistic influence in the individual child's development or from input in Singapore English, a contact variety strongly influenced by Chinese (Gupta, 1994). Similarly, several studies have found that Spanish-English bilingual children use fewer null subjects in their Spanish than monolingual children. This could either be due to cross-linguistic influence from English to Spanish or to the variety of Spanish to which the children are exposed (Paradis & Navarro, 2003).

Another point made by Unsworth and Blom (2010, p. 216) is that bilingual children can serve as their own controls when it comes to testing input effects: "child-internal factors, such as IQ and age, are held constant, as are many child-external factors, such as social class." Such input effects on the acquisition of Welsh-English are discussed in Gathercole and Thomas (2005) among others.

6.2 Methodological Issues

Studying bilingual children requires attention to methodological issues deriving from the study of child language at large, as well as from research on adult bilingualism. In addition, certain methodological issues are specific to bilingual development (Hoff & Rumiche, 2011). For example, in selecting bilingual children for longitudinal or cross-sectional studies, in addition to the usual variables such as gender, birth order, and socio-economic status, one must consider the patterns of language input to which the children are exposed. These patterns include one parent–one language, one parent–two languages, one environment–one language, one environment–two languages, etc (Romaine, 1995). Due to the wide variability in children's backgrounds, care should be taken to examine the input conditions in each child which will have implications for their patterns of dominance and development.

6.2.1 Language pairs

Among the many possible permutations, some language pairs are genetically and/ or typologically distant, while some are closer. If the languages being acquired are genetically related and/or have a history of contact, there will be cognate lexical items, such as German *mein* and Swedish *min* "my." Such cognates may facilitate, hinder or otherwise affect development: they are thought to function as triggers for code-mixing, for example (Kootstra, Van Hell, & Dijkstra, 2012). If the languages share typological affinities, there will be points of structural overlap between them, which may be loci of code-mixing and/or cross-linguistic influence. For example, Chinese and Japanese have similar prenominal relative clauses, which can influence each other developmentally (Yabuki-Soh, 2007). Chinese and English are both SVO languages with several points of overlap which facilitate syntactic transfer (Yip & Matthews, 2007, p. 208). Conversely, typologically distant pairs such as English and Japanese have relatively few points of overlap. This may be a factor in the lack of cross-linguistic influence observed in studies of Japanese-English development such as Mishina-Mori (2002), since structural overlap appears to be a prerequisite for transfer (Hulk & Müller, 2000; see also Chapter 7).

Just as English and other Indo-European languages are over-represented in linguistics at large, so in bilingual development an overwhelming number of studies include English as one of the target languages, while an even higher percentage involves one or more European languages. For example, among five seminal studies of the 1980s cited by De Houwer (2009, p. 13), the language pairs involved were German–French, French–English, Norwegian–English, Spanish–English, and Dutch–English. This is far from being a representative sample, and it may have given us an incomplete picture of aspects of bilingual development. Childhood bilingualism will be better understood when investigated against a rich background of linguistic diversity, extending the database from pairing English and European languages to typologically unrelated languages with very different structures. For example, properties of Chinese such as lexical tone, topic prominence, word order, classifiers, and null arguments raise new possibilities for interaction between a child's developing linguistic systems (Yip & Matthews, 2010).

In practice, the choice of a language pair to be studied is usually determined by the availability of participants (as in the case of parent-researchers) and other practical concerns. In order to make original contributions, such studies need to be designed to exploit the properties of the language pair being acquired. Another requirement is to consider the development of both languages. Studies of bilingual children have often focused on one language, such as English in the case of immigrant children. To provide a fuller picture of bilingual acquisition in such cases, aspects of both English and the home language should be investigated since both languages are developing concurrently.

6.2.2 Language mode

Among the many contributions made to bilingualism research by François Grosjean, the notion of language mode is especially fundamental. Grosjean's model sees bilinguals as operating along a continuum from a monolingual mode (in which one language is activated and in use) to a bilingual mode (in which two or more languages are activated and in use.) The model assumes that there is always a "base" language A in which the speaker is primarily operating in a particular context. This base language need not correspond to a bilingual's dominant language, but is determined by the communicative situation. At the monolingual end of the continuum, language A is fully activated while language α is activated to the minimum degree (Grosjean assumes that it can never be entirely "turned off"). At the bilingual end, language α is strongly activated (but not as strongly as the base language A, the language being produced or perceived). In between these two extremes, intermediate positions are possible in which language α is partly activated (Grosjean, 2008, p. 41). According to this model, a speaker operates in a bilingual mode when speakers of both languages are present (either in the form of bilinguals or monolingual speakers of different languages), and the bilingual's behavior will differ accordingly: in particular, the speaker will be more likely to code-mix when in a bilingual mode (Grosjean, 2008, p. 72). The bilingual is in a monolingual mode when interacting with monolinguals, reading in a single language, etc. Crucially, since the bilingual's mechanisms for production and comprehension contain two distinct systems, in order to operate monolingually one system needs to be deactivated or inhibited so as to prevent code-mixing or production of an utterance in the "wrong" language. This inhibition appears to underlie bilinguals' superior ability to ignore distracting stimuli (see Chapter 9).

Relatively little research has applied the distinction between language modes to child bilingualism, and Grosjean (1998, 2008) suggests that studies should control for language mode. In studies such as Yip and Matthews (2007), two researchers were each assigned to speak a different language to the child in each recording session, and attempted to act as monolingual speakers: for example, they would pretend not to understand when the children used the other language. However, the researchers were in fact bilingual and the children often showed awareness of this. Consequently, it cannot be assumed that a child interacting in English was in a monolingual mode. Instead of "feigning" monolingualism, Grosjean suggests, a true monolingual researcher needs to be involved in order to ensure that a participant is operating in a monolingual mode. A bilingual mode can readily be induced by having bilingual researchers from the same community as the participants being studied.

Children's ability to produce language appropriately with different interlocutors suggests that they are able to switch between modes in much the same way as adults do (Deuchar & Quay, 2000; Lanza, 2004). Bilingual parents will also shift along the continuum. For example, some parents intentionally adopt a monolingual mode, "feigning" monolingualism and refusing to accept code-mixing by the child. Other parents may operate in a bilingual mode, responding to code-mixing with the "move on" strategy and possibly code-mixing themselves (see Section 6.2.3 on parental discourse strategies).

6.2.3   Language choice

The ability to choose the appropriate language to speak is remarkable in bilingual children who have two or more languages in their repertoire. Choosing which language to speak at a given time is determined by a range of factors including the interlocutor, the linguistic context, the topic of conversation, etc. Bilingual children develop sensitivity to these factors at an early age (Sinka & Schelletter, 1998; De Houwer, 2009, p. 145).

Children may differ in the degree to which they are sensitive to the factors governing language choice, but they are generally able to switch to the language appropriate to the speech situation. An important factor here is how the adult's language choice is made in the environment that the bilingual child is exposed to (Mishina, 1999): What is the expectation for the child to speak which language in which context? Do parents cue the child about the wrong language choice using certain discourse strategies? (Lanza, 2004).

6.2.4   Language dominance

It is often the case that one of the languages acquired by the bilingual child develops faster and/or shows greater complexity then the other at a given age. Such a language is termed the dominant language. Measures of language dominance include Mean Length of Utterance (MLU), Upper Bound, and lexical diversity in the two languages. Bilingual children with different dominance patterns need to be sorted out in order for comparisons among them to be meaningful. Patterns of language dominance may vary over time during the course of development (Romaine, 1995).

Dominance is a traditional notion which remains part of many theories of bilingualism and bilingual development. Its status has been questioned on a number of grounds, including problems of measurement as well as conceptual necessity (Müller, 2003; De Houwer, 2009). In response, Lanza (2004) and Grosjean (2008) reaffirm the psycholinguistic status of language dominance. In view of these questions, many recent studies have referred instead to a child's "stronger" and "weaker" languages. These are purely descriptive terms which avoid any commitment to dominance as an abstraction.

A number of studies have referred to contrasts in Mean Length of Utterance (MLU) as an indication of language dominance (Müller, 2003; Cantone, 2007). MLU can be calculated easily using the MLU command in CLAN (MacWhinney, 2000) but this depends on the transcripts used: in particular, the decisions made on what is a word and what constitutes an utterance. Moreover, a higher MLU indicates a dominant language only if the languages are comparable in areas such as overall morphological complexity. In response to these concerns, Yip and Matthews (2006, 2007) propose using MLU differentials (the difference between MLU values for a child's two languages) as a *relative* measure of the development of each language.

Upper Bound (UB) is a measure of the longest (and presumably most complex) utterance in a sample. UB is used alongside MLU by Bernardini and Schlyter (2004) to quantify the difference between Swedish as the stronger language and French or Italian as the weaker language in the children studied.

Another approach is to use on-line methods. For example, the Hawaii Assessment of Language Access (HALA) test developed by O'Grady, Schafer, Perla, Lee, and Wieting (2009) measures the time taken to name a basic vocabulary item displayed on a screen in each language. This assessment tool was developed for speakers of heritage and endangered languages, but is also feasible for use with young children.

6.2.5   Methods of data collection

In early studies such as that of Leopold (1939–49), the researchers kept a diary in which children's utterances were noted down. The disadvantages of this method are clear: choosing utterances to write down results in a selective, not a representative, sample, effectively precluding quantitative analysis. While superseded for many purposes by more powerful methods using corpora and experiments, the diary method still has its merits. Particularly for parent-researchers, continuous access to the child means that even relatively rare features can be recorded which might not occur at all in corpora (such as relative clauses in the study by Yip & Matthews, 2007).

Longitudinal studies are generally conducted using corpora, compiled by regular audio and/or video recording and transcription. The CHILDES database uses a standard format which facilitates searching and analysis using the CLAN program. For bilingual studies, corpora documenting the monolingual development of each language serve as controls (see Section 6.2.6).

An expanding repertoire of experimental methods is available to test children's perception, comprehension, and production. The methods applicable to bilingual children include essentially all those developed for first language acquisition (see McDaniel, McKee, & Cairns, 1996; Blom & Unsworth, 2010). Three methods testing infants' receptive language abilities including the visual fixation procedure, the head-turn preference, and the preferential looking procedure are discussed in Johnson and Zamuner (2010). Eye tracking as a technique to integrate the study of representation and real-time processing in child language acquisition research is reviewed in Sedivy (2010). Although functional Magnetic Resonance Imaging (fMRI) is not suitable for preschool children, Event-Related Potential (ERP) can be used on children of any age to study brain waves in response to linguistic stimuli (see Friederici & Thierry, 2008).

6.2.6   Controls

In order to explain some developmental feature in terms of bilingualism, reference needs to be made to a comparable monolingual data set serving as a control. For example, two nontarget features observed in bilingual children's Cantonese (Yip & Matthews, 2007) are dative sentences such as (1) in which the indirect object *keoi5* "him" is misplaced, and prepositional phrases following the verb (where Cantonese requires it to precede the verb), as in (2):

(1) Bei2   keoi5   zyu1gwu1lik1   laa1
    Give   him   chocolate   SFP
    "Give him chocolate!"   (Timmy 2;07;04)[1]

(2) Ngo5   daa2   din6waa2   hai2   li1dou6
    I   call   telephone   at   here
    "I'm making a call here."   (Llywelyn 2;08;08)

In principle, these could be developmental errors general to Cantonese-speaking children, or English-influenced features specific to Cantonese-English bilinguals. Comparison of bilingual and monolingual corpus data shows that feature (1) is a

---

[1] The age of the child is given in years, months, and days following the child's name. For example, (Timmy 2;07;04) indicates that the child is at two years, seven months, and four days.

general developmental feature of child Cantonese (Chan, 2010), whereas (2) is not (Yip & Matthews, 2007). Further complicating the comparison, the error in type (1) occurs more frequently in bilinguals, and persists for a longer period. In order to establish these points, comparable monolingual data are called for to serve as a baseline for comparison with bilingual data. For many languages (including Cantonese) such corpora are available through the CHILDES database; if they are not, this may constitute a major limitation on the bilingual study. Unsworth and Blom (2010) discuss how such comparisons can be used to address theoretical and practical questions.

6.3   Early Developmental Stages and Language Differentiation

Much evidence has shown that children develop distinct systems for their two languages. Recent work has shown that language differentiation is evident from the very earliest stages of development.

6.3.1   Speech perception in bilingual infants

A fascinating area of investigation in early bilingualism is speech perception and language discrimination. While bilingual children generally attain the same language milestones as their monolingual counterparts at the macrostructure level, there are differences in the microstructure of acquisition (Werker, Byers-Heinlein, & Fennell, 2009). Bilinguals must tackle unique challenges posed by bilingual input in language discrimination and separation, speech perception, phonetic and phonotactic development, word recognition, word learning, and aspects of conceptual development that underlie word learning.

Despite these challenges, bilingual infants show no delay in speech perception compared to monolinguals. In fact, bilingual exposure to rhythmically close languages enhances the child's ability to differentiate languages relative to monolinguals before the age of 5 months (Sebastián-Gallés, 2010). For example, Bosch and Sebastián-Gallés (2001) demonstrated the remarkable ability of infants at 4.5 months to distinguish between Spanish and Catalan, two rhythmically similar languages to which they are exposed in the environment.

Studies of early infant speech perception have examined how infants discriminate speech sounds from two languages. Monolingual infants show an early "language-general" sensitivity for phonetic perception in different languages, but this sensitivity becomes "language-specific" toward the end of the first year as native language experience accrues. A study of American infants exposed to Mandarin by Kuhl, Tsao and Liu (2003) highlights the importance of social interaction together with early exposure in mastering speech perception. The American infants were exposed to

Mandarin in two conditions: Live exposure vs. DVD exposure. In the Live exposure condition, 9-month-old infants were exposed to Mandarin through interaction with native speakers; in the DVD exposure condition, infants of the same age were exposed to recorded speech via videotapes or audiotapes of the same speakers and same speech material. Following the experimental sessions, the children's ability to discriminate Mandarin syllables was tested. Infants in the Live exposure condition showed significant effects of learning as evidenced in their syllable discrimination scores after 12 exposure sessions, whereas infants in the DVD exposure condition showed no effects of learning. These findings indicate that for successful second language phonetic learning to occur, it is crucial to have interpersonal social interaction between the infant and the native speaker.

6.3.2   Bilingual babbling

Given that babbling shows phonological features of the target language, it is possible to see language differentiation as early as the babbling stage, and even to identify a dominant language in bilingual infants' babbling. For example, studying 13 infants between of 10 and 14 months exposed to both French and English, Poulin-Dubois and Goodz (2001) found that those of French-speaking mothers showed consonantal characteristics of French in their babbling. Similarly, Maneva and Genesee (2002) found that infants aged 10–15 months showed different babbling patterns depending on the language of the speaker with whom they were interacting.

6.3.3   First words and the lexicon

The question of language differentiation arises regarding the child's first words: do they have two lexicons from the outset? A child developing a single lexicon incorporating words from both languages is not expected to have translation equivalents, but studies have shown that children do have translation equivalents from the earliest stages (Deuchar & Quay, 2000).

Another question is whether, like monolinguals, some bilingual children show a vocabulary spurt. Several studies have found a spurt in the child's dominant language: children for whom Cantonese is dominant show a spurt in their Cantonese (Yip & Matthews, forthcoming). Another possibility is that the spurt occurs later in the weaker language. As in monolinguals, the vocabulary spurt is subject to individual variation, occurring at a similar rate in both monolingual and bilingual children (Pearson & Fernández, 1994).

6.4   Cross-linguistic Influence

Effects of one language on the other are known collectively as cross-linguistic influence (CLI), a term which encompasses the traditional notions of transfer and interference (see Chapter 1, Section 1.5.2). While such phenomena have been reported, their status and prevalence are matters of debate. The Separate Development Hypothesis (SDH, De Houwer, 1990) holds that each language develops separately, much as it does in monolingual children acquiring the same languages. The main alternative is the Interdependent Development Hypothesis formulated by Paradis and Genesee (1996) who consider the following phenomena as signs of interdependent development:

1. delay, i.e., the acquisition of a property later than expected as a result of development in the other language;
2. acceleration, i.e., the acquisition of a property earlier than expected as a result of development in the other language;
3. transfer, i.e., "incorporation of a grammatical property from one language into the other."

Evidence has been adduced to support both hypotheses. Several studies based on European languages have argued for separate development (De Houwer, 1990, 2009; Meisel, 1994, 2001). Interdependent development has been observed by Döpke (2000), Silva-Corvalán and Montanari (2008), Yip and Matthews (2000, 2007) among others. The conflicting claims and findings can be explained on a number of grounds. Firstly, CLI is most often observed when the children involved have a dominant or stronger language, as in Yip and Matthews' (2007) study where the children's Cantonese as the stronger language influences their English extensively. Secondly, there are issues involving the interpretation of the data. For example, Mishina-Mori (2005) documents both separate development and instances of CLI between English and Japanese, but De Houwer (2009, pp. 350–351) interprets this study as supporting the SDH. A third possibility is that CLI occurs in some domains but not in others. Several attempts have been made to specify the domains in which cross-linguistic influence may occur. An influential proposal by Hulk and Müller (2000) specifies two conditions:

(a) the structure in question involves an interface such as that between syntax and pragmatics;
(b) there is surface overlap between the two languages, with language A allowing one option and language α allowing two (one of which overlaps with language A).

An example of the interface condition (a) involves dislocated sentences, a syntactic pattern which serves pragmatic purposes such as foregrounding and backgrounding of sentence constituents. This construction is especially productive in French and, accordingly, French-English bilingual children produce significantly more dislocations in their English than monolingual children, including qualitatively different and ill-formed examples such as (3) where the subject *this* is "dislocated" to the right; similarly, French-Dutch bilingual children transfer the

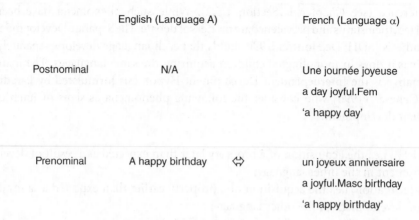

Figure 6.1: Structural overlap between English and French in adjective placement.

construction from French to their Dutch, as in (4) where *dat* "that" appears in the dislocated position (Notley, Van der Linden, & Hulk, 2005):

(3) Is a big one this?   (JER 2;05;11)
(4) Is Winnie the Pooh dat   (THO 2;8)
     Is Winnie the Pooh that
     "That's Winnie the Pooh."

An example of the overlap condition involves adjective placement in English and French. While English has only preverbal adjectives, French allows adjectives both before and after the noun. The overlap between the English option and the second French option fulfils the condition for transfer (Figure 6.1).

Based on the overlap condition, we expect influence from English to French, and indeed French-English bilingual children show signs of being influenced by the English option, namely prenominal adjective placement, in their French (Nicoladis, 2006).

Given that CLI occurs, the next question is how to interpret these phenomena. In particular, to what extent are they systematic? Adopting the Chomskyan distinction between competence and performance, CLI could apply at either level, or at both. For Paradis and Genesee (1996), systemic influence is "influence at the level of representation or competence, sustained over a period of time." Nicoladis (2006) outlines a performance account for the cases of CLI observed in her study cited above. While it is likely that CLI can occur as a performance phenomenon, Matthews and Yip (2011) argue that CLI must apply at the level of (transitional) competence in categorical cases of transfer. For example, 100% of Sophie and Alicia's *where*-questions in the corpus showed wh-in situ under the influence of Cantonese, as in:

(5) [with lotion on palm] Put in where?   (Sophie 2;06;20)

In the same children, Mok (2011) found evidence for CLI between Cantonese and English in speech rhythm. Cantonese is a syllable-timed language, with syllables spaced at approximately equal intervals, while English is stress-timed. In the bilingual children's English, syllables are more evenly spaced than in monolingual children, with a rhythm closer to that of Cantonese. At the same time, the bilingual children's Cantonese also differs subtly from that of monolingual children, showing a tendency toward simpler syllable structures in Cantonese. This pattern of asymmetrical influence is consistent with that seen in syntactic development in the same children, with Cantonese being the dominant language (Yip & Matthews, 2007).

6.5　Code-mixing

Bilingual children naturally mix their languages: that is, they use both languages in a single sentence. This is known as code-mixing (which can involve borrowing or code-switching, as described in Chapter 1, Section 1.5). In a typical example from Lanza (2004, p. 353), the child inserts an English noun *hair* into an otherwise Norwegian utterance, adding the suffixed definite article *-et*:

(6) Du　　vaske　hairet　　　(Siri 2;06)
　　you　　wash　hair-DEF
　　"You wash your hair"

Importantly, language mixing in young bilinguals is not necessarily evidence of attrition of a weaker language or failure of inhibitory control (Halmari, 2005). Rather than being a sign of lack of differentiation between the two linguistic systems, code-mixing proves to be quite systematic, subject to principles that govern when and where to mix languages. In recent work, code-mixing is seen as a resource which children exploit to express themselves more fully and effectively. This positive view, however, conflicts with parental and educational views which still tend to disapprove of code-mixing.

6.5.1　Code-mixing and input

Being a feature of most bilingual societies, and a behavior practiced by most bilingual individuals, code-mixing forms part of the input to most children developing bilingual competence. Even parents who claim not to mix themselves are unlikely to be able to avoid it consistently.

A close relationship between input and output can be seen qualitatively and quantitatively. In data from the Hong Kong Bilingual Child Language Corpus, we regularly find children producing code-mixing following adult input using the same mixed item. In a typical example from Yiu (2005), the child follows the adult investigator's lead in inserting the noun *turtle*:

(7) Adult: Ngo5dei6   waan2-zo2 # *turtle* sin1 laa1, hou2-mou2   aa3
            We   play-ASP turtle   first SFP good-not-good SFP
            "Let's play with the turtle first, shall we?"
    Child: Ngo5dei6 jau5 [/] jau5   loeng5   go3   *turtle* gaa3
            We   have   have   two   CL   turtle SFP
            "We have two turtles!"
                                                          (Kathryn 3;02;19)

In the Hong Kong data there is an asymmetry in the direction of mixing: mixing is
more common in Cantonese transcripts – such as the sample in (7) – than English
ones. This holds true even for Cantonese-dominant children, who might be expected
to have more need for code-mixing when producing English. This asymmetry
reflects the fact that code-mixing is common in adult Cantonese as used by English-
educated bilinguals (Chan, 1998, 2003; Li, 1996), whereas it is relatively rare to insert
Cantonese words or phrases while speaking English.

Further evidence for the relationship between input and code-mixing comes
from the French-English environment of Québec. Comeau, Genesee, and Lapaquette
(2003) manipulated the rate of code-mixing in the input by having researchers
interact with the same children using different degrees of code-mixing. A close
relationship was found between rates of mixing produced by the adults and
children.

6.5.2   Caregiver responses to code-mixing

Another factor in the development of code-mixing involves the responses of parents/
care-givers to mixing by children. Various parental "discourse strategies" are identified by Lanza (2004):

1. Minimal Grasp strategy: the parent indicates lack of understanding of the
   child's mixed utterance (*What did you say?*)
2. Expressed Guess strategy: the parent reformulates the child's mixed utterance
   by way of a guess (*Is that what you mean?*)
3. Repetition: the parent reformulates the child's mixed utterance in the target
   language without code-mixing.
4. Move on: the parent continues the interaction without "flagging" the child's
   mixing in any way.
5. Code-switching: the parent switches into the language which the child has
   introduced by means of code-mixing.

Parental use of these strategies is related to views of code-mixing in particular
societies and families. In some European contexts, such as the Norwegian-English
families studied in Lanza (2004), strategies (1–3) which question or correct the
child's mixing are often used. In Cantonese-English code-mixing the *move on* strategy is common, because such mixing is widespread and accepted in society at large.

The *Expressed Guess* strategy is also found, as in the following exchange, where the child inserts the English word *ant* into a Cantonese sentence, which is immediately queried by the adult investigator who prompts the child with the Cantonese equivalent *ngai* "ant":

(8) Child: Ngo5   zek3   ant   le1
                I   CL   ant   SFP
                "Where's my ant?"
     Adult: ant?
     Child: ant   hai6   gam2joeng2   gaa3
                ant   is   like that   SFP
                "Ants are like that."
     Adult: Ngai5   hai6   mai6   aa3
                ant   be   not-be   SFP
                "You mean ants?"   (Sophie 2;03;14)

6.5.3   Structural aspects of code-mixing

Many studies have shown adult code-mixing to be systematic, and this proves to be true of children's code-mixing too. In the Québec context (French-English), for example, Paradis, Nicoladis, and Genesee (2000) found that children follow the same constraints as adults. An initial structural question involves the direction of language mixing: does a child insert English words while speaking Spanish, and/or Spanish elements when speaking English? The Matrix Language Frame (MLF) model (Myers-Scotton, 1993, 2006) assumes that one language serves as the matrix language into which the other may be inserted as the embedded language. For example, in (7) and (8) Cantonese would be the matrix language and English the embedded language.

One of the proposed constraints, the System Morpheme Principle, holds that lexical but not functional morphemes can be inserted as embedded language elements (Myers-Scotton, 1993). Thus when inserting an English verb into a Cantonese utterance, children (like adults) use Cantonese aspect markers, as in (9) where the perfective aspect marker *zo2* is attached to the verb *plant*:

(9) Hai6 aa3 keoi5dei6 plant-zo2 go2 di1 gaa3 laa3
    yes   SFP they   plant-ASP that CL SFP SFP
    "Yes, they have planted those."   (Kathryn 3;06;18)

While this model can usefully be applied to bilingual children, it has weaknesses both in general (MacSwan, 2000) and specifically in bilingual development (Cantone, 2007). One difficulty is that in two-word utterances it may not be feasible to identify a matrix language at all. For example, the following synonymous questions were produced by the same child (Yip & Matthews, 2007, p. 122):

   (10) Where's dang6?
        where's chair
        "Where's the chair?"   (Charlotte 1;10;09)
   (11) Bin1dou6   chair?
        where   chair
        "Where's the chair?"   (Charlotte 1;11;05)

In (10), if English is the matrix language, the insertion of a Cantonese noun *dang* "chair" is consistent with the model, but in (11) this would mean inserting a Cantonese function word, *bin1dou6* "where" into an English utterance, which is both inconsistent with adult usage and theoretically unexpected: the System Morpheme Principle (Myers-Scotton, 1993) requires such functional elements to be supplied by the matrix language. Alternatively, if we consider (11) to be a Cantonese utterance with the English noun *chair* inserted, this would be a rare example of fronting of *wh*-words being applied to Cantonese (Yip & Matthews, 2007, p. 122).

An additional variable involves the balance between the child's languages. Several studies have hypothesized that children tend to resort to words from the stronger language while speaking the weaker language. The *Dominant Language Hypothesis* (Petersen, 1988) states that the grammatical morphemes from the dominant language may co-occur with lexical morphemes of either language, whereas the grammatical morphemes of the non-dominant language cannot co-occur with the lexical morphemes of the dominant language. Petersen (1988) found that an English-Danish bilingual child used English morphology with Danish lexical items but not vice versa; this asymmetry was attributed to dominance of English, that is, the inflectional morphology of the dominant language is used with lexical morphemes of the non-dominant language. A related proposal, the Ivy-Hypothesis (Bernardini & Schlyter, 2004) hypothesizes that functional elements of the stronger language are retained when speaking the weaker language. For example, a child may combine a determiner from the stronger language (Swedish) with a lexical item from the weaker language (Italian):

   (12) en   bacca
        DET (Sw)   N (It)
        "a berry"   (Lukas 2;0)

The Ivy-Hypothesis sees the weaker language "growing" on a scaffolding of functional categories provided by the stronger language. In the case studies from Sweden, Swedish is the stronger language and French or Italian the weaker language. While this represents a possible developmental pattern, the applicability of the Ivy-Hypothesis may be limited by the language pairs (European languages with moderately complex inflectional morphology) as well as the balance of the two languages (strongly unbalanced, with a MLU differential of around 1 point: see Bernardini & Schlyter, 2004, p. 58).

6.5.4   Motivations for code-mixing

Motivations for code-mixing are already many and varied in adult language (see Chapter 1, Section 1.5): in the case of Hong Kong these include economy, identity, and humor (Li, 1996). A similar range of motivations may underlie code-mixing in bilingual children's language. One possibility is that in speaking Language A the child uses a word from Language α when she lacks the word in Language A. Montanari (2009, p. 510) argued that mixed utterances produced by a Tagalog-Spanish-English child were generally caused by vocabulary gaps. As noted in Section 6.5.1, in the Hong Kong data mixing is more common when children are conversing in Cantonese than in English. While the insertion of English words into Cantonese sentences can be attributed to patterns of code-mixing in the input, the reverse (mixing of Cantonese items when conversing in English) may be due to lexical gaps. For example:

> (13) Lei5 bump into my *fei4 tou5laam5*
>   "You bump into my fat belly."   (Kathryn 4;00;15)

The word *tou5laam5* is not a neutral body part term, but refers specifically to a protruding belly, and English lacks such a word (*beer belly* being still more specific). In addition, the Cantonese word is colloquial and inherently "cute," so that the example (13) is invariably amusing to Cantonese speakers. This illustrates how humor may be an additional motivation for code-mixing (Siegel, 1995).

Another possibility is that mixing could be "triggered" in specific circumstances. For example, a prior instance of code-mixing (whether produced by the child or an interlocutor) may lead to subsequent code-mixing by the child. Possible mechanisms for triggering are investigated in Kootstra, Van Hell, and Dijkstra (2012).

6.6   Extensions and Applications

Following a spate of research in recent decades, bilingual first language acquisition is beginning to be understood in some depth and detail. There are many logical extensions and applications for such work. Here the extension from two languages to three will be briefly discussed, followed by a note on applications to clinical settings.

6.6.1   From bilingual to trilingual acquisition

Beyond two languages, the field of bilingual development extends naturally to children with three or more languages. Research on trilingual children has begun to probe the limits of the child's language faculty. While the principles involved may be essentially the same for trilingual as for bilingual development, interactions between the developing language systems are necessarily more complex. Principles developed for bilingual development, such as structural overlap and input ambiguity, can be extended to the trilingual context but their implementation becomes correspondingly more elaborate. Three-way interactions raise new questions: for example, can two similar languages "gang up" to influence the third? What is the role of typological differences and similarities in predicting and accounting for transfer? How is language dominance manifested in trilingual individuals and what effects does it have? Is there trilingual delay, and if so, does this effect differ from bilingual delay?

A typology of trilingual children based on patterns of exposure is proposed in Hoffman (2001). Based on both quantitative and qualitative differences between bilingual and trilingual speakers, Hoffman suggests that trilingual competence is distinct from bilingual competence. Assuming that trilingualism is simply an extension of bilingualism would miss many important differences, notably in the possible interactions between language systems. Developmental outcomes are also different: although case studies show that trilingual development resulting in productive competence is possible, other attested outcomes include passive competence and/ or attrition in one or more of the three languages.

Several successful cases of trilingual development have been described in which the parents speak different languages and a third language is spoken in the community. In Cruz-Ferreira's (2006) study, the parents speak Portuguese and Swedish, respectively, and the three siblings acquire English from their environment and schooling in Singapore and elsewhere. In Wang's (2008) case study, the mother is a native speaker of Mandarin, the father of French, and the family lives in New York. The two siblings show the ability to distinguish between the three languages from as early as 1;06. The children's Chinese showed some of the same phenomena reported in bilingual development, such as overgeneralization of the default classifier *ge* to nouns which do not take the classifier in Mandarin, as in *wu ge tian* "five CL day" where the classifier is redundant between the numeral and the noun (Wang, 2008, p. 79).

6.6.2 Bilingual children in clinical settings

An important practical question is how bilingual development interacts with speech and language disorders. In particular, Specific Language Impairment (SLI), in which impaired development of language is not accompanied by general cognitive impairment, raises a range of theoretical and practical problems (Paradis, 2010). The challenges include disentangling the effects of bilingualism and SLI, and diagnosing SLI in bilingual populations (see Armon-Lotem, 2012 and related papers in the same volume).

In the case of bilingual children with SLI and other language-related problems, parents often wonder whether bilingualism imposes an additional burden. An outdated view, deeply entrenched in some parts of the world and sometimes expressed by teachers or speech therapists, is that one of the languages should be withheld in order to reduce the burden on the child. This practice is not supported by research, which shows that bilingualism does not exacerbate any of the problems posed by speech disorders. The current view from professional experts is therefore not to withdraw one of the languages from the environment (Genesee, Paradis, & Crago, 2005). Far from being a burden, bilingualism may well be advantageous: just as bilingualism brings cognitive advantages to bilingual children without impairment, it can similarly be expected to offer bilingual children with SLI cognitive advantages. While such effects have been convincingly demonstrated in experiments with typical bilingual children (see Bialystok, this volume), the nature and extent of the cognitive advantages of bilingualism in children with various forms of language impairment await future research.

Research Questions

1. In order to control for language mode, Grosjean suggests that monolingual investigators must be involved in experiments or elicitation situations that are intended to elicit data in a particular speech context. How could this be achieved in a multilingual environment such as Singapore or India in which monolinguals are rare or nonexistent?
2. Some people are skeptical about the ability of infants and children to keep two languages apart, thinking that they may be confused. What kind of experimental evidence would demonstrate language differentiation at each stage of development?
3. Consider how to respond to the following question from a concerned parent:
   "What's the impact on a child's language development if the parents or playgroup teachers speak a mixture of languages to the child? For example, mixing languages in a sentence or alternating between languages in different sentences? Would this be an impediment to their language learning?"

Further Readings

Genesee, Fred, Paradis, Johanne, & Crago, Martha. 2004. *Dual Language Development and Disorders*. Baltimore, MD: Brokes.

McCardle, Peggy & Hoff, Erika (eds). 2006. *Childhood Bilingualism: Research on Infancy through School Age*. Clevedon, UK: Multilingual Matters.

Yip, Virginia & Matthews, Stephen. (forthcoming). *Bilingual Development*. Cambridge: Cambridge University Press.

References

Armon-Lotem, Sharon. 2012. Introduction: Bilingual children with SLI – the nature of the problem. *Bilingualism: Language and Cognition* 15. 1–4.

Bernardini, Petra & Schlyter, Suzanne. 2004. Growing syntactic structure and the weaker language: The Ivy-Hypothesis. *Bilingualism: Language and Cognition* 7. 49–69.

Blom, Elma & Unsworth, Sharon (eds). 2010. *Experimental Methods in Language Acquisition Research*. Amsterdam: John Benjamins.

Bonnesen, Matthias. 2007. The status of the "weaker" language in unbalanced French/German language acquisition. *Bilingualism: Language and Cognition* 12. 177–192.

Bosch, Laura & Sebastián-Gallés, Núria. 2001. Evidence of early language differentiation abilities in infants from bilingual environments. *Infancy* 2. 29–49.

Bosch, Laura & Sebastián-Gallés, Núria. 2003. Simultaneous bilingualism and the perception of a language-specific vowel contrast in the first year of life. *Language and Speech* 46. 217–243.

Cantone, Katja Francesca. 2007. *Code-switching in Bilingual Children*. Dordrecht, The Netherlands: Springer.

Chan, Angel Wing-Shan. 2010. The Cantonese double object construction with *bei2* "give" in bilingual children: The role of input. *International Journal of Bilingualism* 14. 65–85.

Chan, Brian Hok-Shing. 1998. How does Cantonese-English code-mixing work? In Martha Pennington (ed.), *Language in Hong Kong at Century's End*, pp. 191–216. Hong Kong: Hong Kong University Press.

Chan, Brian Hok-Shing. 2003. *Aspects of the Syntax, the Pragmatics, and the Production of Code-switching*. New York: Peter Lang.

Chomsky, Noam. 1980. *Rules and Representations*. New York: Columbia University Press.

Comeau, Liane, Genesee, Fred, & Lapaquette, Lindsay. 2003. The Modeling Hypothesis and child bilingual codemixing. *International Journal of Bilingualism* 7. 113–126.

Cruz-Ferreira, Madalena. 2006. *Three is a Crowd? Acquiring Portuguese in a Trilingual Environment*. Clevedon, UK: Multilingual Matters.

De Houwer, Annick. 1990. *The Acquisition of Two Languages from Birth: A Case Study*. Cambridge: Cambridge University Press.

De Houwer, Annick. 2009. *Bilingual First Language Acquisition*. Clevedon, UK: Multilingual Matters.

Deuchar, Margaret & Quay, Suzanne. 2000. *Bilingual Acquisition: Theoretical Implications of a Case Study*. Oxford: Oxford University Press.

Döpke, Susan (ed.). 2000. *Cross-linguistic Structures in Simultaneous Bilingualism*. Amsterdam: John Benjamins.

Francis, Norbert. 2011. Imbalances in bilingual development: A key to understanding the faculty of language. *Language Sciences* 33. 76–89.

Friederici, Angela D. & Thierry, Guillaume. (eds). 2008. *Early Language Development: Bridging Brain and Behavior*. Amsterdam: John Benjamins.

Gathercole, Virginia C. Mueller & Hoff, Erika. 2007. Input and the acquisition of language: Three questions. In Erica Hoff & Marilyn Shatz (eds), *The Handbook of Language Development*, pp. 107–127. Malden, MA: Blackwell.

Gathercole, Virginia C. Mueller & Thomas, Enlli Môn. 2005. Minority language survival: Input factors influencing the acquisition of Welsh. In James Cohen, Kara T. McAlister, Kellie Rolstad, & Jeff MacSwan (eds), *Proceedings of the 4th International Symposium on Bilingualism*, pp. 852–874. Somerville, MA: Cascadilla Press.

Gauthier, Karine & Genesee, Fred. 2011. Language development in internationally adopted children: A special case of early second language learning. *Child Development* 82 (3). 887–901.

Genesee, Fred, Paradis, Johanne, & Crago, Martha. 2004. *Dual Language Development and Disorders*. Baltimore, MD: Brokes.

Grosjean, François. 1998. Studying bilinguals: Methodological and conceptual issues. *Bilingualism: Language and Cognition* 1(2). 131–149.

Grosjean, François. 2008. *Studying Bilinguals*. Oxford/New York: Oxford University Press.

Gupta, Anthea F. 1994. *The Step-tongue: Children's English in Singapore*. Clevedon, UK: Multilingual Matters.

Halmari, Helena. 2005. "I'm forgetting both": L1 maintenance and codeswitching in Finnish-English language contact. *International Journal of Bilingualism* 9. 197–433.

Hoff, Erica & Rosario Luz Rumiche. (2011). *Studying bilingual children*. In Erica Hoff (ed.), *Research Methods in Child Language: A Practical Guide*. Wiley-Blackwell.

Hoffman, Charlotte. 2001. Towards a description of trilingual competence. *International Journal of Bilingualism* 5. 1–17.

Hulk, Aafke & Müller, Natascha. 2000. Bilingual first language acquisition at the interface between syntax and pragmatics. *Bilingualism: Language and Cognition* 3. 227–244.

Johnson, Elizabeth & Zamuner, Tania. 2010. Using infants and toddler testing methods in language acquisition research. In Elma Blom & Sharon Unsworth (eds), *Experimental Methods in Language Acquisition Research*, pp. 201–222. Amsterdam: John Benjamins.

Kootstra, Gerrit Jan, Van Hell, Janet G., & Dijkstra, Ton. (2012). Priming of code-switches in sentences: The role of lexical repetition, cognates, and language proficiency. *Bilingualism: Language and Cognition*.

Kuhl, Patricia K., Tsao, Feng-Ming, & Liu, Huei-Mei. 2003. Foreign-language experience in infancy: Effects of short-term exposure and social interaction on phonetic learning. *Proceedings of the National Academy of Sciences of the United States of America* 100. 9096–9101.

Lanza, Elizabeth. 2004. *Language Mixing in Infant Bilingualism: A Sociolinguistic Perspective*. Oxford: Oxford University Press.

Leopold, Werner. 1939, 1947, 1949a, 1949b. *Speech Development of a Bilingual Child: A Linguist's Record* (Vols 1–4). Evanston, IL: Northwestern University Press.

Li, David. 1996. *Issues in Bilingualism and Biculturalism: A Hong Kong Case Study*. New York: Peter Lang.

MacWhinney, Brian. 2000. *The CHILDES Project: Tools for Analyzing Talk*. (3rd edition). Mahwah, NJ: Lawrence Erlbaum.

Maneva, Blagovesta & Genesee, Fred. 2002. Bilingual babbling: Evidence for language differentiation in dual language acquisition. In Barbora Skarabela, Sarah Fish, & Anna Do (eds), *BUCLD26: The Proceedings of the 26th Boston University Conference on Language Development*, pp. 383–392. Somerville, MA: Cascadilla Press.

Matthews, Stephen & Yip, Virginia. 2011. Unbalanced bilingual acquisition as a mechanism of grammatical change. *Bilingualism: Language and Cognition* 14. 159–161.

McDaniel, Dana, McKee, Cecile, & Cairns, Helen Smith (eds). 1996. *Methods for Assessing Children's Syntax*. Cambridge, MA: MIT Press.

McLaughlin, Barry. 1978. *Second Language Acquisition in Childhood*. Hillsdale, NJ: Lawrence Erlbaum.

MacSwan, Jeff. 2000. The architecture of the bilingual language faculty: Evidence from intrasentential codeswitching. *Bilingualism: Language and Cognition* 3. 37–54.

Meisel, Jürgen (ed.). 1994. *Bilingual First Language Acquisition: French and German Grammatical Development*. Amsterdam: John Benjamins.

Meisel, Jürgen. 2001. The simultaneous acquisition of two first languages: Early differentiation and subsequent development of grammars. In Jasone Cenoz & Fred Genesee (eds), *Trends in Bilingual Acquisition*, pp. 11–41. Amsterdam: John Benjamins.

Mishina, Satomi. 1999. The role of parental input and discourse strategies in the early language mixing of a bilingual child. *Multilingua* 18. 1–30.

Mishina-Mori, Satomi. 2002. Language differentiation of the two languages in early bilingual development: A case study of Japanese/English bilingual children. *International Review of Applied Linguistics* 40. 211–233.

Mishina-Mori, Satomi. 2005. Autonomous and interdependent development of two language systems in Japanese/English simultaneous bilinguals: Evidence from question formation. *First Language* 25. 291–315.

Mok, Peggy. 2011. The acquisition of speech rhythm by three-year-old bilingual and monolingual children: Cantonese and English. *Bilingualism: Language and Cognition* 14. 458–472.

Montanari, Simona. 2009. Multi-word combinations and the emergence of differentiated ordering patterns in early trilingual development. *Bilingualism: Language and Cognition* 12(4). 503–519.

Montrul, Silvina. 2008. *Incomplete Acquisition in Bilingualism: Re-examining the Age Factor*. Amsterdam: John Benjamins.

Müller, Natascha. 1998. Transfer in bilingual first language acquisition. *Bilingualism: Language and Cognition* 1. 151–71.

Müller, Natascha (ed.). 2003. *(In)vulnerable Domains in Multilingualism*. Amsterdam: John Benjamins.

Myers-Scotton, Carol. 1993. *Duelling languages: Grammatical structure in codeswitching*. Oxford: Clarendon Press.

Myers-Scotton, Carol. 2006. *Multiple Voices: An Introduction to Bilingualism*. Oxford: Blackwell.

Nicoladis, Elena. 2006. Cross-linguistic transfer in adjective-noun strings by preschool bilingual children. *Bilingualism: Language and Cognition* 9. 15–32.

Notley, Anna, Van der Linden, Elizabeth, & Hulk, Aafke. 2005. Crosslinguistic influence in bilingual children: The case of dislocation. In Sergio Baauw, Frank Drijkoningen, & Manuela Pinto (eds), *Roman Languages and Linguistics Theory 2005*, pp. 229–258. Amsterdam: John Benjamins.

O'Grady, William. 2005. *Syntactic Carpentry: An Emergentist Approach to Syntax*. Mahwah, NJ: Lawrence Erlbaum.

O'Grady, William, Schafer, Amy, Perla, Jawee, Lee, On-Soon, & Wieting, Julia. 2009. A psycholinguistic tool for the assessment of language loss: The HALA project. *Language Documentation and Conservation* 3. 100–112.

Paradis, Johanne. 2010. The interface between bilingual development and specific language impairment. *Applied Psycholinguistics* 31. 227–252.

Paradis, Johanne & Genesee, Fred. 1996. Syntactic acquisition in bilingual children: Autonomous or interdependent? *Studies in Second Language Acquisition* 18. 1–25.

Paradis, Johanne & Navarro, Samuel. 2003. Subject realization and crosslinguistic interference in the bilingual acquisition of Spanish and English: What is the role of the input? *Journal of Child Language* 30. 371–393.

Paradis, Johanne, Nicoladis, Elena, & Genesee, Fred. 2000. Early emergence of structural constraints on code-mixing: Evidence from French-English bilingual children. *Bilingualism: Language and Cognition* 3. 245–261.

Pavlenko, Aneta & Jarvis, Scott. 2002. Bidirectional transfer. *Applied Linguistics* 23. 190–214.

Pearson, Barbara Zurer & Fernandez, Sylvia C. 1994. Patterns of interaction in the lexical development in two languages of bilingual infants. *Language Learning* 44. 617–653.

Petersen, Jennifer. 1988. Word-internal code-switching constraints in a bilingual child's grammar. *Linguistics* 26. 479–493.

Poulin-Dubois, Dianne & Goodz, Naomi. 2001. Language differentiation in bilingual infants: Evidence from babbling. In Jasone Cenoz & Fred Genesee (eds), *Trends in Bilingual Acquisition*, pp. 95–106. Amsterdam: John Benjamins.

Romaine, Suzanne. 1995. *Bilingualism*. Oxford: Basil Blackwell.

Schlyter, Suzanne. 1993. The weaker language in bilingual Swedish-French children. In Kenneth Hyltenstam & Åke Viberg (eds), *Progression and Regression in Language*, pp. 289–308. Cambridge: Cambridge University Press.

Sebastián-Gallés, Núria. 2010. Bilingual language acquisition: Where does the difference lie? *Human Development* 53. 245–255.

Sedivy, Julie. 2010. Using eyetracking in language acquisition research. In Elma Blom & Sharon Unsworth (eds), *Experimental Methods in Language Acquisition Research*, pp. 115–138. Amsterdam: John Benjamins.

Siegel, Jeff. 1995. How to get a laugh in Fijian: Code-switching and humor. *Language in Society* 24 (1). 95–110.

Silva-Corvalan, Carmen & Montanari, Simona. 2008. The acquisition of *ser, estar* (and *be*) by a Spanish-English bilingual child: The early stages. *Bilingualism: Language and Cognition* 11. 341–360.

Sinka, Indra & Schelletter, Christina. 1998. Morphosyntactic development in bilingual children. *International Journal of Bilingualism* 2(3). 301–326.

Unsworth, Sharon & Blom, Elma. 2010. Comparing L1 children, L2 children and L2 adults. In Blom, Elma & Sharon Unsworth (eds), *Experimental Methods in Language Acquisition Research*, pp. 201–222. Amsterdam: John Benjamins.

Volterra, Virginia & Taeschner, Traute. 1978. The acquisition and development of language by bilingual children. *Journal of Child Language* 5. 311–326.

Wang, Xiao-lei. 2008. *Growing Up with Three Languages: Birth to Eleven*. Clevedon, UK: Multilingual Matters.

Werker, Janet F., Byers-Heinlein, Krista, & Fennell, Christopher T. 2009. Bilingual beginnings to learning words. *Philosophical Transactions of the Royal Society of London – Series B: Biological Sciences* 364. 3649–3663.

Wölck, Wolfgang. 1987/1988. Types of natural bilingual behavior: A review and revision. *The Bilingual Review/La Revista Bilingüe* 14. 3–16.

Yabuki-Soh, Noriko. 2007. Teaching relative clauses in Japanese: Exploring alternative types of instruction and the projection effect. *Studies in Second Language Acquisition* 29. 219–252.

Yip, Virginia & Matthews, Stephen. 2000. Syntactic transfer in a Cantonese-English bilingual child. *Bilingualism: Language and Cognition* 3. 193–208.

Yip, Virginia & Matthews, Stephen. 2006. Assessing language dominance in bilingual acquisition: A case for Mean Length Utterance differentials. *Language Assessment Quarterly* 3. 97–116.

Yip, Virginia & Matthews, Stephen. 2007. *The Bilingual Child: Early Development and Language Contact*. Cambridge: Cambridge University Press.

Yip, Virginia & Matthews, Stephen. 2010. The acquisition of Chinese in bilingual and multilingual contexts. *International Journal of Bilingualism* 14. 127–146.

Yip, Virginia & Matthews, Stephen. (forthcoming). *Bilingual Development*. Cambridge: Cambridge University Press.

Yiu, Sze-Man Emily. 2005. Asymmetrical language mixing in a Cantonese-English bilingual child. Paper presented at the 5th International Symposium on Bilingualism, Barcelona.

Chapter 7

Successive Language Acquisition
Ping Li

Unlike the situation with simultaneous language acquisition, which is defined by some scholars as "exposure to both languages from birth or within the first year" (see Chapter 6), successive acquisition of two languages can occur across the lifespan, in adolescence, in adulthood, as well as childhood. However, given that bilingual language learning is a complex continuum, the distinction between simultaneous versus successive language acquisition is necessarily arbitrary, as pointed out earlier. Nevertheless, this discussion does provide a convenient way to talk about different types of bilingual experiences and to examine different theoretical questions associated with different learning situations.

Because the study of simultaneous bilingual acquisition focuses on childhood, the theoretical issues there tend to be similar or closely related to the issues addressed in the domain of first or child language acquisition. Researchers are often reluctant to call the bilingual child's two languages "first language" (L1) versus "second language" (L2), given the nature of simultaneous acquisition. In contrast, the theoretical questions in the study of successive language acquisition are more closely related to those addressed in the domain of second language acquisition. Here, there is a relatively clear distinction between the learner's first language and second language. In most cases, the first language is the native language, the dominant, more frequently used, and stronger language, whereas the second language is the nonnative language, the less dominant, less frequently used, and weaker language. In addition, the age at which the second language is acquired varies greatly from individual to individual, and this variation and its impact on the speed and outcome of language acquisition has been a matter of intense theoretical debate for the last several decades. In this chapter, we will examine this "age of acquisition" effect and its theoretical implications.

This chapter is organized into three sections. In Section 7.1, we provide a review of the contentious critical period hypothesis and the different theoretical perspectives. In Section 7.2, we examine speech learning in infants, children, and adults, along with a brief discussion of the variables that could influence success in speech learning. In Section 7.3, we examine how the two languages influence one another in the mental representation of the bilingual learner during successive language acquisition, and how cross-language influences might surface not only in the direction from L1 to L2, but also from L2 to L1.

7.1   Age Effects in Second Language Acquisition

In an increasingly globalized world, knowing two or more languages confers distinct social, economic, and even cognitive benefits (see Chapter 9). Researchers and laymen alike are interested in second language acquisition for a variety of intellectual and pragmatic reasons. But anyone who has experience learning a second language will probably be struck by the apparent child-adult difference: while most children appear to be at ease acquiring multiple languages simultaneously or learning additional languages successively, adult learners appear to have significant difficulties, sometimes even with rudimentary aspects of new languages, after years of struggle. Such age-related differences in L2 learning have motivated researchers to look for explanations, and led to decades of intense debates on the cognitive and neural mechanisms of second language acquisition.

7.1.1   The critical period hypothesis

Perhaps no other domain in second language acquisition has generated so much public attention, debate, and controversy as the critical period hypothesis (CPH). Indeed, understanding of the critical period for language learning has been listed among the top 125 big science questions for the next quarter century in the 125th anniversary issue of *Science* (vol. 309, July 1, 2005). According to the original formulation of the CPH by Lenneberg (1967), the automatic acquisition of a language in the natural setting (e.g., from mere exposure to a given language) takes place only during a critical period (age 2 to puberty), after which language learning proceeds more slowly, and ultimately proves less successful (Lenneberg, 1967: see Long, 1990 for a review). Lenneberg linked this critical time window to constraints in brain development, and the endpoint of that period coincides with puberty, at which time, it was believed, brain lateralization is complete, that is, the language function is settled in the left hemisphere (for over 90% of people). This formulation and explanation of why children are better language learners than adults attracted a great deal of interest for its simplicity and conformity to intuition based on folk wisdom, and the idea that there is a fixed biological timetable for language development also accorded well with nativist views of language such as those championed by Noam Chomsky (1988).

While early work did not question this view of the CPH, few studies were actually devoted to experimentally testing the biological basis of the critical period in humans. Progress was made, however, in understanding the critical period of learning and maturation in other species, particularly in songbirds, perhaps because it was possible to isolate animals from their natural environment for extended periods, something that is naturally unethical and illegal with humans. In one study (Marler, 1970), researchers put baby white-crowned sparrows in acoustic isolation for a given period of time, and then exposed the birds to the normal songs their species. The amount of time in isolation for these birds varied from a few days to a few weeks to a few months. The longer the birds were in isolation, the worse their songs were when they grew up, compared to the song patterns of the normal white-crowned sparrows. The findings were clear: songbirds that did not get early exposure to their native tongue (bird songs) were unable to sing "natively." These data suggest that age of acquisition, at least in learning bird songs, is the determining factor for success in reaching a native level of vocal production.

7.1.2 Experimental studies of the critical period in successive language acquisition

While the CPH based on biological explanations seemed at first a highly viable account, in the 1980s researchers started to question this line of thinking by comparing children's and adults' linguistic performance with regard to both learning speed and ultimate attainment in the context of second language acquisition. In a series of comprehension and production tasks (e.g., auditory discrimination of sounds, translation), Snow and Hoefnagel-Höhle (1978) studied native English speakers who spent a year in the Netherlands learning Dutch, and showed that older children (12–15 years of age) had a faster rate of learning than the younger groups of children (3–5, 6–7, 8–10 years of age). This study, although limited in its scope (e.g., testing over a short period of time), countered the argument that older language learners are worse than younger learners. Further counter evidence to the biological account of the critical period is that lateralization appears to occur early in children, definitely much earlier than puberty, a time stipulated by Lenneberg for the end of the critical period. Many researchers felt uncomfortable with the use of "critical" for critical period, and instead adopted the term "sensitive period." The use of "sensitive" suggests more of a window of opportunity rather than a time period beyond which language acquisition becomes impossible (see Long, 1990 for discussion). More recently, researchers have adopted the term "age of acquisition" (AoA) to refer more generally to age-related differences in language acquisition, including effects of critical or sensitive periods.[1]

[1] The term AoA has been used in three distinct ways in the literature to refer to different age effects: the age at which a lexical item is acquired by monolingual speakers, the age at which L2 learning begins, and the age at which skills are acquired in nonlinguistic domains (see Hernandez & Li, 2007 for a review). Further complicating the picture is the use of AoA along with other terms to refer to overlapping concepts with slightly different focus, including critical period, sensitive period, age-related difference, age of onset (AoO), and age of arrival (AoA).

In 1989 Johnson and Newport published a study that later became highly influential. In that study, 46 successive language learners were tested on their knowledge of L2 grammar. They were native speakers of Chinese or Korean who learned English as a second language at various points in life. Johnson and Newport used "age of arrival" in the US as a measure of when the participants were first exposed to English, which varied from age 3 to age 39. They also used "length of residence" in the US to measure the participants' amount of English experience, which varied from 3 to 26 years by the time of the study. Participants were asked to listen to English sentences and make grammaticality judgments (i.e., judge whether a sentence was grammatical or not). Half of the sentences contained morphosyntactic errors such as lack of plural marking (e.g., *the farmer bought two pig at the market*) or wrong past tense (e.g., *a bat flewed into our attic last night*), and half were grammatical sentences. The sentence judgment scores were used as an index of a participant's performance in English, compared with judgment scores for the same set of sentences by native speakers of English. Findings from this study indicated that participants' age of arrival was a key factor in determining performance, when compared with other variables such as length of residence, motivation, and cultural identification. For learners who arrived in the US early (before age 16), performance in sentence judgments decreased linearly as age of arrival increased, whereas for those who arrived in the US late (after age 16), performance in sentence judgments was generally poor, but highly variable, and unrelated to age of arrival.

Johnson and Newport's study provided experimental grounds for the CPH, but also showed that the original CPH needed to be modified, in at least two respects. First, their data indicated that, contrary to common belief, the "critical period" has no sharp boundary before which performance is uniformly good and after which performance is uniformly bad. There is a linear decline before the critical period, such that the earlier the L2 is learned, the better the learner will perform in the L2. Second, there are large individual variations after the cutoff point (age 16), such that some learners do very well while others do poorly. One individual, even at the age of arrival of 23, could perform as well as native speakers. Such individual differences may be attributed to a number of cognitive, motivational, and social-cultural factors (including level of education, as demonstrated by Hakuta, Bialystok, & Wiley, 2003).

While Johnson and Newport's study contributed significantly to the understanding of the critical period for language acquisition, some subsequent studies were inconsistent with the general claim about the contrasting patterns for the early versus the late learner groups. Birdsong & Molis (2001), for example, attempted to replicate Johnson and Newport's study with Spanish learners, and found that early and late learners similarly showed negative correlations between L2 performance and age of acquisition. Other researchers found more complex, nonlinear patterns of development associated with age of acquisition. Liu, Bates, and Li (1992) tested Chinese learners of English who arrived in the US at varying ages, as in Johnson and Newport's study. They examined L2 learners' processing strategies in thematic role assignment in sentences (i.e., determining who does what to whom) rather than their knowledge of morphosyntax. Liu *et al.*'s data indicated that the late learners tended to show forward transfer, that is, they used L1 processing strategies for L2 comprehension, whereas early learners, depending on the age of L2 acquisition, showed either backward transfer (using L2 strategies for L1 comprehension) or differentiation (distinct patterns for L1 versus L2). Interestingly, in contrast to Johnson and Newport's findings, their data showed no linear decline even within the critical period, indicating that there is no single critical point for successful language learning, and that a positive outcome can rise and fall at different developmental points. Such data constitute further evidence against the existence of a simple, clearly bounded, and monotonically developing, critical period.

7.1.3 The cognitive and neural bases of the critical period

Johnson and Newport's (1989) contribution lay not only in their experimental evidence for a refined view of the critical period, but also in the theoretical proposal the authors advanced. The biological account as proposed by Lenneberg attributes the critical period to brain maturation, specifically brain lateralization, whereas Johnson and Newport relied on the interplay between learning mechanisms and other cognitive capacities in explaining age of acquisition effects. They suggested the "less is more" hypothesis: the less well developed cognitive capacity in children actually confers learning advantages: young learners tend to be engaged in piecemeal, gradual, and implicit learning whereas adults, because of formal operational abilities, tend to use explicit analytic procedures in dealing with complex aspects of language. When faced with complex linguistic stimuli, children perform only a limited number of componential analyses of the possible form-meaning mappings because they do not have the capacity (e.g., a large working memory) to compute the complete set of data or perform complex form-to-meaning (sounds-to-semantic relations) mappings. Such componential analysis turns out to be advantageous to children as they are not overwhelmed from the beginning. This "less is more" hypothesis coincides with patterns from computational modeling (Elman, 1993), according to which connectionist networks (see Chapter 10) are able to learn complex grammar only if the network first receives simple sentences and then moves on to complex ones, or alternatively, if the network is provided with limited memory windows early on so that initial componential analysis is efficient and successful.

The "less is more" hypothesis has remained largely a hypothesis for the past 20 years, as there is scant experimental evidence (other than from connectionist modeling) for the negative relationship between cognitive resources and L2 acquisition. An alternative view is to look at the critical period effects in relation to the competition between the two languages, more specifically to the "entrenchment" created by the varying degrees of consolidation of L1 at different points of learning (Hernandez, Li, & MacWhinney, 2005). As knowledge and skills of L1 become more established, its representational structure becomes increasingly resistant to change ("entrenched") in the face of new input, or new data. Connectionist simulations in which L2 was introduced at different time points relative to L1 learning (Zhao & Li, 2010) have shown that these entrenchment effects are observed in both phonological and lexical representation systems, in that at later stages of acquisition, a parasitic L2 representation develops, resting upon the L1 representation (for discussion of connectionist models in L2, see Chapter 10, Section 10.3). This is because when structural consolidation in L1 has reached a point of entrenchment, organization of the L2 will have to tap into existing representational resources as well as its structure. Entrenchment is accompanied by changes in neural plasticity, particularly in sensorimotor integration, such that highly flexible neural systems for developing fine-grained articulatory motor actions and for sequences processing are no longer available, while these skills are critical for early phonological processing and grammatical acquisition. Once the neural system settles into stable states for learned patterns (rather than for brain lateralization), radical changes become difficult even if the new language requires such changes (see Hernandez & Li, 2007 for discussion of the "sensorimotor integration hypothesis"; Figure 10.4 also offers an illustration of the L1 and L2 competition in connectionist models of lexical learning).

A recent theoretical framework articulated by MacWhinney (2012), the Unified Competition Model (UCM), has attempted to account for critical period effects in L2 by reference to a host of neural, cognitive, and social variables formulated as risk factors of L2 learning. Consistent with the above perspective on the dynamic interplay between the competing languages, the UCM model assumes that the underlying learning mechanisms for L1 acquisition and L2 acquisition are not fundamentally different, contrary to what the CPH posits. How do we then account for the different outcomes due to age of acquisition? According to the united model, such differences arise from a set of risk factors: negative transfer from L1, entrenchment as discussed above, parasitism (dependency of L2 on L1 including positive and negative transfer), mismatched connectivity (incorrect connections between processing areas in the brain), and social isolation of the L2 learner. To achieve successful L2 acquisition (or to overcome the critical period effect), the adult successive learner must strive to use the same core mechanisms available to the child (e.g., implicit learning, embodied experience), as well as a set of protective factors: positive (rather than negative) transfer from L1 to L2, social participation or immersion (rather than social isolation), active thinking in the L2, reorganization through resonance (interactive activation for relevant processing sites), and internalization (using L2 for inner speech). Successive learners who are able to maximize the benefits of these protective factors will show better and faster learning than learners who are highly susceptible to the risk factors. A major challenge in future research will be to identify how the various risk factors unfold in development and how they affect different domains of linguistic processing.

7.2   Speech Learning in Successive Language Acquisition

Although MacWhinney's (2012) unified model assumes no fundamental differences in the learning mechanisms underlying first language and second language acquisition, it does take into consideration the very different experiences that children and adults have in acquiring single or multiple languages. In Chapter 6 we saw how language acquisition unfolds in a context in which young children are exposed to both languages simultaneously. In Section 7.1.3 above, we discussed how the representation of L2 might depend on the entrenchment effects due to consolidation of the L1 and its influence on L2. In this section, we examine in some detail the differences between simultaneous and successive language acquisition, and how the competing languages might interact dynamically with one another to impact the representation and acquisition of the bilingual's two languages. We will focus on speech, hence the expression "speech learning," and more precisely on the perception and discrimination of speech sounds in L2 learners.

7.2.1   Speech learning in children and adults

Young children spend at least three quarters of their first year actively listening to environmental sounds, including speech input, before they take on the major task of speaking (they typically produce their first words around their first birthday). Adults rarely have the luxury of concentrating first on the second language phonology for an extended period of time and then moving on to other aspects of language (e.g., lexicon and grammar), and moreover, they already have a first language phonological system in place. Such differences could have profound implications for why the acquisition of a native-like, accent-free, second language phonology is so difficult. Both speech perception and speech production involve fine-grained sensorimotor coordination and integration, from the accurate processing of phonemes, tones, and intonations, to the rapid and precise control of tongue, lips, and larynx movements. Neuroimaging evidence suggests that a frontal-striatal circuit may play a significant role in the relevant sensorimotor processes, and children may have both the time and the neuroplasticity to develop sensorimotor processes necessary for native phonological perception and production (see Hernandez & Li, 2007 for a discussion). By contrast, adults in general lack the neural resources to radically change learned systems (L1 phonology) or to develop new phonological categories in the second language to be sufficiently differentiated from those in the first language (Flege, 1995). Connectionist models (see the discussions in Section 7.1.3 and Chapter 10) provide mechanistic accounts of such age of acquisition effects, in that if the connections in the model are fully committed to the learned structure (i.e., functionally specified in weights), the model will be less open to radical changes in terms of the updating of connection weights, rendering the model an entrenched system that is resistant to adaptation.

In studies of early infant speech perception, researchers have examined how bilingual babies, compared with monolingual babies, are able to handle speech sounds from both languages if they are exposed to both early on (see a discussion in Chapter 6, Section 6.3.1). By contrast, adult learners often fail to acquire a native-like phonological system. It has been found that speech accent is the most difficult aspect to overcome for immigrant L2 learners (e.g., Yeni-Komshian, Flege, & Liu, 2000). Why do adults have so much difficulty in speech learning, as compared with children? Flege (1995) proposed the Speech Learning Model (SLM), according to which L2 learners establish phonetic categories according to the degree to which the phonological system of the target language resembles that of their native language; for example, similar but nonidentical phonemes, such as English vowels /æ/, /ɒ/, and /ʌ/ (as in *hat*, *hot*, and *hut*, respectively), present more difficulties to second language learners than totally different phonemes. In both Spanish and Chinese, these English vowels would be mapped onto a single vowel /a/, and hence L2 learners easily confuse them. Importantly, child learners can create new phonetic categories more easily than adult learners, and these child-adult differences are due to the degree to which the phonetic representations of the L1 vs. that of L2 are stabilized over the lifespan of learning. The SLM's account of speech learning differences with respect to both cross-linguistic overlap and L1-L2 interaction is highly consistent with our discussion in terms of the impact of L1 consolidation on L2 (Hernandez *et al.*, 2005) and the sensorimotor integration hypothesis (Hernandez & Li, 2007), as discussed in Section 7.1.3. An interesting aspect of the SLM, in fact, is the hypothesis that age differences may be linked to changes in perceptual and sensorimotor processes involved in learning, although this hypothesis has never been directly put to the test empirically. Obviously, the articulation of sounds must be a sensorimotor process, and the accuracy of L2 as well as L1 pronunciation must depend on the speaker's motor control and coordination of the articulatory apparatus (tongue, lips, jaw, larynx, etc.).

Another important aspect of the SLM theory is that cross-language similarity creates different effects with respect to the ease of speech learning in a second language. Although the details of the SLM are concerned with speech learning, researchers have found that the degree to which L1 and L2 overlap in phonology, grammar, and the lexicon will all lead to cross-language transfer or interference. A Chinese learner of Spanish will need to form a complex set of grammatical rules (such as gender agreement) which is absent in Chinese, whereas a Spanish learner of Chinese will need to avoid the interference of lexical stress when learning lexical tones. Previous research has shown that native speakers of European languages tend to show a higher level of L2 proficiency in English, all other things being equal, compared with native speakers of Chinese who learn English as the L2 (see Birdsong & Molis, 2001; Jia, 2006). In Chapter 10, we will discuss the neural correlates of cross-language similarity or overlap in bilingual representation and processing. Here it suffices to say that learners whose native language does not make a given phonological distinction will have more difficulty in learning a language that makes that distinction.

A widely studied phonemic distinction is that between /r/ and /l/ in English, a distinction that is not made in Japanese. Japanese learners of English have great difficulty in accurately perceiving or producing the phonemic contrast between English /r/ and /l/: for example, the words /load/ and /road/ would be considered the same by native Japanese speakers. In two experiments Aoyama, Flege, Guion, Akahane-Yamada, and Yamada (2004) tested native Japanese children and adults who resided in the US and had learned English. In Experiment 1, 16 children (mean age = 10) and 16 adults were asked to listen to triads of words that contained the consonants /r/, /l/, and a few other consonants. The participants' task was to indicate if one of the three words differed from the other two. In Experiment 2, the same 32 participants were asked to name pictures whose English names began with the /l/, /r/, or /w/ consonants. Native English speakers then made judgments on the words produced by the learners. In both experiments, the children and adults were tested twice (Time 1 and Time 2), one year apart, in order to assess their improvement in learning. Results from Experiment 1 showed that, compared with native English speakers, both Japanese children and adults performed worse for the /r/-/l/ contrast. In addition, the adult learners improved their performance only slightly from Time 1 to Time 2 of testing, whereas child learners improved significantly within the same period. Results from Experiment 2 indicated similar patterns, in that the child learners improved significantly over the 1-year period, whereas adults showed little improvement. Interestingly, adult learners started out with better performance at Time 1 in both perception and production, but their performance did not improve at Time 2. Furthermore, children's improvement was observed mainly with /r/ rather than /l/, and Aoyama *et al.* interpreted this finding as being consistent with the SLM model discussed above: previous studies have found that the English /r/ is perceptually more dissimilar from the Japanese /r/ than is English /l/ for native Japanese speakers. Since Japanese learners did better with English /r/, this confirmed that more dissimilar phonemes are easier to learn than more similar ones, as suggested by the SLM model.

7.2.2 Age of acquisition effects and individual differences in speech learning

The study of Aoyama *et al.* showed a clear difference between child and adult learners in discriminating non-native phonemes in the second language, and the age of L2 acquisition (L2 AoA) clearly is a very important variable here. The children tested in their study were on average 10 years of age, and with experience, they were able to perform well in the phonemic perception and production tasks, although not to a native level. Archila-Suerte, Zevin, Bunta, and Hernandez (2012) further tested Spanish-English bilinguals' perception of speech sounds in a similarity-judgment task, in which syllables that contrasted in English vowels (e.g., *saf, sef, sof, suf*) were presented to participants in pairs and participants were asked to rate how similar the two syllables were. These syllables were also digitally edited so that many tokens (examples) of the same syllable were created that varied in intonation, timbre, and duration. The bilingual participants were all native speakers of Spanish and learned English as a second language at varying AoA and had varying levels of English proficiency. Unlike the Aoyama *et al.* study that examined only two groups (child vs. adult learners), the Archila-Suerte *et al.* study divided the participants into three groups based on the bilinguals' L2 AoA: early (mean L2 AoA = 3.6), intermediate (mean L2 AoA = 6.9), and late (mean L2 AoA = 14.5). The results indicated that only the early learners performed similarly to native monolingual English speakers, not only in perceiving the different categories associated with different syllables, but also in ignoring the variability (e.g., intonation) of the different tokens of the same syllable.

Archila-Suerte *et al.*'s study was significant in two ways. First, age of L2 acquisition is important in determining whether the learners will end up with native-like performance in speech perception. Their intermediate and late learners did not perform like native speakers. In addition, the early learners who performed as native speakers learned English after age 3, which is inconsistent with the hypothesis that language-specific speech perception occurs already at the end of the first year (see Chapter 6, Section 6.3.1). It appears from these data that there is considerable plasticity for learning in the early childhood years for native-like speech performance. It is important to note that age 3–4 is still very young (mean AoA was 3.6 in Archila-Suerte *et al.*) compared with the critical period originally thought to end around puberty (Lenneberg, 1967) or age 16 (Johnson & Newport, 1989). Thus, the learning of phonology, as compared with that of grammar or lexicon, might impose an earlier time constraint for native-like performance. Second, the learner's language proficiency also plays an important role in determining speech perception. A high level of proficiency in the second language helped the intermediate and late learners to correctly discriminate phonemic boundaries between pairs of syllables. The difference between these learners and the early learners is that the intermediate and late learners could not ignore the acoustic changes (e.g., different intonation, timbre, or duration) that are irrelevant for the target language phonemic categories, often treating different tokens of a syllable with minor changes as belonging to different phonemic categories. Perhaps the late learners, due to their increased attentional and cognitive executive abilities, employ different, more controlled, processing strategies as compared with early child learners, and therefore cannot ignore irrelevant details in speech perception. This conjecture is consistent with the "less is more" hypothesis (see Section 7.1.3) with respect to the performance outcome of speech learning. It would be interesting to see in future research whether such different styles of processing are reflected in the different brain systems used by children and adults.

If the success of L2 speech learning is determined by age of second language acquisition as discussed, can we see individual differences in how well learners with the same L2 AoA perform in speech learning? In other words, do different learners have different perceptual abilities such that these differences also determine how successful L2 speech learning will be? Researchers are increasingly interested in such individual differences: two learners, with the same language background, same length of residence in the target language country, or even starting at the same age of L2 learning, may end up with very different learning outcomes as well as speed of learning. What factors determine such differences? This question has been traditionally asked by L2 researchers interested in language aptitude, including the study of learner differences in motivation of learning, learning strategies, and cognitive style (see Dörnyei, 2005). Cognitive scientists have also been interested in whether executive control abilities such as working memory and processing speed might predict individual learners' success in a second language (see Miyake & Friedman, 1998). In a recent study, Diaz, Baus, Escera, Costa, and Sebastián-Gallés (2008) specifically addressed the individual difference question by examining Spanish-Catalan bilinguals who learned the Catalan phonetic /e/-/ɛ/ contrast not present in Spanish (Spanish has only /e/). The participants were native Spanish speakers who all started to learn Catalan at age 4, and based on their performance with discriminating the /e/-/ɛ/ sounds, participants were divided into the good performers (GP) versus the poor performers (PP).

Diaz *et al.* were specifically interested in whether the differences between GP learners and PP learners stemmed from general perceptual variability in detecting basic acoustic differences, or whether their differences reflected only speech-specific abilities. The researchers generated nonspeech acoustic contrasts such as tones that vary in duration and frequency, and speech material that contrasted in vowel space (e.g., /o/-/e/). By collecting participants' ERP responses to speech and nonspeech contrasts presented (see discussion of the ERP method in Chapter 10), Diaz *et al.* found that the GP and PP learners did not differ in discriminating the acoustic variations, but did differ in discriminating both native and non-native speech sounds. The authors therefore concluded that poor L2 speech perception performance is correlated with speech-specific discriminatory abilities, not with general perceptual psychoacoustic abilities. More specifically, phonetic abilities in the native language may predict one's success in learning the phonetic contrasts in a second language. However, it remains an open question whether such conclusions would apply to the learning of speech contrasts involving consonants (only vowels were studied by Diaz *et al.*) and suprasegmental features such as lexical tones in Chinese. Evidence from other phonetic training studies has suggested that better acoustic processing abilities are correlated with faster speech learning and such correlations are reflected in neuroanatomical differences between faster or successful versus slower or less successful learners involving the superior temporal gyrus and the parieto-occipital brain areas (e.g., Golestani, Paus, & Zatorre, 2002; Wong, Perrachione, & Parrish, 2007; see Chapter 10 for discussion of neuroscience approaches).

7.3 Dynamic Interaction between First Language and Second Language

Although the Speech Learning Model (Flege, 1995; see discussion in Section 7.2.1) was developed to account for phonological acquisition, the basic premises of the model are relevant to other aspects of successive language acquisition. In particular, the SLM model argues for the importance of cross-language interaction and child-adult differences in perceiving and producing speech sounds in a second language. Building on the original cross-linguistic Competition Model (Bates & MacWhinney, 1987), the Unified Competition Model (MacWhinney, 2012; see discussion in Section 7.1.3) highlights the core principles of competition, cross-language variation, and child-adult differences in the acquisition of both first and second languages. Importantly, the UCM model does not view the underlying learning mechanisms for L1 and L2 acquisition as fundamentally different, but rather attributes the child-adult differences to a set of risk factors (e.g., negative transfer from L1 and entrenchment; see Section 7.1.3). In Chapter 6, syntactic transfer and code-mixing in simultaneous learners were used as evidence of cross-language interaction at a very early age. In the remainder of this chapter, we discuss how cross-language lexical and grammatical interactions occur with successive learners.

7.3.1   Patterns of cross-language lexical interaction and competition

A major task in learning a second language is the acquisition of new lexical items in the target language. This task may appear daunting to an adult successive learner, considering how many words there are in a dictionary, and how fast the child learner acquires the vocabulary in his or her native language.[2] The situation is further complicated by cross-language mismatches in phonology, grammatical use, and semantic nuances. A significant challenge to the L2 learner is then to figure out not only how to correctly produce the words, but also how to use them grammatically in a sentence and appropriately in a speech context. Thus, words of the two languages cannot simply be lined up as translation equivalents. Moreover, even many seemingly equivalent words are not truly equivalent, as illustrated in Figure 7.1.

The English words *chair* and *sofa* can be easily translated into the Chinese words *yizi* and *safa*, respectively. However, Figure 7.1 shows that the two languages are in disagreement as to which word should be used to refer to the object in the middle. In English, padded, upholstered seats for one person receive the same name as hard wooden seats for one person (*chair*), whereas in Chinese they receive the same name as padded, upholstered seats for several people (*safa*) (see the arrows in Figure 7.1). In other words, English assigns more weight to size and Chinese gives more weight to the material of the object in naming. Interestingly, in German the three objects in Figure 7.1 would receive three separate names, *stühl*, *seßel*, and *sofa*, respectively. This situation shows significant differences in how words from different languages may carve up the world differently (see Bowerman & Choi, 2001, for a discussion of such cross-linguistic differences in the use of spatial prepositions and verbs).

---

[2]   An average 6-year-old may have a passive vocabulary of 14,000 words, according to some estimates (e.g., Carey, 1978).

L1:

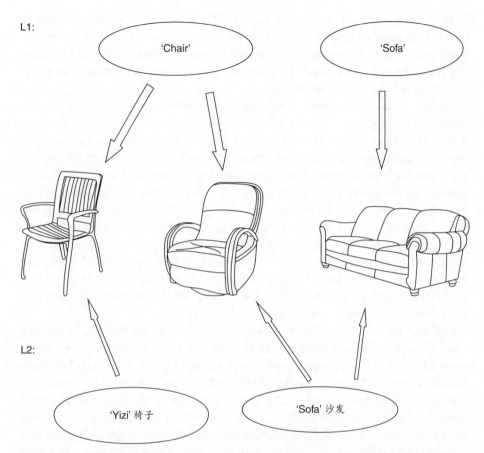

L2:

Figure 7.1: Cross-language differences in object naming. In English (designated as L1 here), size or shape of the object is important in calling something a chair or a sofa, whereas in Chinese (designated as L2 here), material of the object (e.g., having soft cushions) is more important. Speakers will name the middle object differently depending on whether the language pays attention to size or to material.

In successive language acquisition, the first possible pattern of cross-language interaction is the influence from L1 to L2. With respect to the situation depicted in Figure 7.1, an English learner of Chinese as L2 would be more likely to call the middle object *yizi*, due to influence of *chair* in L1 English. Similarly, a Chinese learner of English as L2 would be more likely to call a mug or a glass a *cup*, because in Chinese the word *beizi* is used to refer to all objects covered by the three English terms. As in speech learning, the degree to which such L1 to L2 influences occur may depend on the semantic distance between L1 and L2 items. If word meanings are totally different, the negative impact from L1 to L2 could be smaller, as compared with cross-language overlaps such as those described in the English-Chinese examples. This prediction is quite similar to that espoused by the SLM model with regard to the impact of cross-language phonetic similarities on speech learning.

There is some empirical evidence for this prediction: for example, Malt and Sloman (2003) found that L2 English learners showed naming patterns for common household objects that did not match those of native speakers, but some lexical categories (e.g., jars) showed better matches than others (e.g., containers), perhaps due to different degrees of L1 to L2 influence.

Studies of second language acquisition have traditionally focused on how L1 influences or impacts L2, but not on how L2 could influence L1 (but see Grosjean & Py, 1991). More recent evidence suggests that our first language is more permeable than traditionally thought, and that such L2 to L1 influences not only exist in early, simultaneous, bilingual language acquisition (as discussed in Chapter 6), but also in late, successive language learning (e.g., Linck, Kroll, & Sunderman, 2009; Pavlenko & Malt, 2011). That is, the influence of the later learned language could exert significant impact on one's native language, and such influences may be observed first in L1 lexical uses that are deviant from those of monolingual speakers. In extreme cases, significant L2 -> L1 influence may be accompanied by language attrition in the L1 (i.e., loss of productive use of L1) or a shift in the speaker's language dominance from L1 to L2 (i.e., the L2 becomes the dominant language; see also Chapter 1, Section 1.3 and Chapter 6, Section 6.2).

Pavlenko and Malt (2011) provided clear empirical evidence that late L2 learning may influence L1 in the domain of lexical usage. They tested three groups of immigrant Russian-English bilingual speakers who learned English as L2: early bilinguals (mean L2 AoA = 3.6 years), childhood bilinguals (mean L2 AoA = 11.7 years), and late bilinguals (mean L2 AoA = 22.8 years). Like Malt and Sloman (2003), they tested the bilingual as well as the monolingual participants' naming of common household objects, particularly drinking containers like cups, mugs, and glasses that varied in size, height, volume, and material (e.g., glass, paper or ceramic; see Figure 7.2 for examples). They counted how often participants would use different words to name a given object, and the results indicated that first, there were clear cross-language differences in the naming patterns produced by monolingual native speakers of English versus Russian. The three Russian words *chashka*, *kruzhka*, and *stakan* are generally translated into English as *cup*, *mug*, and *glass*, respectively, but the naming data indicated that each language assigns different weights to different meaning features of words. English, for example, distinguishes *cup* from *glass* based on the material that the container is made of, whereas Russian distinguishes *chashka* from *stakan* more on the basis of the size or height of the container. Such differences mean that bilinguals need to learn to focus on the right features in using names for objects. Second, the researchers found, as in Archila-Suerte *et al.* (2012; see discussion in Section 7.2.2), that there was a strong AoA effect in the L2 -> L1 interactions. The early bilinguals showed the strongest L2 influence in their L1, and the late bilinguals the least influence. This makes sense especially in light of the fact that the early bilinguals considered English (L2) to be their dominant language.

Pavlenko and Malt found that the L1 shift toward L2 entailed attrition of some L1 words as well as changes in the usage of others. There has been growing interest in L1 lexical attrition in recent years (see Schmid & Köpke, 2009), but for the most

cup (90%)   cup (85%)
stakan (100%)   chashka (75%)

glass (95%)   glass (70%)
stakan (90%)   stakan (25%)

mug (95%)   mug (95%)
kruzhka (75%)   chashka (90%)

Figure 7.2: Stimulus examples of drinking containers used by Pavlenko and Malt (2011). Below the picture of each object is the dominant name produced by native speakers of English and Russian, respectively, along with the percentage of speakers who produced the name. (Reproduced with author permission.) Copyright © 2010 Cambridge University Press.

part, research on language attrition has been a descriptive enterprise limited often to case studies of individuals who have stopped using L1 for an extended period of time. To simulate the developmental changes in language attrition, Zinszer and Li (2010) implemented a computational model of L1 lexical attrition based on the DevLex connectionist model (see Chapter 10, Section 10.3.2 for a discussion), in which 116 Chinese words and 116 English words were the learning targets. The advantage of the model was that L2 AoA could be systematically manipulated, as well as the age at which L1 training ceases. The Zinszer and Li model was trained in such a way that it stopped L1 learning at varying time points when L2 learning began, so that effects of L2 influence on L1 (specifically lexical attrition) could be observed as a function of L2 AoA. Figure 7.3 illustrates how this can be done in the model by changing the L2 onset time and the L1 attrition time (this is just one scenario in which the model could be manipulated; in other cases, L1 training can continue after L2 exposure begins; see Zhao & Li, 2010).

The modeling results indicated a nonlinear pattern of lexical attrition (defined as the lack of correct activation of the L1 words after L2 learning starts). In particular, there was a stronger L1 attrition when L2 learning occurred early, becoming weaker up to a certain point (halfway through the entire training), after which attrition slowed down. These patterns, when considered along with L2 learning, make great sense. Recall the data in Johnson and Newport's (1989) study that indicated a linear decline of L2 performance up to a given age, after which no clear patterns existed. Increases in L1 attrition and corresponding decreases in L2 performance reflect the wax-and-wane competition and dynamic interplay between the two languages, showing that the earlier the L2 is learned, the less complete the L1 may be (for some bilinguals at least), and the more susceptible the L1 is to attrition. The modeling results provided the first systematic computational evidence that is complementary to the majority of previous modeling work focused on L1 to L2 influences or simultaneous bilingual processing (see the discussion in Chapter 10, Section 10.3).

7.3.2   Grammatical acquisition in the second language

So far we have seen the complex cross-language interaction and competition occurring in the domains of second language phonological acquisition and lexical acquisition. A large body of relevant research has also been conducted in second language grammatical acquisition, including the acquisition of tense and aspect that we illustrate in this section as an example.

In first language development, the ability to talk about time is one of the earliest tasks that children learn. Speakers use tense markers to indicate that a given event that occurred in the past is occurring in the present, or will occur in the future. By contrast, aspect is a grammatical means with which the speaker marks the temporal contour of a situation described, for example, presenting the speaker's view of a situation or an event as ongoing or as completed. Temporal reference can be encoded in a variety of ways in different languages (see Klein, 2009, for a discussion of how

(a)

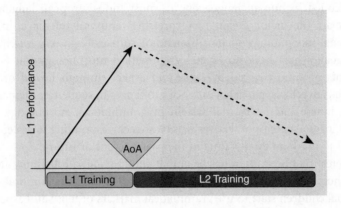

(b)

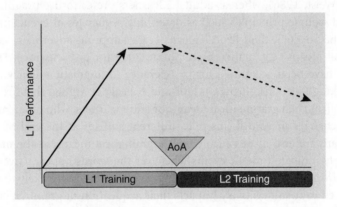

(c)

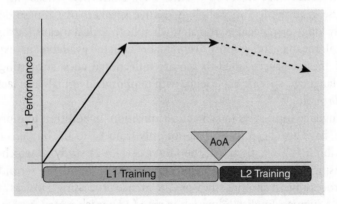

Figure 7.3: Illustration of how L1 lexical attrition is simulated as a function of L2 AoA in a computational model. (a) Early L2 AoA: L1 learning is stopped in the model at an early point in model training, and severe L1 attrition occurs; (b) Intermediate L2 AoA: L1 reached a consolidated level and training is stopped mid-course, with some L1 attrition occurring; and (c) Late L2 AoA: L1 is further entrenched before L2 begins and only limited L1 attribution occurs.

time is encoded in human languages). In most Indo-European languages, tense and aspect are the major means for expressing temporal reference, in the form of inflectional morphology such as prefixes or suffixes (e.g., -*ed*, -*ing* in English). Other languages may have no formal grammatical morphology but can express the concepts of time covered by tense and aspect through lexical or discourse devices (e.g., adverbials, particles, order of utterances in sequence; Klein, 2009). For example, Chinese has no formal system of grammatical morphology for tense. Instead, Chinese uses temporal adverbials (words corresponding to yesterday, today, tomorrow) to mark an event's time in the past, present or future.[3]

One interesting observation has been that children and adults show clear differences in their preferences for different means of encoding temporal reference: monolingual children start to use grammatical markers of tense and aspect as early as 1.5 years, many months before they systematically use lexical means of temporal reference (Weist, 1986), whereas adult L2 learners prefer to use pragmatic means first (e.g., discourse principles such as describing sequences of events in the order in which they occur), then lexical means (e.g., temporal adverbials), and finally grammatical means (e.g., suffixes; see Shirai, 2009 for a discussion). Such L1-L2 differences have been accounted for by reference to linguistic saliency and attentional blocking (see Ellis, in press). Ellis and colleagues argued that lexical means are more salient than grammatical means for adult learners, who often fail to detect the subtle changes in verb forms (e.g., different suffixes at the end of the verb). Lexical means are also more reliable than grammatical means, as the meanings of words clearly indicate time of events whenever the words appear. Given the lexical repertoire adults have for temporal reference, they are more likely to use lexical means, which in turn negatively impacts their acquisition of grammatical markers (i.e., lexical means block grammatical means). Experimental evidence indicates that such blocking effects are most clearly reflected in L2 learners whose native language does not use grammatical morphology. Native speakers of Chinese demonstrate most clearly long-term negative transfer: when both lexical means (adverbials) and grammatical means (inflections) were made equally available in experimental conditions, these learners failed to acquire inflectional cues, suggesting effects of long-term language-specific experience with temporal adverbials and lack of grammatical morphology.

Cross-language influences in syntactic acquisition, in addition to morphological acquisition, have also been identified, not only from L1 to L2, but also from L2 to L1. In Section 7.1.2, we discussed the Liu *et al.* (1992) study in which backward transfer (using L2 processing strategies for L1) was found for second language sentence processing. In another study of L2 sentence processing, Dussias and Sagarra (2007) asked Spanish-English bilinguals to read L1 Spanish sentences that contained relative clauses, such as *El policía arrestó a la hermana del criado que estaba enferma*

---

[3]   Chinese does have a grammatical system of aspect, not through morphological markers, but through bound morphemes of lexical units (e.g., the aspect markers -*le*, -*zhe*, -*guo*; see Li & Bowerman, 1998; Li & Shirai, 2000).

desde hacía tiempo (the police arrested the sister of the servant who had been ill for a while; see Chapter 4, Section 4.4.1 for a more detailed discussion of the study). For the English version of the sentence, native speakers prefer to attach the relative clause to the second NP (*servant*), interpreting the servant as the one who is ill. Native Spanish speakers, when faced with such sentences, prefer to attach the relative clause to the first NP (*sister*), interpreting the sister as the one who is ill. In the specific Spanish example, the sentence was disambiguated by the gender marking on the adjective (i.e., *enferma*), marked with female gender morphology that agrees with the first NP. The participants were monolingual Spanish speakers plus two groups of Spanish-English bilinguals who differed in their L2 (English) immersion experience and in self-rated L2 proficiency. Analyses of the participants' eye movements during the reading of the sentences indicated that the bilinguals with limited immersion experience performed similarly to monolingual Spanish speakers, in that they spent more reading time on the sentences with relative clauses modifying the second NP, whereas the bilinguals with more immersion experience spent more time on sentences with relative clauses modifying the first NP.

Dussias and Sagarra's data point to an important aspect we discussed with cross-language lexical interaction: bilinguals with more immersion experience may change processing strategies in reading their own native language, due to their experience with and proficiency in the second language. In this set of data, the bilinguals with immersion experience may have adopted the second NP interpretation strategy preferred by native speakers of English (their L2). The data further confirm that the L1 syntactic comprehension system is also permeable, as is the lexical representation. Thus, language immersion and proficiency may have similar effects as AoA on bilingual performance: increased proficiency in the L2 grammar may be associated with more L2-native like performance but may also be accompanied by an increased loss of access to L1 processing strategies, just as younger AoA leads to better performance in the L2 and worse performance in the L1 (see Liu *et al.*, 1992 and Jia, 2006 for reviews).

In Chapters 4 and 10, we see how researchers can use electrophysiological (ERP) methods to study second language morphosyntactic processing with learners of different L2 AoA and language proficiency. By using ERP in combination with behavioral tasks (such as the "grammaticality judgment" as used by Johnson & Newport, 1989), researchers are able to tap into the L2 learner's use of grammatical knowledge during on-line processing (i.e., as it happens in real time). Reviewing a number of behavioral and ERP studies, Clahsen and Felser (2006) suggested that child L1 and adult L2 learners employ fundamentally different mechanisms in grammatical processing, in contrast to what has been suggested by the Unified Competition Model (see Section 7.1.3). Specifically, Clahsen and Felser suggested the "shallow structure hypothesis," which states that when adult L2 learners process syntactic structures in the non-native language, they are unable to construct a detailed syntactic representation for comprehension. Such detailed syntactic representations may include complex hierarchical relations involving multiple relative clauses (e.g., *the nurse the doctor argued that the rude patient had angered is refusing to work late*), representations that native speakers can compute and use rapidly on-line for comprehension. Contrary to Dussias and Sagarra (2007), Clahsen and Felser cited studies that failed to find relative clause attachment preferences in the L2 (for either the first NP or the second NP). As evidence for the shallow structure hypothesis, the authors argued that:

(1)   ERP waveforms (e.g., left anterior negativity) that are supposed to reflect early automatic grammatical analysis are absent; and

(2)   Cross-grammatical processing strategies due to cross-language influence from L1 to L2 are also absent (but see the counter evidence discussed in this section and in Chapter 10).

Clearly, there are many unresolved questions with regard to whether and how grammatical acquisition differs in L1 versus L2, and whether and how native language-specific experience interacts with L2 properties and age of L2 acquisition in influencing the process and outcome of successive language acquisition. But it is clear that we are starting to understand the critical period effects better, and that effects of age of acquisition depend on language-specific characteristics and cross-language interactions. There is overwhelming evidence that it is the complex and dynamic interplay between languages, and between the learner and the environment, that determines the success and the neurocognitive representation of single and multiple languages.

Research Questions

1.   The critical period hypothesis (CPH) has been a popular hypothesis but data obtained from successive language acquisition suggest that the original CPH is likely to be wrong. What problems does it have when explaining second language acquisition?

2.   What are the alternatives to the CPH in explaining the apparent age-related differences in successive language acquisition? What evidence is there that the CPH may be outdated?

3.   Cross-language influence occurs at many levels for second language learners. Discuss one example each from phonological learning, lexical learning, and grammatical learning that illustrate some common principles of cross-language influences.

4.   We believe that our first language is stable because it is our native language, but evidence suggests that it is also susceptible to change (permeable). Give some examples that support the idea of L1 permeability. Can you also think of personal examples (from yourself or bilinguals you know) that support this idea?

Further Readings

Bialystok, Ellen. 2001. *Bilingualism in Development: Language, Literacy, and Cognition*. Cambridge: Cambridge University Press.

Li, Ping. 2009. Lexical organization and competition in first and second languages: Computational and neural mechanisms. *Cognitive Science* 33. 629–664.

Pavlenko, Aneta. 2009. Conceptual representation in the bilingual lexicon and second language vocabulary learning. In Aneta Pavlenko (ed.), *The Bilingual Mental Lexicon: Interdisciplinary Approaches*, pp. 125–160. Bristol, UK: Multilingual Matters.

Snow, Catherine. 1998. Bilingualism and second language acquisition. In Jean Berko Gleason & Nan Bernstein Ratner (eds), *Psycholinguistics* (2nd edition), pp. 453–481. Fort Worth, TX: Harcourt Brace.

References

Aoyama, Katsura, Flege, James Emil, Guion, Susan G., Akahane-Yamada, Reiko, & Yamada, Tsuneo. 2004. Perceived phonetic dissimilarity and L2 speech learning: The case of Japanese /r/ and English /l/ and /r/. *Journal of Phonetics* 32. 233–250.

Archila-Suerte, Pilar, Zevin, Jason, Bunta, Ferenc, & Hernandez, Arturo E. 2012. Age of acquisition and proficiency in a second language independently influence the perception of non-native speech. *Bilingualism: Language and Cognition* 15. 190–201.

Bates, Elizabeth A. & MacWhinney, Brian. 1987. Competition, variation and language learning. In Brian MacWhinney (ed.), *Mechanisms of Language Acquisition*, pp. 157–193. Hillsdale, NJ: Erlbaum.

Birdsong, David & Molis, Michelle. 2001. On the evidence for maturational constraints in second-language acquisition. *Journal of Memory and Language* 44. 235–249.

Bowerman, Melissa & Choi, Soonja. 2001. Shaping meanings for language: Universal and language-specific in the acquisition of spatial semantic categories. In Melissa Bowerman & Stephen Levinson (eds), *Language Acquisition and Conceptual Development*, pp. 475–511. Cambridge: Cambridge University Press.

Carey, Susan. 1978. The child as a word learner. In Morris Halle, Joan Bresnan, & George Miller (eds), *Linguistic Theory and Psychological Reality*, pp. 264–239. Cambridge, MA: MIT Press.

Chomsky, Noam. 1988. *Language and Problems of Knowledge: The Managua Lectures*. Cambridge, MA: MIT Press.

Clahsen, Harald & Felser, Claudia. 2006. Grammatical processing in language learners. *Applied Psycholinguistics* 27. 3–42.

Díaz, Begoña, Baus, Cristina, Escera, Carles, Costa, Albert, & Sebastián-Gallés, Núria. 2008. Brain potentials to native phoneme discrimination reveal the origin of individual differences in learning the sounds of a second language. *Proceedings of the National Academy of Sciences of the United States of America* 105. 16083–16088.

Dörnyei, Zoltan. 2005. *The Psychology of the Language Learner*. Mahwah, NJ: Lawrence Erlbaum Associates.

Dussias, Paola E. & Sagarra, Nuria. 2007. The effect of exposure on syntactic parsing in Spanish-English bilinguals. *Bilingualism: Language and Cognition* 10. 101–116.

Ellis, Nick. 2012. Learned attention and blocking. In Peter Robinson (ed.), *The Encyclopedia of Second Language Acquisition*. pp. 360–363. London: Routledge.

Elman, Jeffrey. 1993. Learning and development in neural networks: The importance of starting small. *Cognition* 48. 71–99.

Flege, James. 1995. Second-language speech learning: Theory, findings, and problems. In Winifred Strange (ed.), *Speech Perception and Linguistic Experience: Theoretical and Methodological Issues*, pp. 233–277. Baltimore, MD: York Press.

Golestani, Narly, Paus, Tomás, & Zatorre, Robert. 2002. Anatomical correlates of learning novel speech sounds. *Neuron* 35. 997–1010.

Grosjean, François & Py, Bernard. 1991. La restructuration d'une première langue: l'intégration de variantes de contact dans la compétence de migrants bilingues. *La Linguistique* 27. 35–60.

Hakuta, Kenji, Bialystok, Ellen, & Wiley, Edward. 2003. Critical evidence: A test of the critical-period hypothesis for second-language acquisition. *Psychological Science* 14. 31–38.

Hernandez, Arturo, Li, Ping, & MacWhinney, Brian. 2005. The emergence of computing modules in bilingualism. *Trends in Cognitive Science* 9. 220–225.

Hernandez, Arturo & Li, Ping. 2007. Age of acquisition: Its neural and computational mechanisms. *Psychological Bulletin* 133. 638–650.

Jia, Gisela. 2006. Second language acquisition by native Chinese speakers. In Ping Li, Li-Hai Tan, Elizabeth A. Bates, & Ovid J. L. Tzeng (eds), *The Handbook of East Asian Psycholinguistics (Vol. 1: Chinese)*, pp. 61–69. Cambridge: Cambridge University Press.

Johnson, James S. & Newport, Elissa. 1989. Critical period effects in second language learning: The influence of maturational state on the acquisition of English as a second language. *Cognitive Psychology* 21. 60–99.

Klein, Wolfgang. 2009. How time is encoded. In Wolfgang Klein & Ping Li (eds), *The Expression of Time*, pp. 39–81. Berlin: Mouton de Gruyter.

Lenneberg, Eric H. 1967. *Biological Foundations of Language*. New York: Wiley.

Li, Ping & Bowerman, Melissa. 1996. The acquisition of lexical and grammatical aspect in Chinese. *First Language* 18. 311–350.

Li, Ping & Shirai, Yasuhiro. 2000. *The Acquisition of Lexical and Grammatical Aspect*. Berlin & New York: Mouton de Gruyter.

Linck, Jared, Kroll, Judith, & Sunderman, Gretchen. 2009. Losing access to the native language while immersed in a second language: Evidence for the role of inhibition in second-language learning. *Psychological Science* 20. 1507–1515.

Liu, Hua, Bates, Elizabeth, & Li, Ping. 1992. Sentence interpretation in bilingual speakers of English and Chinese. *Applied Psycholinguistics* 13. 451–484.

Long, Michael H. 1990. Maturational constraints on language development. *Studies in Second Language Acquisition* 12. 251–285.

MacWhinney, Brian. 2012. The logic of the Unified Model. In Susan Gass & Alison Mackey (eds), *The Routledge Handbook of Second Language Acquisition*, pp. 211–227. New York: Routledge.

Malt, Barbara C. & Sloman, Steven A. 2003. Linguistic diversity and object naming by non-native speakers of English. *Bilingualism: Language and Cognition* 6. 47–67.

Marler, Peter. 1970. A comparative approach to vocal learning: Song development in white-crowned sparrows. *Journal of Comparative and Physiological Psychology Monographs* 71. 1–25.

Miyake, Akira & Friedman, Naomi P. 1998. Individual differences in second language proficiency: Working memory as language aptitude. In Alice F. Healy & Lyle E. Bourne (eds),

Foreign Language Learning: Psycholinguistic Studies on Training and Retention, pp. 339–364. Mahwah, NJ: Lawrence Erlbaum Associates.

Pavlenko, Aneta & Malt, Barbara C. 2011. Kitchen Russian: Cross-linguistic differences and first-language object naming by Russian-English bilinguals. *Bilingualism: Language and Cognition* 14. 19–45.

Schmid, Monika, & Köpke, Barbara. 2009. L1 attrition and the mental lexicon. In Aneta Pavlenko (ed.), *The Bilingual Mental Lexicon: Interdisciplinary Approaches*, pp. 209–238. Bristol, UK: Multilingual Matters.

Shirai, Yasuhiro. 2009. Temporality in first and second language acquisition. In Wolfgang Klein & Ping Li (eds), *The Expression of Time*, pp. 167–194. Berlin: Mouton de Gruyter.

Snow, Catherine E. & Hoefnagel-Höhle, Marian. 1978. The critical period for language acquisition: Evidence from second language learning. *Child Development* 49. 1114–1128.

Weist, Richard. 1986. Tense and aspect. In Paul Fletcher & Michael Garman (eds), *Language Acquisition* (2nd edition), pp. 356–374. Cambridge: Cambridge University Press.

Wong, Patrick C. M., Perrachione, Tyler K., & Parrish, Todd B. 2007. Neural characteristics of successful and less successful speech and word learning in adults. *Human Brain Mapping* 28. 995–1006.

Yeni-Komshian, Grace, Flege, James, & Liu, Serena H. 2000. Pronunciation proficiency in the first and second languages of Korean-English bilinguals. *Bilingualism: Language and Cognition* 3. 131–149.

Zhao, Xiaowei & Li, Ping. 2010. Bilingual lexical interactions in an unsupervised neural network model. *International Journal of Bilingual Education and Bilingualism* 13. 505–524.

Zinszer, Benjamin & Li, Ping. 2010. A SOM model of first language lexical attrition. In Stellan Ohlsson & Richard Catrambone (eds). *Proceedings of the 32nd Annual Conference of the Cognitive Science Society*, pp. 2787–2792. Austin, TX: Cognitive Science Society.

IV
Cognition and the Bilingual Brain

Chapter 8

Bilingual Memory

Annette M.B. de Groot

The word "memory" has a number of different senses: It is used to refer to the place where memory information is kept, to the stored information itself, and to the processing involved in storing new information in memory and retrieving it when needed later. A distinction is made between "long-term memory" and "working memory." Long-term memory stores information for long periods of time (and perhaps permanently) while working memory retrieves information from long-term memory and holds (and manipulates) it for the duration it is needed to perform some mental operation.

Long-term memory is divided into two subsystems called "declarative memory" and "non-declarative memory." Declarative memory contains knowledge that is explicit, accessible to consciousness. In contrast, knowledge contained by non-declarative memory (also called "procedural memory") is implicit, unavailable to consciousness. It is expressed in behavior rather than by conscious recollection and can be acquired without the individual being aware of what is being learned. Two common forms of memory information contained by non-declarative memory are skills and habits (see Squire, Knowlton, & Musen, 1993 for further details).

This chapter deals exclusively with long-term declarative knowledge. Declarative memory contains both general, factual knowledge that we share with other people, and personal knowledge that reflects our individual past experiences. These two types of knowledge are usually called "semantic" and "episodic" or "autobiographical" respectively, and the systems that hold them are called "semantic" and "episodic" memory. Our mental lexicon – that is, the words we know, their form and meaning – constitutes a major component of semantic memory, but also general facts like *the longest river on earth is the Nile*, and *Prince Willem Alexander is married to Maxíma Zorreguieta* are part of semantic memory. In contrast, episodic or autobiographical memory stores our memories of specific events that happened to us in our past lives. I may, for instance, remember talking to Princess Maxíma about her

The Psycholinguistics of Bilingualism, First Edition. François Grosjean and Ping Li.
© 2013 Blackwell Publishing Ltd with the exceptions of Chapter 1, Chapter 2, Chapter 3, Chapter 7, Chapter 10 © 2013 François Grosjean and Ping Li. Published 2013 by Blackwell Publishing Ltd.

daughters' bilingualism at a reception held in the administrative building of the University of Amsterdam on the occasion of the university's foundation day.

Semantic and episodic knowledge are closely interrelated. On the one hand, semantic knowledge is built up from a process of generalization and abstraction from personal experiences and the memory traces left by them. For instance, our knowledge of what the word "dog" means is based on our personal experiences with individual dogs and summarizes the core of those experiences. On the other hand, what we experience is given meaning by information in semantic memory.

The aim of this chapter is to familiarize the reader with methods and outcomes of research on bilingual declarative memory, both semantic and episodic/autobiographical. The part of bilingual semantic memory that will be focused on is the bilingual's mental lexicon. Section 8.1 discusses various views on how the mental representations of (1) the form of an L1 word, (2) the form of its translation in L2, and (3) the meaning associated with these word forms are connected with each other and how the connections develop with increasing fluency in L2. In addition, it introduces the notion of meaning "nonequivalence" of translation pairs and its consequences for the representation of meaning. In the relevant literature the meaning representations of words are usually called "conceptual representations" or, simply, "concepts," and all of the mental lexicon's conceptual representations together constitute "conceptual memory." In this literature the word-form representations are often called "lexical representations" and all of these lexical representations together constitute "lexical memory." This latter nomenclature can be confusing at times because the adjective "lexical" can also refer to the mental lexicon as a whole, containing the representations of both the forms *and* meanings of words. For clarity's sake, in Section 8.1 of this chapter I will consistently use the term "conceptual representation" and "form representation" to refer to the representation of word meaning and word form, respectively.

Following the presentation of the various models of the organization of words' form and conceptual representations in the bilingual mental lexicon in Section 8.1, Section 8.2 then looks more closely at conceptual representations. From here on these are simply called "concepts" (because they are no longer discussed in relation to the form representations). Section 8.2 presents studies that examine whether, how, and why the L1 and L2 concepts in bilinguals differ from one another and from the corresponding concepts in monolingual native speakers of the languages concerned. Finally, Section 8.3 deals with bilingual episodic/autobiographical memory, specifically posing the question whether the language spoken at the time of a past event is encoded in the memory trace of that event and what this means for retrieving the memory at some later point in time.

8.1   The Organization of the Bilingual Mental Lexicon

Exactly 60 years ago Weinreich (1953/1968) described three organizations of word knowledge in a bilingual's mental lexicon: "coordinative," "compound," and

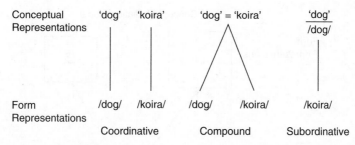

| Conceptual Representations | 'dog' | 'koira' | 'dog' = 'koira' | 'dog' /dog/ |

Figure 8.1: Three organizations of vocabulary knowledge in bilingual memory as proposed by Weinreich (1953/1968).

"subordinative" (see Chapter 1, Section 1.6). They are illustrated in Figure 8.1. In bilinguals of the coordinative type a word in L1 and its translation in L2 not only have separate form representations in memory but also separate conceptual representations. In contrast, in compound bilinguals an L1 word and its translation in L2 have separate form representations but share one and the same conceptual representation. Finally, in subordinative bilinguals the form representation of an L2 word does not map directly onto a conceptual representation. Instead, it maps onto the corresponding L1 form representation and exploits the latter's conceptual representation. In other words, in subordinative bilingualism access from an L2 word to conceptual memory is indirect, proceeding via the form representation of the corresponding L1 word. Weinreich suggested that this type of representation might hold during an early stage of L2 learning and that with increased learning a transition takes place from subordinative to coordinative bilingualism.

Weinreich's compound and subordinative memory systems are equivalent to the "Concept Mediation Model" and the "Word Association Model" examined by Potter, So, Von Eckardt, and Feldman (1984) in a study that set the stage for many studies on bilingual memory organization in the years that followed. Common illustrations of these two models are shown in Figure 8.2. Instead of showing the concept-mediation and word-association organizations for individual translation pairs (as Weinreich did), in agreement with common convention these two organizations are now shown for the bilingual mental lexicon as a whole. The different sizes of the L1 and L2 form stores reflect the fact that in (unbalanced) bilinguals the L1 vocabulary is usually larger than the L2 vocabulary.

An unfortunate consequence of illustrating the concept-mediation and word-association organizations for the system as a whole is that it can easily lead to the misguided inference that all structures within a bilingual's mental lexicon are necessarily of one and the same kind. Although few authors explicate whether or not this is the stance they take, such an assumption would be unjust in at least a number of cases. The possibility that different types of structures coexist within a bilingual's memory was already suggested by Weinreich (1953/1968) and is explicit in some of the more recent work as well (e.g., De Groot, 1993; Dufour & Kroll, 1995).

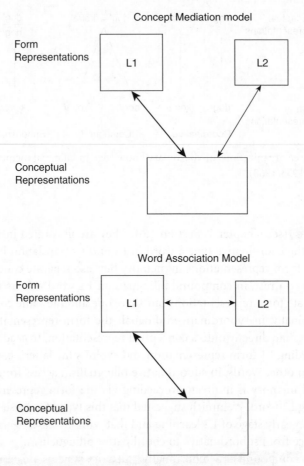

Figure 8.2: The Concept Mediation Model and Word Association Model (Potter *et al.*, 1984).

In their seminal study, Potter *et al.* examined the possibility that the form representations of new L2 words first get directly connected to those of the corresponding L1 words and that "this association is used in understanding and speaking the second language" (p. 23). So, just like Weinreich, they hypothesized that during an early stage of L2 learning the memory structures are of the word-association type (called "subordinative" by Weinreich). They furthermore hypothesized that with increased L2 learning, direct links between the L2 form representations and the conceptual representations (shared between L1 and L2) develop, replacing the word-association connections. In other words, whereas Weinreich assumed a development from word-association structures to coordinative structures, Potter *et al.* hypothesized a development from word-association to compound structures.

They tested this hypothesis by comparing the performance of two groups of L2 speakers on two tasks. One group consisted of L1-Chinese speakers relatively proficient in L2 English. The second group consisted of L1-English speakers with a relatively poor mastery of L2 French. The critical comparison was between each group's performance on a task that required the participants to translate L1 words into L2 and a second task in which they had to name pictures in L2. On the basis of a careful analysis of the type and number of mental processing steps involved in both tasks – in terms of either the Word Association Model or the Concept Mediation Model – the authors argued that response times should be equally long in both tasks if the Concept Mediation Model held, whereas they should be shorter for translation than for picture naming if the Word Association Model applied. In both groups translating from L1 to L2 and picture naming in L2 took equally long. Based on this finding the authors concluded that concept mediation holds not only for bilinguals with a relatively high level of L2 proficiency but also for less proficient bilinguals. In other words, the direct connections between L2 form representations and the conceptual representations that enable concept mediation already seem to be in place early on during L2 acquisition.

However, a small set of subsequent studies (e.g., Chen & Leung, 1989; Kroll & Curley, 1988) indicated that this conclusion does not apply to L2 speakers with an even lower level of L2 proficiency than the less fluent group in Potter *et al.* (1984). These less fluent L2 speakers showed the data patterns predicted by the Word Association Model. The combined studies thus suggest that increases in L2 fluency are accompanied by changes in the linkage patterns between the form and conceptual representations in the bilingual mental lexicon. The time it takes for these changes to take place is likely to be a function of frequency of word use: The more often an L2 word will be used, the sooner a direct link between its form and conceptual representation will be in place. This claim implies that within a bilingual's memory, different types of structures may coexist: At a given stage of L2 fluency a bilingual has developed more direct connections between the form representations of frequently used L2 words and the corresponding conceptual representations than between the form representations of infrequently used L2 words and their conceptual representations (De Groot, 1993). In other words, at this stage of L2 learning concept-mediation and word-association processing will take place for relatively many frequent and infrequent L2 words, respectively.

The "Revised Hierarchical Model" (e.g., Kroll, 1993; Kroll & Stewart, 1994) integrates these views on the development of bilingual memory representations into a single model that combines the Word Association and Concept Mediation Models and extends the integrated model with some new features. The model, as shown in Figure 8.3, assumes both direct links between the form representations of a translation pair (as in the Word Association Model) as well as direct connections between each of the form representations and a shared conceptual representation (as in the Concept Mediation Model). The extension of this combined model concerns two modifications: Two unidirectional instead of one bidirectional link between the L1 and L2 form representations are hypothesized, and the various connections are assumed to differ in strength. Specifically, the direct link from the L2 form representation to the L1 form representation is stronger than the one in the reverse direction, and the direct link between the L1 form representation and the shared

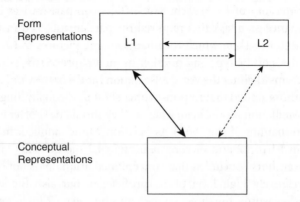

Form
Representations

L1

L2

Conceptual
Representations

Figure 8.3: The Revised Hierarchical Model (Kroll & Stewart, 1994).

conceptual representation is stronger than the direct link from the L2 form representation to this shared representation. Note that in Figure 8.3 solid and dashed lines represent strong and weak links, respectively.

An important reason for developing this model was the authors' observation that translating L1 words into L2 often takes longer than translating L2 words into L1. After excluding the possibility that this translation asymmetry results from a difference between L1 and L2 words in pronunciation difficulty, they hypothesized that it reflects the use of two different translation routes: L2 to L1 translation comes about by tracing the strong direct connection between the L2 and L1 form representations whereas L1 to L2 translation uses the indirect route from the L1 form representation, via the shared conceptual representation, to the corresponding L2 form representation. The latter route takes more time to complete because it is the longer of the two. As suggested by the authors, a reason why the direct link from the L2 form representation to the L1 form representation is relatively strong may be that "second language words are frequently taught by associating them to first language words [. . .] but not vice versa" (Kroll, 1993, p. 70). With increasing L2 use, the direct connections between the L2 form representations and the common conceptual representations gradually become stronger so that ultimately they are strong enough to enable direct access to the conceptual representations from the L2 form representations (in comprehension) and direct retrieval of the L2 form representations following the activation of a conceptual representation (in production). The consequence of these developmental changes is that the above translation asymmetry should only hold for the earlier stages of L2 acquisition.

The Revised Hierarchical Model is supported by various sets of data (e.g., Kroll & Stewart, 1994; Sholl, Sankaranarayanan, & Kroll, 1995). For instance, Kroll and Stewart replicated the above translation asymmetry but provided another source of evidence as well: Clustering the words to be translated into semantic categories (e.g., clothing, body parts, musical instruments) as opposed to presenting them in random order slowed down L1-to-L2 translation but not L2-to-L1 translation. This effect presumably results from fierce competition between the conceptual representations of semantically related words caused by semantic clustering. The fact that the effect only occurred in L1-to-L2 translation thus suggests the involvement of conceptual representations in L1-to-L2 translation but not in L2-to-L1 translation.

But counterevidence has also been gathered, such as the finding that the predicted difference in translation time for the two translation directions does not always materialize. This finding is unproblematic for the model if the participants in the pertinent studies are equally proficient in both languages. In fact, equally long translation times for both translation directions are expected under those circumstances. It *is* problematic, however, in cases where the participants' L2 is clearly much weaker than their L1. Similarly, the opposite pattern of *shorter* L1-to-L2 translation times, even in bilinguals nonfluent in L2, cannot be accounted for in terms of the model. Yet both these findings have been obtained (De Groot & Poot, 1997; La Heij, Hooglander, Kerling, & Van der Velden, 1996). Obviously then, the model requires revision (see Brysbaert & Duyck, 2010, and Kroll, Van Hell, Tokowicz, & Green, 2010, for discussions).

Excepting Weinreich's coordinative model, an unrealistic suggestion of the models of the bilingual mental lexicon presented so far is that the L1 and L2 terms of a translation pair are implicitly assumed to have exactly the same meaning. Contrary to this suggestion, it is well known that complete meaning equivalence of a pair of translations rarely exists. Instead, in addition to the shared meaning aspects, each member of a translation pair typically has meaning aspects specific to the language it belongs to. Furthermore, different types of words (e.g., concrete vs. abstract words; cognates vs. noncognates) may differ in the amount of meaning they share with their translations. Further noteworthy characteristics of word meanings are that they are not static but change over time and differ between individuals (Pavlenko, 1999). The Distributed Conceptual Feature Model (De Groot, 1992, 1993; Van Hell & De Groot, 1998) explicitly acknowledges that a pair of translations may not share meaning completely and that the degree of meaning nonequivalence may vary across word types (see Figure 8.4). This model does not represent a word's meaning in a single memory unit (models that do so are called "localist" models) but assumes "distributed" representations, where the word's meaning is spread out over a number of more elementary conceptual units. The two terms in a translation pair may share many or fewer of these conceptual units between them. This idea is illustrated in the figure, which shows the fictitious memory structure for a pair of translations that share all conceptual elements and another structure for a pair that shares fewer, while each member of the pair contains language-specific conceptual elements as well.

The Distributed Conceptual Feature Model is supported by the fact that the response patterns to different types of words (e.g., concrete vs. abstract words; cognates vs. noncognates) systematically differ in various bilingual research paradigms, such as word translation, between-language semantic priming, and bilingual word association (see De Groot, 1992; Van Hell & De Groot, 1998 for reviews). In particular, the results obtained by means of the bilingual word-association

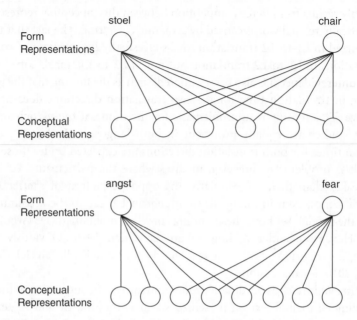

Figure 8.4: The Distributed Conceptual Feature Model (De Groot, 1992).

paradigm strongly support the model, because it is known that the generation of word associations generally exploits the words' conceptual representations (not the form representations) in memory. The bilingual participants in these studies (e.g., Van Hell & De Groot, 1998) are presented with a series of words and have to give a single word association to each of them. In a within-language condition, the responses must be in the language of the presented words; in a between-language condition, the responses must be in the other language. The critical dependent variable is the response equivalence of the responses to one and the same word in the within- and between-language conditions. If, for instance, a Dutch-English participant is shown the word "skirt" and responds with "dress" in the within-language English condition and with "jurk" in the between-language condition, this counts as an equivalent response ("jurk" is Dutch for *dress*). If, instead, he responds with "dress" in the within-language English condition but with "vrouw"(*woman*) in the between-language condition, this counts as a nonequivalent response. The crucial finding is that the responses in the within- and between-language conditions are more often equivalent for concrete words and cognates than for abstract words and noncognates, respectively. This finding suggests that the conceptual representations of concrete and cognate translation pairs share more conceptual units in bilingual memory than those of abstract and noncognate translation pairs. By implication, this indicates that full meaning equivalence does not hold for all translation pairs (and, in fact, it may never hold).

More recent models similarly acknowledge that translation pairs generally do not share meaning completely. One of these, the Shared Distributed Asymmetrical

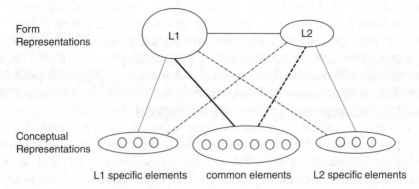

Form
Representations

Conceptual
Representations

L1 specific elements   common elements   L2 specific elements

Figure 8.5: The Shared Distributed Asymmetrical Model. (Based on Dong *et al.*, 2005, with permission from Cambridge University Press.)

Model (Dong, Gui, & MacWhinney, 2005) incorporates the assumptions of the Distributed Conceptual Feature Model that (1) the representation of word meaning is distributed over a set of elementary conceptual units, (2) the two members of a translation pair minimally share a subset of these units, and (3) each member of a translation pair is associated with a number of language-specific conceptual units as well (see Figure 8.5). To this set of assumptions the authors add a fourth: The connections between the L2 form representations and the conceptual representations are assumed to be weaker than the connections between the L1 form representations and the conceptual representations (cf. the Revised Hierarchical Model). During the advancement of L2 learning these strength differences will gradually become smaller. A fifth assumption of the model is that during the early stages of L2 learning the L2 form representations are not only connected to the conceptual units they share with L1, but also to the L1-specific conceptual units and that with increasing levels of L2 proficiency the latter type of connections gradually weaken (while the links between L2 form representations and L2-specific conceptual units gradually strengthen). Figure 8.5 illustrates these assumptions for one level of L2 proficiency (so it ignores the model's developmental assumptions).

Dong *et al.* (2005) obtained support for the latter characteristics of the model in an experiment wherein Chinese learners of L2 English produced semantic-similarity ratings to word sets. Four groups of L2 learners were tested, two consisting of first-year English majors, the remaining two of third-year English majors. One of the two groups at each of these levels of English rated sets of English words; the second rated the closest Chinese translations of the words in the English sets. In addition, groups of English and Chinese monolinguals (one of each) performed the task on the English sets and the Chinese sets, respectively. Each word set consisted of a "head word" and seven words that were all semantically related to the head word but in different ways and to different degrees. The participants were asked to rank the closeness of the head word to each of the other words in the set. Similarity analyses were then performed between the ratings of all six groups of participants. These analyses showed, first, that the ratings of the two monolingual groups differed significantly from one another, thus substantiating the present general claim that translation equivalents do not share meaning completely. Secondly, the L2 English learners' ratings on the English sets deviated from those of the English monolinguals and the more advanced learners produced ratings that were closer to those of the English monolinguals than the less advanced learners. These findings suggest that the learners' L2 gradually becomes more native-like. In terms of the model, they suggest the gradual weakening of the links between the L2 form representations and the L1-specific conceptual units. Thirdly, the ratings that the L2 English learners produced on the L1 Chinese sets deviated from the corresponding ratings of the Chinese monolinguals on these sets, and the deviance was relatively large for the more advanced learners. This finding supports the model's assumption that during L2 learning connections between the L1 form representations and the L2-specific conceptual units are formed.

A final model to present here is Pavlenko's (2009) Modified Hierarchical Model. Like the Shared Distributed Asymmetrical Model and the Distributed Conceptual Feature Model it assumes that conceptual representations do not have to be fully shared between a bilingual's two languages but may be partially shared as well. This implies distributed instead of unitary, localist conceptual representations. But a unique feature of this new model is that it explicitly posits the existence of conceptual representations that are *completely* language specific, thus acknowledging that not all words in one of the bilingual's languages can be translated by means of a single word in the other language (but require a circumlocution instead). Another way of saying this is that these words are not "lexicalized" in the other language. Examples of such words are *frustration* and *privacy*, which have no equivalent in Russian (Pavlenko's examples).

A further central feature of Pavlenko's (2009) model is that it tries to account for the phenomenon of "conceptual transfer," where the complete conceptual content associated with an L1 word is assigned to ("transferred to") a translation "equivalent" word in L2, including meaning aspects not typically associated with the L2 word. For instance, an L1 English speaker of L2 Russian may call a cup-shaped drinking container made of paper and without a handle a *chaska* despite the fact that this Russian word for cup never refers to containers of this type (in Russian, paper cups without a handle are named with the Russian word for little glasses: *stakanchiki*). This naming flaw suggests that this learner has transferred the complete concept of English *cup* to Russian *chaska*, including *cup*'s L1-specific conceptual elements (e.g., the fact that cups can be made of paper and do not necessarily have handles). Notice that this idea rephrases the assumption in Dong *et al.*'s (2005) model above, that L1-specific meaning units are linked to L2 word forms. L2 learning involves chipping off the L1-specific parts of the L2 conceptual representations (and adding the L2-specific parts). This process of redefining L2 *chaska* implicates the redefinition of other words as well (in this case, of *stakanchiki*). In other words, learning the exact reference of a word requires "conceptual restructuring" in the L2 lexicon. A third main feature of Pavlenko's model is that it implements the idea that a main goal of L2 vocabulary learning is conceptual restructuring such that the L2 conceptual representations will ultimately be as native-like as possible.

To summarize, the various models of the bilingual mental lexicon presented in this section differ from one another in the type of conceptual representations that they assume, unitary or distributed. A correlated difference between the models is whether or not they assume the presence of language-specific elements in the conceptual representations. In addition, they differ in the way the form and conceptual representations are connected. Finally, some of the models explicate how the conceptual representations and the links between the form and conceptual representations change when a bilingual gradually becomes more fluent in the L2 whereas others do not say anything about this.

8.2   Bilingual Concepts

We have just seen that the two terms in a translation pair may not refer to exactly the same set of things (the *cup-chaska* example). Another way of saying this is that the concepts associated with a pair of word translations differ from one another. (Recall that from here on we will no longer talk about "conceptual representations" but about "concepts.") This does not only hold for concrete words like *cup*, but even more so for abstract words (Van Hell & De Groot, 1998; see also Section 8.1). We have also seen that not all words have a close lexical equivalent in the other language at all because this language may lack the associated concepts altogether. These facts about cross-language conceptual nonequivalence raise the question of what information bilinguals' concepts contain exactly. This question has been examined both for late bilinguals, who started to learn an L2 when the L1 was already (largely) in place, and for simultaneous bilinguals, exposed to two languages from birth or soon after. In these studies the bilinguals' L2 concepts were compared with the corresponding concepts of monolingual native speakers of that language and/or with the corresponding L1 concepts in these very same bilinguals.

Major questions posed in these studies are whether or not an L2 speaker will ever attain native-like L2 concepts and, if not, what causes the L2 concepts to remain nonnative-like. One possible reason is that during L2 learning, the meaning associated with an L2 word's closest translation equivalent in L1 is transferred completely to the L2 word, a process called "conceptual transfer" in Section 8.1 (e.g., Pavlenko, 2009, where the meaning of L1 English *cup* was transferred to L2 Russian *chaska*). The consequence of this process is that bilinguals' L2 word use exhibits a "semantic accent": A particular L2 word might be used where a native speaker would not use it and, conversely, the word might not be used where a native speaker *would* use it. While conceptual transfer from L1 would lead to nonnative-like L2 word use, bilinguals' L1 word use should remain native-like, indistinguishable from word use in monolingual speakers of this language. Nonnative-like concepts may also result from a process during which the L1 and L2 concepts are merged into one concept that is used for both languages (e.g., Pavlenko, 2005). Because this one concept contains both L1- and L2-specific meaning nuances, bilinguals' word use in *both* L1 and L2 will be semantically accented. These issues have been examined for various types of concepts, including object concepts, color concepts, and the concepts of time, space, and motion. Due to space limits I will confine my discussion to object concepts (see Pavlenko, 2005, for a more complete discussion).

8.2.1 Object concepts and word naming

The term "object concepts" refers to the concepts associated with common artifacts such as combs, keys, and cups. In one of the studies examining these concepts (Malt & Sloman, 2003), three groups of L2 speakers of American English were tested. The groups differed between them with respect to the number of years they had been immersed in an American English language environment (from 2.3 years to 13.5 years on average for the least experienced and most experienced group, respectively). The participants were asked to give the English names for 60 photographed containers (the "bottles set") and for 60 photographed household objects for preparing and serving food (the "dishes set"). An earlier study had shown that native speakers of American English most commonly used the words *bottle, jar,* or *container* to describe the objects in the bottles set and *dish, plate,* or *bowl* to describe those in the dishes set. Following the naming session, the participants were asked to judge each object's typicality as an instance of these subclasses. They were, for instance, first presented with a photograph from the bottles set together with the word *bottle* and had to indicate the typicality of the depicted object as a bottle on a scale ranging from 0 (not a member of the bottle subclass) to 7 (very typical of the bottle subclass). Next, they were presented with the same photograph again, now with the word *jar*, and had to indicate the object's degree of "jarness," again on a 7-point scale. Finally, the same photograph was presented with the word *container* and the subjects rated how typical a container the object was. An earlier set of data obtained from American native speakers of English was used for comparison with the L2 speakers' data.

Following data gathering the researchers calculated the overlap between the native speakers' naming scores and the naming scores of each group of L2 speakers. In addition, they correlated the typicality judgments provided by the native speakers with those given by the groups of L2 speakers. The naming- and typicality-judgment patterns observed for the least experienced L2 speakers differed substantially from the native speakers' patterns. The analyses furthermore showed that the response patterns of the L2 speakers were more native-like the larger their L2 experience. But interestingly, even in the most experienced L2 speakers, deviations from the native speakers' response patterns remained. These findings indicate that L2 concepts differ from the corresponding concepts in native speakers and that this still holds after a long period of immersion in the L2 environment. Because the participants did not perform the tasks in their L1, it is impossible to tell whether their L1 might have developed an accent as a result of acquiring an L2.

A similar study (Ameel, Storms, Malt, & Sloman, 2005) tested balanced simultaneous bilinguals instead of late L2 speakers. The participants had all grown up with two languages, Dutch and French, from birth. The materials and procedure were largely similar to those used by Malt and Sloman (2003), except that the participants now named the objects twice, once in each language. Their naming performance in both language conditions was compared to the performance of Dutch and French monolingual control groups. Whereas the monolingual control groups showed language-specific naming patterns, the French and Dutch naming patterns of the bilinguals converged toward a common pattern, suggesting merged concepts. The authors concluded that "through the mutual influence of the two languages, the category boundaries in each language move toward one another and hence diverge from the boundaries used by the native speakers of either language" (Ameel *et al.*, 2005, p. 60).

The likely source of these cross-language differences between object concepts is a rather trivial one: For no other reason than mere habit, native speakers of a particular language refer to this specific object by this specific name and this habitual naming pattern just happens to differ between languages. If a particular object is usually called *bottle* by speakers of English whereas speakers of Dutch most often call it *flacon* (which is closer to English *flask*), the *bottle* concept in native speakers of English will come to differ, however slightly, from the *fles* concept in Dutch native speakers (*fles* is the closest Dutch translation equivalent of *bottle*). Grammatical differences between languages constitute a further, more interesting, source of cross-language differences between object concepts. One of these concerns a difference between languages in their use of grammatical gender. A second is a difference in the way they mark grammatical number.

8.2.2   Grammatical gender and object concepts

"Grammatical gender" refers to a grammatical distinction that marks common nouns as "masculine," "feminine," and "neuter." Contrary to the suggestion conveyed by these adjectives, in many languages that exploit grammatical gender the relation between grammatical and biological gender is largely arbitrary. This follows clearly from the fact that the word for one and the same object may be feminine in one language and masculine in another (and neuter in a third). For instance, the word for a key is masculine in German (*der Schlüssel*, where *der* indicates grammatical masculinity) but feminine in Spanish (*la llave*, where *la* indicates grammatical femininity). Of course, it also follows from the fact that inanimate objects such as keys are, by their very nature, all sexless.

Boroditsky, Schmidt, and Phillips (2003) wondered whether talking about inanimate objects such as keys as if they were masculine or feminine might mislead people into thinking that inanimate objects have a gender. If so, in the process of acquiring the associated concepts, native-language learners may look for specific object properties that match the object name's gender. For example, for an L1 German learner the hardness of the key's material may be especially noticeable (hardness having a masculine connotation), while an L1 Spanish learner may notice the key's smallness (a feminine connotation). The properties noticed this way will likely be included in the developing concept while those that go unnoticed will not be included. In other words, if two languages denote a particular inanimate object by different grammatical genders, the associated concepts will differ between the languages (e.g., hardness and smallness will be included in the L1 German and L1 Spanish concepts of a key, respectively). If comparisons of monolingual speakers of such languages would show this to be the case, a next question is what information is contained in an L2 speaker's concepts for common nouns to which the L2 does not assign gender while this L2 speaker's L1 does do so.

To answer this question, Boroditsky *et al.* (2003) examined the L2 English concepts for inanimate objects in German-English and Spanish-English bilinguals. The participants, all highly proficient in L2 English, were presented with a set of English common nouns and were asked to name for each of them, in English, the first three adjectives that came to mind. All nouns referred to inanimate objects and their translations in German and Spanish had opposite genders (but they were all non-gendered in English; after all, English does not use gender marking on nouns). The question of interest was whether the grammatical gender of the objects' names in L1 influenced adjective naming in non-gendered L2 English: Would English object names with a feminine translation equivalent in L1 evoke relatively many adjectives with a feminine connotation whereas those with a masculine L1 translation equivalent would evoke relatively many with a masculine connotation? The data showed this to be the case. For example, to English *key* (with a masculine translation in German and a feminine translation in Spanish), the L2 speakers with German as L1 produced, among others, *hard, heavy,* and *metal,* while the L2 speakers with Spanish as L1 generated the adjectives *little, lovely,* and *shiny.* These findings suggest that (1) the grammatical gender system of L1 influences the content of the L1 object concepts, and that (2) conceptual transfer occurs from L1 to L2.

Whereas Boroditsky *et al.* looked at the effect of a gendered L1 (German or Spanish) on the content of object concepts in a non-gendered L2 (English), in an Italian-German study Bassetti (2007) examined the consequences for the content of bilingual concepts of mastering two languages that both exploit grammatical gender but that assign opposite genders to particular object nouns. While the participants in Boroditsky *et al.*'s study were adult late bilinguals, Bassetti tested balanced-bilingual 9-year-olds that had either been exposed to both Italian and German from birth or exclusively to Italian at first but subsequently (before age 4) also to German. In addition, a group of monolingual Italian 9-year-olds was included for comparison. The experimental materials were drawings of familiar objects. Half of these had masculine names in Italian and feminine names in

German whereas for the other half the opposite held. An experimental procedure suitable for 9-year-olds was developed: The participants saw the object while hearing a sentence spoken by a male and then saw the object a second time accompanied by the same sentence but now spoken by a female, or vice versa. The participants were asked to imagine the object could talk and to choose the voice that belonged to the object, male or female. All testing was done in Italian. The results showed that the Italian monolingual children tended to attribute sex to the objects consistent with the grammatical gender of the objects' Italian names. This tendency was considerably weaker in the bilingual children, and detailed analyses indicated that their responses were influenced by the objects' German names. Apparently, the contrasting grammatical gender of the objects' names in Italian and German had given rise to object concepts that differ from the corresponding concepts in monolingual children.

8.2.3 Grammatical number and object concepts

A second grammatical difference between languages that appears to influence the content of object concepts concerns the way languages mark grammatical number. In English and many other languages, both nouns that refer to living beings ("animate" nouns) and nouns referring to inanimate objects take an obligatory plural marker when more than one of their referents is implied (e.g., *three dogs, two bottles*). In contrast, nouns that have an inanimate, non-countable referent ("mass nouns") cannot take a plural marker and require some unit of measurement (a "unitizer") to be quantified (*two bags of flour*). In other languages, for instance in Japanese, nouns referring to inanimate objects cannot take a plural marker and, just like English mass nouns, are quantified by means of a unitizer. In other words, these languages talk about inanimate objects as if they were substances (Boroditsky, 2003). In these languages plural marking of animate nouns is optional rather than obligatory.

To acquire the grammatical-number system of the ambient language, learners of different languages must attend to different aspects of the living beings, things, and substances that surround them. On the assumption that what is attended to will become part of the developing concepts, the consequence of language-dependent attention allocation is that the ensuing concepts will differ between speakers of different languages. If so, the question of present interest is what information is contained by the analogous concepts of bilinguals whose two languages have different number systems. Athanasopoulos and Kasai (2008) examined this question in a Japanese-English study in which they compared object categorization by intermediate and advanced Japanese learners of L2 English with that by Japanese and English monolinguals. Adopting a theoretical analysis by Lucy and Gaskins (2001), Athanasopoulos and Kasai hypothesized that a focus on the shape of a noun's referent in particular is conducive to developing the English grammatical-number system (because shape is a marker of individuation, and individuation is required for using plural marking properly), while this strategy is not particularly suitable for learning the Japanese system (see the original studies for details). If learners of English indeed rely strongly on the referent's shape, with a growth in L2 English, shape should become a more prominent feature in the object concepts of Japanese L1 speakers who are learning L2 English.

On each trial, the participants in Athanasopoulos and Kasai (2008) were presented with a picture that showed three artificial objects (drawings of irregular shapes), one object being the target, the other two the "alternates." One of the alternates was identical to the target in shape but printed in a different color; the second was identical to the target in color but had a different shape. The participants were asked to indicate which of the two alternates they thought was "the same as" the target. The advanced Japanese learners of L2 English behaved like the English monolinguals, selecting the shape match in the vast majority of cases (about 90% of the time). In contrast, the intermediate Japanese learners of L2 English behaved like the Japanese monolinguals, selecting the shape match less often than the other two groups (about 65% of the time). In other words, the advanced Japanese learners of L2 English, but not yet the intermediate ones, had learned to categorize objects the way English monolinguals do, namely, predominantly on the basis of shape. This difference in categorization behavior between the two groups of L2 English learners confirmed the hypothesis that, with a growth in L2 English, shape had become a more prominent feature in the learners' object concepts.

To summarize, the studies by Boroditsky *et al.* (2003) and Malt and Sloman (2003) suggest that late L2 speakers transfer L1 object concepts to the L2 with the effect that L2 speakers exhibit a semantic accent when speaking about the concerned objects in L2. In contrast, the study by Athanasopoulos and Kasai (2008) indicates that with extensive L2 use the L2 object concepts of late L2 speakers can become native-like, suggesting that cognitive restructuring has taken place. Furthermore, the studies that tested simultaneous bilinguals (Ameel *et al.*, 2005; Bassetti, 2007) indicate that bilinguals of this type develop object concepts that merge the concepts specific to their two languages. The result of this process of merging is that the object concepts in these bilinguals, in both languages, differ from the corresponding native speakers' concepts. The joint results of the above studies also indicate that both arbitrary naming conventions and systematic grammatical differences between languages influence concept formation and that the grammatical cross-language differences in question exert their effect on concept formation by having language learners allocate their attention to specific aspects of the environment.

8.3 Bilingual Autobiographical Memory

So far we discussed one type of declarative knowledge, namely, semantic knowledge. Recall that this concerns general knowledge such as knowing what the word *cup* means and that Maxíma Zorreguieta is the wife of Prince Willem Alexander. In the previous sections we have dealt with the former of these two types of general semantic knowledge, that is, vocabulary knowledge, focusing on the special case of the bilingual who knows two sets of words.

As mentioned in the introduction, a second type of declarative knowledge is "episodic" knowledge. This concerns personal memories of events that happened to us in our past lives. These episodic memories typically contain information on the time the event took place, where it took place, and perceptual details of the event. Because such memories are autobiographical records of our own experiences they are called "autobiographical memories" as well. The study of autobiographical memory tries to answer such questions as:

(1)   What types of encoding processes are going on when a person experiences some event?
(2)   Which aspects of the event get stored in the memory trace of this event?
(3)   How can this memory trace be accessed and the information on it retrieved when we try to recall the event at some later moment in time?

Tulving and Thompson (1973) posited an influential theory that addressed these questions. A central component of the theory is the Encoding Specificity Principle (ESP). It states that an event can only be recalled successfully if the information contained by the retrieval cue (the prompt that is presented to trigger recall of the event) is actually encoded in the memory trace of that event. If it is not, retrieval fails. If ESP is correct, the content of memory traces can be charted by varying the type of retrieval cues presented to the participants in memory experiments and seeing which ones are effective and which ones are not. Using this procedure it has, for instance, been discovered that information about the physical environment in which an event took place and the mood of the person experiencing the event are encoded in the event's memory trace (e.g., Godden & Baddeley, 1975).

If language is involved in an event, this aspect of the event might also be imprinted in the memory trace. If so, bilinguals' autobiographical memory may contain a subset of memories with their one language encoded onto them and a subset with their other language imprinted on them (in addition to memories with both languages encoded on them, plausibly resulting from events that involved frequent language switching). ESP then predicts that in cuing autobiographical memories in bilinguals by means of words, different memories will pop up depending on the language of the cues. A specific prediction regarding immigrant late bilinguals is that when a word from their L1 serves as the retrieval cue, relatively many memories from the remote past will be retrieved because during their younger years this was the only language they experienced and, thus, the only language to become imprinted in the memory traces.

Several researchers have tested these ideas and the collective data suggest that language is indeed encoded in the memory trace of an event and that immigrant late bilinguals' two languages trigger memories from different life periods. The participants in one of the relevant studies (Schrauf & Rubin, 2000) were older L1 Spanish/L2 English bilinguals who had immigrated to the United States around the age of 28 and had lived there for 38 years on average. The researchers used a common word-prompt technique, in an English session and then in a Spanish session (or vice versa) that were held on two separate days. In each language session the participant was first given a set of prompt words in the language of that session and was asked to come up with a specific event from his personal past for each of them and to write a few words about that memory in the language of that session. Immediately after completing the description of the event, the participant was asked to determine whether the memory had seemed to come in no language, in Spanish, in English, or in both languages. With this procedure the researchers could, among other things, distinguish between "congruent" and "crossover" memories. A congruent memory was defined as one that had come to the participant in the same language as the prompt word (that is, in the language of the session) whereas in a crossover memory the language of the prompt word and that of the memory differed from one another. In addition, the participants were asked to date their memories, that is, to indicate what age they were when they experienced the event. A similar earlier study by these same researchers (Schrauf & Rubin, 1998) used a somewhat different procedure in which only the occurrence of crossover memories was determined.

In the vast majority of cases (about 80%) the participants in Schrauf and Rubin (2000) indicated that the memory had come to them in one or more languages. This finding per se supports the idea that language is encoded in the memory trace of an event. But of particular interest was the finding that in both studies the crossover memories that were recalled internally in Spanish dated back to events that happened earlier in life (on average 30 and 27 years in the 1998 and 2000 studies, respectively) than those recalled in English (47 and 53 years, respectively). The same held for the congruent memories in the 2000 study: The average age at which the remembered event occurred was 29 years for congruent Spanish memories and 48 years for congruent English memories. Both these findings confirm the hypothesis that language is encoded in the memory trace of an event.

Schrauf and Rubin (1998) had also predicted that Spanish and English prompts would trigger relatively many older and more recent memories, respectively (specifically, from before and after the age at immigration, respectively). This hypothesis was not confirmed: The mean age of the participants at the time of the recalled event was around 40 for both English and Spanish prompts. Marian and Neisser (2000) suggested this result may have been due to the fact that the participants in Schrauf and Rubin's (1998) study were relatively old and had lived in the United States the larger part of their lives, possibly using *both* languages frequently after immigration. Because of the large number of post-immigration years at the moment of testing, not only events from the pre-immigration period will then have been encoded in L1 Spanish, but also relatively many post-immigration events. This may be the reason why Spanish prompts did not trigger relatively more Spanish memories from early in life.

To circumvent this problem, in an L1-Russian/L2-English study, Marian and Neisser (2000) used a slightly different methodology and tested subjects with a lower chronological and immigration age (on average 22 and 14 years, respectively). After collecting two sets of memories by means of the usual word-prompt procedure, one set in an all-Russian interview and a second in an all-English interview, the subjects were asked to indicate "the language they had spoken, had been spoken to in, or were surrounded by, at the time when each recalled event took place and to estimate their age at the time" (Marian & Neisser, 2000, p. 364). The participants reported more "Russian memories" (i.e., memories of events in which the language used at the time was Russian) when prompted with Russian words (in the Russian interview) while they reported more English memories when prompted with English words (in the English interview). Importantly, in the Russian interview more memories from an earlier age were reported (13 years on average) than in the English interview (16 years on average).

In conclusion, the joint findings of the above studies confirm the hypotheses that language is encoded in the memory trace of an event, that bilinguals' autobiographical memory therefore contains a subset of memories with their one language encoded into them and a second set that encodes their other language, and that immigrant late bilinguals' two languages trigger memories from different life periods.

Research Questions

1. According to the Revised Hierarchical Model, L1-to-L2 word translation is slower than L2-to-L1 translation because the two translation directions use different translation routes. Try to think of other reasons why L1-to-L2 translation is relatively slow.
2. The conceptual representations of an abstract word and its closest translation in another language generally differ more than the conceptual representations of a concrete pair of translations. Try to think of a reason why this is the case.
3. Bilinguals often report that speaking two languages is accompanied by the feeling of living in two different worlds. How can the studies on bilingual autobiographical memory account for this phenomenon?

Further Readings

Altarriba, Jeanette. 2003. Does *cariño* equal "*liking*"? A theoretical approach to conceptual nonequivalence between languages. *The International Journal of Bilingualism* 3. 305–322.

Athanasopoulos, Panos. 2009. Cognitive representation of colour in bilinguals: The case of Greek blues. *Bilingualism: Language and Cognition* 12. 83–95.

Matsumoto, Akiko & Stanny, Claudia. 2006. Language-dependent access to autobiographical memory in Japanese-English bilinguals and US monolinguals. *Memory* 14. 378–390.

References

Ameel, Eef, Storms, Gert, Malt, Barbara, & Sloman, Steven. 2005. How bilinguals solve the naming problem. *Journal of Memory and Language* 53. 60–80.

Athanasopoulos, Panos & Kasai, Chise. 2008. Language and thought in bilinguals: The case of grammatical number and nonverbal classification preferences. *Applied Psycholinguistics* 29. 105–123.

Bassetti, Benedetta. 2007. Bilingualism and thought: Grammatical gender and concepts of objects in Italian-German bilingual children. *International Journal of Bilingualism* 11. 251–273.

Boroditsky, Lera. 2003. Linguistic relativity. In Lynn Nadel (ed.), *Encyclopedia of Cognitive Science*, pp. 917–921. London: MacMillan.

Boroditsky, Lera, Schmidt, Lauren, & Phillips, Webb. 2003. Sex, syntax, and semantics. In Dedre Gentner & Susan Goldin-Meadow (eds), *Language in Mind: Advances in the Study of Language and Thought*, pp. 61–79. Cambridge, MA: MIT Press.

Brysbaert, Marc & Duyck, Wouter. (2010). Is it time to leave behind the Revised Hierarchical Model of bilingual language processing after fifteen years of service? *Bilingualism: Language and Cognition* 13. 359–371.

Chen, Hsuan-Chih & Leung, Yuen-Sum. 1989. Patterns of lexical processing in a nonnative language. *Journal of Experimental Psychology: Learning, Memory, and Cognition* 15. 316–325.

De Groot, Annette. 1992. Bilingual lexical representation: A closer look at conceptual representations. In Ram Frost & Leonard Katz (eds), *Orthography, Phonology, Morphology, and Meaning*, pp. 389–412. Amsterdam: Elsevier.

De Groot, Annette. 1993. Word-type effects in bilingual processing tasks: Support for a mixed-representational system. In Robert Schreuder & Bert Weltens (eds), *The Bilingual Lexicon*, pp. 27–51. Amsterdam/Philadelphia: John Benjamins.

De Groot, Annette & Poot, Rik. 1997. Word translation at three levels of proficiency in a second language: The ubiquitous involvement of conceptual memory. *Language Learning* 47. 215–264.

Dong, Yanping, Gui, Shichun, & MacWhinney, Brian. 2005. Shared and separate meanings in the bilingual mental lexicon. *Bilingualism: Language and Cognition* 8. 221–238.

Dufour, Robert & Kroll, Judith. 1995. Matching words to concepts in two languages: A test of the concept mediation model of bilingual representation. *Memory & Cognition* 23. 166–180.

Godden, D. & Baddeley, Allen. 1975. Context-dependent memory in two natural environments: On land and underwater. *British Journal of Psychology* 66. 325–331.

Kroll, Judith. 1993. Accessing conceptual representations for words in a second language. In Robert Schreuder & Bert Weltens (eds), *The Bilingual Lexicon*, pp. 53–81. Amsterdam/Philadelphia: John Benjamins.

Kroll, Judith & Curley, Janet. 1988. Lexical memory in novice bilinguals: The role of concepts in retrieving second language words. In Michael Gruneberg, Peter Morris, & Robert Sykes (eds), *Practical Aspects of Memory: Current Research and Issues, Vol. 2: Clinical and Educational Implications*, pp. 389–395. Chichester, UK: John Wiley & Sons.

Kroll, Judith & Stewart, Erika. 1994. Category interference in translation and picture naming: Evidence for asymmetric connections between bilingual memory representations. *Journal of Memory and Language* 33. 149–174.

Kroll, Judith, Van Hell, Janet, Tokowicz, Natasha, & Green, David. 2010. The Revised Hierarchical Model: A critical review and assessment. *Bilingualism: Language and Cognition* 13. 373–381.

La Heij, Wido, Hooglander, André, Kerling, Robert, & Van der Velden, Esther. 1996. Nonverbal context effects in forward and backward word translation: Evidence for concept mediation. *Journal of Memory and Language* 35. 648–665.

Lucy, John & Gaskins, Suzanne. 2001. Grammatical categories and the development of classification preferences: A comparative approach. In Melissa Bowerman & Stephen Levinson (eds), *Language Acquisition and Conceptual Development*, pp. 465–492. Cambridge, MA: MIT Press.

Malt, Barbara & Sloman, Steven. 2003. Linguistic diversity and object naming by non-native speakers of English. *Bilingualism: Language and Cognition* 6. 47–67.

Marian, Viorica & Neisser, Ulric. 2000. Language-dependent recall of autobiographical memories. *Journal of Experimental Psychology: General* 129. 361–368.

Pavlenko, Aneta. 1999. New approaches to concepts in bilingual memory. *Bilingualism: Language and Cognition* 2. 209–230.

Pavlenko, Aneta. 2005. Bilingualism and thought. In Judith Kroll & Annette de Groot (eds), *Handbook of Bilingualism: Psycholinguistic Approaches*, pp. 433–453. New York: Oxford University Press.

Pavlenko, Aneta. 2009. Conceptual representation in the bilingual lexicon and second language vocabulary learning. In Aneta Pavlenko (ed.), *The Bilingual Mental Lexicon: Interdisciplinary Approaches*, pp. 125–160. Bristol, UK: Multilingual Matters.

Potter, Mary, So, Kwok-Fai, Von Eckardt, Barbara, & Feldman, Laurie. 1984. Lexical and conceptual representation in beginning and proficient bilinguals. *Journal of Verbal Learning and Verbal Behavior* 23. 23–38.

Schrauf, Robert & Rubin, David. 1998. Bilingual autobiographical memory in older adult immigrants: A test of cognitive explanations of the reminiscence bump and the linguistic encoding of memories. *Journal of Memory and Language* 39. 437–457.

Schrauf, Robert & Rubin, David. 2000. Internal languages of retrieval: The bilingual encoding of memories for the personal past. *Memory & Cognition* 28. 616–623.

Sholl, Alexandra, Sankaranarayanan, Aruna, & Kroll, Judith. 1995. Transfer between picture naming and translation: A test of asymmetries in bilingual memory. *Psychological Science* 6. 45–49.

Squire, Larry, Knowlton, Barbara, & Musen, Gail. 1993. The structure and organization of memory. *Annual Review of Psychology* 44. 453–495.

Tulving, Endel & Thomson, Donald. 1973. Encoding specificity and retrieval processes in episodic memory. *Psychological Review* 80. 352–373.

Van Hell, Janet & De Groot, Annette. 1998. Conceptual representation in bilingual memory: Effects of concreteness and cognate status in word association. *Bilingualism: Language and Cognition* 1. 193–211.

Weinreich, Uriel. 1953. *Languages in Contact: Findings and Problems*. New York: Linguistic Circle of New York. [Reprinted 1968, The Hague: Mouton].

Chapter 9
Cognitive Effects
Ellen Bialystok and Raluca Barac

Questions about the effect of bilingualism on cognitive functioning have been asked for almost a century, conveying a long-standing implicit assumption that bilingualism has consequences beyond verbal ability. But the answers to these questions have varied greatly over time, with early studies generally warning about inferior performance by bilingual children, including confusion and mental retardation, and more recent research focusing on large cognitive benefits that come from bilingual experience. Why were the outcomes of these studies so vastly different from each other and why did the interpretation shift from bilingual deficit to bilingual advantage?

One reason pertains to how bilinguals were characterized in the early studies: many aspects of bilingualism were not considered or fully specified, such as level of comprehension and production in the two languages, degree of bilingualism, when and where children started to learn their other language(s), and how often it was used. In addition, early studies paid little attention to the need to carefully match monolingual and bilingual groups, producing comparisons between children who differed in many ways including socio-economic status and their ability to understand English instructions, the language in which testing was usually conducted. For instance, Saer (1923) used the Stanford-Binet test of intelligence to examine the cognitive abilities of a large sample of English monolingual and Welsh-English bilingual school-aged children and reported that bilingual children scored lower than monolinguals, a performance interpreted as a sign of "mental confusion" of the bilingual children. The English proficiency of the bilingual children was not considered.

The change in attitude from believing that bilingualism was a negative experience for children to one in which it is now seen as a positive boost to cognitive functioning began with a study by Peal and Lambert (1962). They gave a battery of intelligence tests to French-speaking children in Montreal who were also fluent English speakers. To their surprise, bilingual children outperformed their monolingual peers on virtually all of the tests, including tests of nonverbal intelligence.

The Psycholinguistics of Bilingualism, First Edition. François Grosjean and Ping Li.

Further analysis revealed that there was little difference between the groups on spatial-perceptual tests, but that the bilingual children showed an advantage on tests requiring symbol manipulation and reorganization. On the basis of these findings, Peal and Lambert suggested that bilingual children may actually show *enhanced* cognitive ability, especially on tests of mental flexibility, perhaps as a consequence of having to switch between their two languages. This was the first evidence that not only was bilingualism not damaging to children's cognitive growth but also that it might be a positive experience that leads to cognitive enhancement.

An active area of research since 2000 has followed up this early evidence for a cognitive advantage in bilinguals by focusing on the set of cognitive abilities known as the executive function. These are the processes responsible for attention, selection, inhibition, shifting, and flexibility that are at the center of all higher thought. Exciting new research is now providing strong evidence that early bilingualism has the power to set in place precocious development of these crucial skills and maintain them at a higher level than found for monolinguals through adulthood and into older age.

The first aim of this chapter is to describe the verbal abilities of bilingual children and adults: Section 9.1 and Section 9.2 will discuss vocabulary size, metalinguistic awareness, and learning to read. The second aim is to offer an overview of the nonverbal consequences of being bilingual, primarily changes in executive function abilities during childhood (Section 9.3) and adulthood (Section 9.4).

9.1 Language and Metalinguistic Abilities

Studies seeking evidence for bilingual effects on development began with the conservative assumption that any detectable effect of a linguistic experience would be found in the domain of linguistic competence. Thus, during the 1970s and 1980s, investigators explored the development of metalinguistic awareness in monolingual and bilingual children. Metalinguistic awareness is the explicit knowledge of linguistic structure and the ability to access it intentionally, abilities that are crucial to children's development of complex uses of language and the acquisition of literacy. In other words, metalinguistic awareness allows children to separate the meaning of the words from their form and make independent judgments about the semantic, syntactic, phonological or morphological aspects of language. But metalinguistic ability also requires cognitive ability; once form and meaning have been separated, controlled attention is required to focus on them separately.

9.1.1 Differences between monolinguals and bilinguals in language proficiency

Children develop metalinguistic abilities gradually during childhood and these abilities are supported by the growth of multiple cognitive and linguistic abilities.

Cognition and the Bilingual Brain

Basic language proficiency, including vocabulary size, is one of these building blocks for metalinguistic abilities. Thus, it is important to examine whether monolingual and bilingual children have similar vocabularies, in other words, whether or not they start out equally.

The evidence is compelling that on average bilingual children know significantly fewer words in each language than comparable monolingual children who speak only that language. A careful investigation of children between 8 and 30 months old which examined the number of words children could understand and produce in each language confirmed that, on average, this number was smaller in each language for bilingual children than for monolingual learners of that language (Pearson, Fernandez, & Oller, 1993). Nevertheless, an analysis of the total number of concepts showed no differences between monolingual and bilingual children (Pearson *et al.*, 1993). The number of words in the total vocabulary of a bilingual child, however, is difficult to estimate: Do proper names count for one language or two? Do cognates (words that are very similar in both languages, such as "table" in English and "la table" in French) count once or twice, especially if the pronunciation is unclear? Do childish sounds that are not quite words count as a word if they have a consistent meaning?

A clearer illustration of the relative vocabulary size of monolinguals and bilinguals comes from a study of children who were older than those in the Pearson *et al.* analysis. Bialystok, Luk, Peets, and Yang (2010) measured the receptive vocabulary of over 1700 children between the ages of 3 and 10. Receptive vocabulary was assessed by the Peabody Picture Vocabulary Test (PPVT-III; Dunn & Dunn, 1997) in which the child is shown a page with four pictures while the experimenter says a word, and the task is to point to the picture that best illustrates that word. All the bilingual children spoke English and another language, with English being the language of the community and school for all children. Across the sample, and at every age studied, the mean standard score on the English PPVT was reliably higher for monolinguals than bilinguals. These results are shown in Figure 9.1. At least in one of the two languages, and importantly, the language of schooling, monolingual children had an average receptive vocabulary score that was consistently higher than their bilingual peers. It is important to note, however, that the disparities were not equivalent for all words. In a subset of 6-year-olds in the sample, all children achieved comparable scores on words associated with schooling (e.g., astronaut, rectangle, writing) but significantly lower scores for words associated with home (e.g., squash, canoe, pitcher). Because all the children attended schools in which English was the language of instruction, their experiences in learning English in this context were more equivalent than their experiences learning words that referred to home and social contexts. This is a reasonable result given that English is not used as extensively in bilingual homes as it is in those of monolinguals. Importantly, school vocabulary for children in the two groups was more comparable. Thus, bilingual children are not typically disadvantaged in academic and literacy achievement (see, for example, Bialystok, Luk, & Kwan, 2005) or academic uses of spoken language (Peets & Bialystok, 2009) because the linguistic basis of those activities is

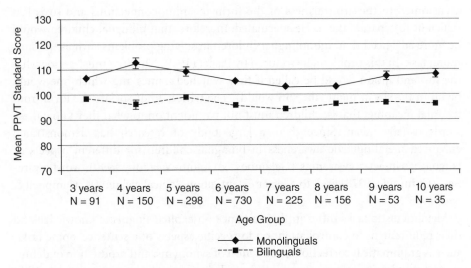

Figure 9.1: Mean Peabody Picture Vocabulary Test (PPVT) standard score by age and language group. Adapted from Bialystok, Luk, Peets, and Yang (2010).

well established. In this sense, the smaller vocabulary for bilingual children in each language is not an overall disadvantage but rather an empirical description that needs to be taken into account in research designs, especially in tasks that involve verbal ability or lexical processing. Moreover, the vocabulary deficit for home words in English in the bilingual children is almost certainly filled by knowledge of those words in the non-English language, making it likely that the total vocabulary for bilingual children is in fact greater than that of monolinguals. Therefore, the nature of the smaller bilingual vocabulary when compared with that of monolingual speakers of each language is complex (Bialystok, Luk, Peets, & Yang, 2010).

9.1.2   Differences between monolinguals and bilinguals in attention to language form

What does it mean to have metalinguistic knowledge of language? Metalinguistic ability allows children to see through the meaning of language to its underlying structure. With metalinguistic ability, children can analyze linguistic representations to extract general grammatical rules and state them explicitly, and control attention to different aspects of a sentence such as its form or its meaning. Tests of metalinguistic awareness, therefore, typically include conflicting information about form and meaning to determine children's understanding that they are separate and to test their ability to attend to them individually.

The first suggestion that bilingualism might affect children's metalinguistic abilities was proposed by Vygotsky (1962). He argued that a bilingual child is more accustomed to the arbitrariness of the form-meaning connections and so is less reluctant to separate them. He speculated, therefore, that bilingual children would be more advanced than monolingual children in solving problems such as the sun-moon task. In this problem, introduced by Piaget (1929), children must decide what the sun and moon would be called if they switched names and which one would be up in the sky at night (the sun would). The trick is to dissociate the form from its usual meaning; that is, children must not pay attention to what they know these words usually mean. Since then, a large body of research has demonstrated enhanced metalinguistic awareness in bilingual children for different aspects of language: syntactic awareness (Galambos & Goldin-Meadow, 1990), word awareness (Cummins, 1978) and, to a lesser extent, phonological awareness (Campbell & Sais, 1995).

Metalinguistic tasks differ in their reliance on explicit linguistic knowledge and their requirement to control attention to specific aspects of a sentence. Some tasks, such as grammatical correction, production of synonyms, and production of definitions depend primarily on the child's knowledge of the linguistic structure. Other tasks, such as counting the number of words in a sentence, the symbol substitution problem in which children are required to substitute arbitrary words into sentences to create nonsense, and the sun-moon problem, depend more on the ability to control attention.

In a series of studies by Bialystok (1986), children were asked to decide if a sentence was said the right way (i.e., grammatically correct) or not, ignoring whether or not it was silly. There were four types of sentences: sentences that were completely correct, grammatically incorrect but meaningful, grammatically correct but silly, or both grammatically and semantically incorrect. Thus a sentence that is grammatically correct but silly, such as "Apples grow on noses," required children to say that it is said the right way. Because meaning is typically the most salient feature of language, it is difficult to ignore the meaning in order to determine that the grammar is intact. Monolingual and bilingual children of between 5 and 9 years old were presented with a scenario in which a puppet character had fallen down the stairs and bumped his head and consequently sometimes said things the wrong way; the child's job was to tell the puppet if he said things "the right way" or "the wrong way." On the difficult condition ("Apples grow on noses,") bilinguals were better than monolinguals at agreeing that the grammar was correct even though the meaning was anomalous. These results were replicated by Ricciardelli (1992) with Italian-English bilinguals and Cromdal (1999) with Swedish-English bilingual children.

An adaptation of this sentence judgment paradigm was created for adults and used in conjunction with electrophysiological data about brain activation in the form of event-related potentials (ERPs) (Moreno, Bialystok, Wodniecka, & Alain, 2010) (see Chapter 10 for an explanation of the ERP methodology). Monolinguals and bilinguals, all young adults, were presented with the same four types of sentences used in the research with children. There were two tasks: in the simple task, the instructions were to decide if the sentence was okay or if there was anything wrong with it ("Apples grow on noses" would be incorrect); in the difficult task based on the children's version, the instructions were to decide only if the sentence was grammatically correct regardless of the meaning ("Apples grow on noses" would be correct). The conflict between form and meaning is only a problem for the difficult task, the one that was solved better by bilingual children than by their monolingual peers. Importantly, on the simple task, monolinguals and bilinguals showed equivalent responses in ERP signals, but on the more difficult conflict task, the bilinguals produced different signals than the monolinguals, indicating less conflict to these sentences on a waveform called the P600 that is known to reflect conflict in syntactic processing. This difference shows that the bilinguals processed the sentence and dealt with the conflict more efficiently than the monolinguals. These findings show that bilingual experience influences brain processing of sentence-level linguistic stimuli and are consistent with the behavioral evidence previously documented in bilingual children. The key component is the ability to control attention to attend to relevant features when there is strongly misleading information that needs to be ignored. Bilinguals find this easier to do than monolinguals.

9.1.3   How general is the bilingual advantage in metalinguistic tasks?

The studies summarized so far show a clear bilingual advantage on tests of metalinguistic knowledge in both children and adults. However, not all studies examining metalinguistic abilities have found improved performance for bilinguals. For instance, some studies reported a hindering effect (e.g., Palmer, 1972) and others reported no effect (Rosenblum & Pinker, 1983) of bilingualism. These inconsistencies can be explained by carefully considering a range of factors related to bilingualism and to the nature of the metalinguistic tasks that may affect performance. For instance, one aspect of metalinguistic awareness is understanding the grammatical and semantic function of morphemes, the small units of meaning that make up language. In addition to basic word forms such as walk or ball, these include the grammatical units such as "-ed" or "-s" that make those forms past tense or plural, respectively. One test of children's morphological awareness in English is the Wugs test developed by Berko (1958). Children are presented with pictures of novel objects, animals, plants or actions, and hear a text that introduces a pseudoword such as "wug" or "kazh." Children need to complete the sentence using the target word by applying English morphology rules for noun plural, past tense, and other aspects of grammar. Figure 9.2 illustrates one of the stimuli used in the Wugs test. In a study by Barac and Bialystok (2012), three groups of bilinguals (Spanish-English, French-English, Chinese-English) and a group of English monolingual children performed this task. All children were 6 years old and all except the French bilingual children were being educated in English. The Chinese-English bilinguals and the French-English bilinguals did not differ from each other (or from the monolinguals), and the best performance, significantly different from the others, was achieved by the Spanish-English bilingual children. For the Spanish group, two

This is a wug

Now there is another one.
There are two of them.
There are two _____.

Figure 9.2: Illustration of Berko's Wug Test taken from Trevor Harley's (2007) *The Psychology of Language*.

aspects were combined to create this advantage: the language of instruction was the same as the language of testing and their two languages had considerable overlap.

These results indicate that bilingualism alone is not sufficient to guarantee a metalinguistic advantage. In fact, children's performance on metalinguistic tasks is influenced by an interaction between bilingualism and factors such as nature of the task, degree of reliance on executive function resources, similarity between the two languages, and correspondence between language of instruction and language of testing. Whether or not bilingualism facilitates children's acquisition and access of linguistic knowledge is a question that has both theoretical and practical implications. Phonological awareness is a precursor to reading and what these results suggest is that children who speak a second language with similar phonological structure and alphabetic orthographic system to English may have some advantage when learning to read in English, whereas those children who speak a second language that is phonologically and orthographically different from English may require additional help in understanding these concepts. Section 9.2 will examine in more detail the acquisition of literacy and academic achievement in bilingual children.

9.2   Acquisition of Literacy

Acquisition of literacy is a crucial milestone in children's development. Children's success in school and more generally, in life, depends to a large extent on how well they acquire this skill. Therefore, evidence that bilingualism modifies the acquisition of literacy would be dramatic. There are at least two reasons to expect there to be a relationship between bilingualism and literacy acquisition. First, bilingual children develop the prerequisite skills that set the stage for literacy, such as oral language proficiency, metalinguistic awareness, and cognitive development, differently from their monolingual peers. Importantly, the nature of the influence of bilingualism on each of these background skills is also different: oral language proficiency is lower in bilingual children whereas some aspects of cognitive development are more advanced. Second, if bilingual children already know how to read in their other language, they have the possibility to transfer what they already know about reading to the new language (Bialystok, Luk, & Kwan, 2005). This section examines how the experience of speaking two languages shapes different aspects of early reading such as the relation between language and print and decoding skills.

9.2.1   Understanding the relation between language and print

Written text is a symbolic representation of spoken language, so learning to read requires an understanding of how the symbolic representations relate to the meaningful language that the child already knows. Different writing systems have different relations to spoken language – symbols can refer to phonemes, syllables or morphemes – but in all cases children need to understand the abstract representational rule that connects spoken and written systems. One part of understanding this relation between language and print is the general representational principle that the meaning is derived completely and exclusively from print and that the symbolic notations are invariant. A way to test children's understanding of this general principle is by using a task called the Moving Word Task (Bialystok, 1997). Children are shown a display including two pictures of common objects such as a dog and a ball, as well as a card with the name of one of the two objects (e.g., "dog") printed on it. Initially, the experimenter tells the child what is written on the card: "This card has the word *dog* printed on it. I am going to put the card right here" and places the card under the image of the object it stands for. Subsequently, once the experimenter and the child agree on what is printed on the card, a puppet creates a mess and the printed word ends up under the card representing the other object, in this case, the ball. This is the key part of the task because the experimenter manipulates the spatial position of the printed card relative to the image of the object it represents to see if children associate that position with changes in meaning. Children are asked again what the card says. If children understand that written text refers to language because written symbols represent words, then they will know that written words are invariably representations for specific words whose meaning cannot change because of contextual variations. Thus to answer the question correctly children must indicate that the word printed on the card is still "dog." Finally, the mess is tidied up, the printed card is returned to the original position under the object it names and children are asked again what the card says. Across two different studies (Bialystok, 1997; Bialystok, Shenfield, & Codd, 2000), three groups of 4-year-old bilingual children (French-English, Chinese-English, and Hebrew-English) showed more precocious understanding of these general properties of the symbolic function of written language than same-age English monolingual children. Thus, bilingual children, regardless of the language combination they spoke, were more likely to attend just to the text, ignore the distracting information when the written word was positioned under the wrong picture, and indicate that the written word is the only source of meaning. In fact, bilingual children were correct in responding to this question over 80% of the time, a level comparable to monolingual children who were one year older than the bilinguals. These studies demonstrate that speaking two languages leads to more advanced understanding of a general representational principle that prepares the child for the process of literacy acquisition.

9.2.2　Early reading: Does bilingualism change anything?

Probably the most important milestone in the process of literacy acquisition is learning to decode words and to read independently. In an alphabetic language, phonological awareness is central to this achievement because it enables children to segment words into sounds and associate those sounds with the appropriate written forms. In fact, at some level reading in any writing system requires phonological analysis because print records spoken language. This relationship between phonological analysis and reading is most apparent at the level of word identification, or word-level reading. However, as discussed in the previous section, when children grow up speaking two languages, their phonological awareness abilities may develop differently than in monolingual children. In some cases, when children speak two languages that are more similar, such as Spanish and English, phonological awareness abilities are improved. But no such advantage is found when the two languages do not have much overlap, such as English and Chinese, and when the language of testing does not correspond to the language in which children receive instruction.

Given that phonological awareness abilities are central to learning how to read and that these abilities develop differently in bilingual children, it is reasonable to expect that the process of learning to read may also unfold differently in bilingual children. A study of these issues was undertaken by Durgunoglu, Nagy, and Hancin-Bhatt (1993). All of the children were native speakers of Spanish and were learning to read in English, their second language. The authors found that children's levels of phonological awareness and word recognition in Spanish predicted how well they were able to recognize words in English, the second language. Summarizing and extending this research, Durgunoglu (1998) reported strong correlations between phonological awareness in English and Spanish for bilingual children as well as significant influences between phonological awareness and word recognition across languages. In other words, the phonological awareness skills developed in one language transferred to reading ability in another language. This is an important result. If children can establish basic concepts of phonological awareness in any language then reading will be facilitated no matter what language initial literacy instruction occurs in.

More recent research, however, has shown that this relationship does not hold generally across different language pairs, and that this pattern of transfer is limited by the relation between the two languages and writing systems. Because different writing systems are based on different sets of symbolic relations, each requires different cognitive skills (Coulmas, 1989). In alphabetic systems, phonemes in words are represented by letters, with different types of alphabetic systems (such as Roman, Semitic, and Cyrillic) using different letters for these sounds. Syllabaries, such as Korean, establish correspondences between consonant–vowel groups and graphemes. These relations place different demands on children's analysis of spoken language and their recording of the language in print. Logographic systems, such as Chinese, select the morpheme as the basic linguistic unit and associate those meaningful segments with characters indicating both semantic and some phonological properties. Because the task of learning to read in each of these writing systems is different, any effect of bilingualism on learning to read will depend on the type of writing system used in each language. In other words, reading skills should transfer from one language to the other only when the two languages use the same writing system.

These were exactly the findings of a study that compared four groups of Grade 1 children (English monolinguals, Cantonese-English bilinguals, Hebrew-English bilinguals, and Spanish-English bilinguals) who received instruction in English (Bialystok, Luk, & Kwan, 2005). Children were given tests of receptive vocabulary, phonological awareness, verbal short-term memory, and decoding. Children in the bilingual Hebrew-English and Spanish-English groups showed more advanced early reading skills in English than Chinese-English bilinguals and English monolinguals. Thus, for some children, being bilingual sped up the acquisition of reading skills, whereas for others it did not bring any changes. The Hebrew and Spanish bilinguals were also the children who showed the highest performance on the phonological awareness task and whose decoding abilities in English were highly correlated with their decoding abilities in the non-English language (Hebrew or Spanish). This finding that for some, but not all, groups of bilinguals reading acquisition is accelerated can be explained by considering the writing system used by their two languages. Hebrew, English, and Spanish are all alphabetic writing systems, although the scripts differ. Therefore, what these results demonstrate is that both facilitation for English reading and transfer of reading across languages was found for bilingual children whose two languages shared a writing system.

These findings support the conclusion that early reading depends on a set of cognitive abilities shared by the two languages plus skills specific to different writing systems. And it is the transfer of these skills specific to different writing systems that explains why some bilingual children perform better than monolinguals, whereas others perform similarly to the latter. Moreover, it is important to emphasize that Chinese-English bilingual children did not perform worse than monolinguals, demonstrating that when the two languages do not share a similar writing system, progress in learning to read is not hindered.

9.3   Developing Executive Control

Bilingualism is essentially a linguistic experience, so a reasonable expectation is that its consequences will be largely linguistic. For this reason, the majority of studies that address bilingualism compare how bilinguals solve linguistic tasks in their two languages. But from early on, there was always the idea that bilingualism could also have cognitive consequences. At first, these consequences were assumed to be negative, specifically, that bilingualism created cognitive confusion, but increasingly it has become clear that the cognitive consequences of bilingualism are entirely positive.

The main impact of bilingualism has been found for a set of processes known as the executive function. These processes include attention, selection, inhibition, monitoring, and flexibility and they develop in parallel with the maturation of the prefrontal cortex. Three main abilities are typically proposed to constitute its core (Diamond, 2006; Miyake, Friedman, Emerson, Witzki, Howerter, & Wager, 2000): inhibitory control (ability to resist a habitual response or information that is not relevant), working memory or updating (ability to hold information in mind and mentally manipulate it), and cognitive flexibility (ability to adjust to changes in demands or priorities and switch between goals).

9.3.1   Executive control abilities affected by bilingualism

In the research on metalinguistic awareness, as was seen earlier, bilingual children and adults outperformed monolinguals when asked to judge whether sentences were grammatically correct but contained a distracting and irrelevant meaning. These sentences required effortful attention to ignore the error in meaning and focus only on the form. For both children and adults, bilinguals found this easier to do than their monolingual counterparts. The process of ignoring salient distraction is part of the function of the executive control system, so it seemed that bilinguals performed this task better than monolinguals because of enhanced executive control for linguistic processing. Thus, research with a metalinguistic task led to the hypothesis that the effect of bilingualism was to enhance the performance of the executive function system, not just for linguistic processing, but for nonverbal processing as well.

A growing number of studies over the past two decades with both children and adults have provided supporting evidence for this idea. For example, Bialystok (1992) reported that bilingual children performed better than their monolingual counterparts on the Embedded Figures Test. In this test, participants must find a simple visual pattern concealed in a larger complex figure. More specifically, children are presented with a complex shape, which is a recognizable picture that contains a simple triangle or a house-shaped configuration and their task is to identify the hidden or embedded shape. Bialystok suggested that the better performance of bilingual children might reflect their superior ability to focus on wanted information and ignore misleading information. That is, the advantage might be one of enhanced selective attention, involving the ability to inhibit irrelevant or unwanted information and the complementary ability to concentrate on relevant aspects.

Typically in this research, the investigator compares performance by monolinguals and bilinguals on tasks that are superficially similar but include one condition that additionally requires some aspect of executive control. An example that illustrates how these processes are used by children is the Dimensional Change Card Sort task (DCCS) developed by Zelazo, Frye, and Rapus (1996). This is a game in which images that vary on two dimensions, usually shape and color, are sorted according to one of them. For example, cards containing either red or blue circles or squares are sorted into containers marked by an image of either a red square or a blue circle. Children are asked to first sort the cards by one dimension – blues in this box and reds in this box – and then to switch to the other – circles in this box and squares in this box. Thus, this problem places two types of rules in conflict and requires children to pay attention to them one at a time. The ability to do this involves several aspects of the executive function – inhibit attending to the irrelevant rule, shift between rules when the game changes, and hold the current rule in mind. The dramatic finding is that young children can easily state the new rule when it changes but continue to sort by the first rule; they have great difficulty overriding the habit set up in the first phase. When this experiment was repeated with bilingual and monolingual children aged between 4 and 5 years, the bilingual children were markedly better at switching to the new rule (Bialystok, 1999; Bialystok & Martin, 2004). This result was obtained despite there being no difference in pre-switch performance. Figure 9.3 presents the scores on the critical post-switch condition in two studies. The researchers thus concluded that the constant need to inhibit the non-used language generalized to more effective inhibition of nonverbal information.

The benefits of the bilingualism experience on children's cognitive development have been documented at various ages ranging from 3 to 8 years. Recently, Kovács and Mehler (2009) extended this pattern to infants. They presented 7-month-old infants with a verbal cue followed by a visual reward. The verbal cue consisted of meaningless trisyllabic cues and the visual reward was a toy that always appeared on the same side of the screen. Infants had to learn that the verbal cue predicted the location of the toy reward. One way to know if infants are able to learn this is by recording their anticipatory looks. That is, if infants learned that the verbal cue predicted the location of the toy on the screen, then they should look at the place where they expect the reward to appear, even before it is shown. Monolingual and bilingual infants were equally good at learning this relation. However, in the second part of the task, the rule was changed so that the toy reward appeared on the opposite side of the screen. Thus, again, infants had to learn that the cues predicted the location of the toy, but to do so they needed to overcome the old response, the tendency to look to the side of the screen that was previously

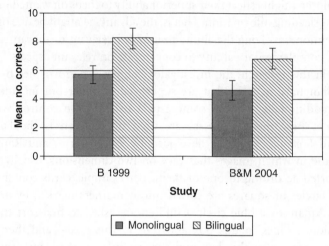

Figure 9.3: Mean number correct (out of 10) and standard error by language group (monolingual or bilingual) in the post-switch condition of the Dimensional Change Card Sort task in two studies. B 1999 = Bialystok (1999); B&M 2004 = Bialystok and Martin (2004). Both figures appeared in Bialystok and Craik (2010).

rewarded. In this sense, infants needed to rely on executive functions in order to be able to switch to the new location. Kovács and Mehler found that 7-month-old infants raised in bilingual households were better able to switch responses after a rule shift than were their peers raised in monolingual households. These results suggest that the experience with two languages changes the cognitive system from very early on.

In an important refinement to the research showing a bilingual advantage in executive function, Carlson and Meltzoff (2008) administered nine different executive function tasks to 50 kindergarten children who were English-speaking monolinguals, English-Spanish bilinguals, or children who were in a language immersion elementary school. The major finding was that the English-Spanish bilingual children performed better on the executive function battery than both other groups, once differences in age, vocabulary, and parents' education and income levels were statistically controlled for. The effects were specific to only some aspects of control: there were no bilingual advantages in the control of impulses (response inhibition) but significant advantages on conditions requiring memory and inhibition of attention to a prepotent response (interference suppression). In other words, on tasks that required children to refrain from peeking at or opening a nicely wrapped gift, bilingual children did not differ from monolinguals. However, on tasks that required children to focus on selected information such as the middle fish in an array of five fish, and ignore the distractors (i.e., the four fish flanking the middle fish), bilingual children surpassed monolinguals. Therefore, the bilingual advantage in executive functioning tasks reflects precocious development in only specific components of executive control.

9.3.2   Is it bilingualism, or it is something else?

Bilingualism is often correlated with other types of experience that may themselves influence performance, so it is difficult to be sure that the performance differences between monolinguals and bilinguals are caused by bilingualism *per se*. For example, claims for cultural effects favoring Asian children on tests of executive control (e.g., Sabbagh, Xu, Carlson, Moses, & Lee, 2006) must be separated from the role of bilingualism in shaping this performance.

Several studies have addressed this issue and demonstrated that bilingualism affects cognitive performance independent of other factors. For instance, two studies have examined the role of culture and immigration history on the cognitive outcomes of bilingualism. In one study, Bialystok and Viswanathan (2009) compared three groups of 8-year-old children on an executive control task called the "faces task." This is a computerized task in which children were presented with schematic faces, with either green or red eyes, that were flanked by two boxes. Once the face disappeared, an asterisk flashed in one of the two boxes and children were instructed to press the key on the same side as the box containing the asterisk if the eyes had been green and the opposite side if the eyes had been red. The task included several manipulations in order to assess various components of executive functions, notably inhibition and shifting. Children were matched on educational experience and social class and were English-speaking monolinguals in Canada, bilinguals in Canada (mixed cultural backgrounds, immigrants) or bilinguals in India (south Asian culture, non-immigrants). The results showed that the two bilingual groups performed as well as each other and both outperformed the monolinguals on the measures of switching and inhibitory control. In the second study, Bialystok, Barac, Blaye, and Poulin-Dubois (2010) compared a group of bilinguals to two monolingual groups – an English-speaking group in Canada and a French-speaking group in France. Again, there was no difference between the two monolingual groups and better performance by the bilinguals on all the executive control tasks that involved conflict resolution. Together, the results from these two studies support the generality of the bilingual effects over the influence of immigration and culture on nonverbal tests of executive control.

Finally, in the study by Barac and Bialystok (2012) described in Section 9.1.3, three groups of 6-year-old bilingual children (Chinese-English bilinguals, French-English bilinguals, Spanish-English bilinguals) who differed from each other in terms of the relationship between the two languages, cultural background, and language of schooling, all showed better executive control than English monolinguals. These results offer strong support for the claim that bilingualism acts independently of variables such as language similarity, cultural background, and language of schooling in influencing nonverbal outcomes. They endorse the conclusion that bilingualism itself is responsible for the increased levels of executive control previously reported.

9.4   Advantages of Bilingualism across the Lifespan

9.4.1   Executive control into adulthood and older age

It is important to establish that bilingual children master the executive control abilities required by the tasks described in the previous sections earlier than monolingual children, but in a short time, all children can perform them. Does that mean that the differences in mastery of executive control disappear in later childhood? Such an outcome would diminish the importance of these differences by confining them to an early developmental period. A more profound case for the effect of bilingualism on cognitive ability requires that these differences in executive control persist into adulthood.

Demonstrations of precocious executive control abilities in children were followed by studies that extended the investigation to adults, using paradigms in which a prepotent response tendency must be inhibited. One example of such a situation is the Simon task. The participants view a screen on which either a red or green square appears; there are two response keys, one for red squares and the other for green squares. Participants are instructed to press the left shift key when they see a green square and the right shift key when they see a red square. The keys are positioned below the sides of the screen, and the squares can appear either immediately above their relevant response key (congruent trials) or above the other key (incongruent trials). Response latencies are longer for incongruent trials, and the difference between incongruent and congruent latencies is the Simon effect. If participants are able to resist the misleading information carried by spatial position in the incongruent trials, the Simon effect will be smaller, and we may conclude that they have well-developed inhibitory control mechanisms; conversely, larger Simon effects imply greater difficulty in suppressing the irrelevant spatial information.

Using this logic, Bialystok, Craik, Klein and Viswanathan (2004) tested groups of younger and older adults who were either monolingual or bilingual on a version of the Simon task. When the colored squares were presented centrally, there was no conflict between the position of the stimulus and side of the appropriate response, and in this case there were no differences in reaction time between monolinguals and bilinguals, although older participants took longer to respond (Figure 9.4a). When the colored squares appeared laterally, however, Simon effects were found, and these were larger for monolinguals – especially older monolinguals (Figure 9.4b). This evidence for a bilingual advantage in inhibitory control in adults extended the results of previous studies on children. Moreover, the bilingual advantage was especially strong in older adults, suggesting that bilingualism may afford some protection against at least some forms of cognitive aging.

Consistent with findings from research with children, bilingual younger adults outperformed monolinguals when the task demanded inhibition and conflict resolution. But what is the range of abilities influenced by the bilingualism experience?

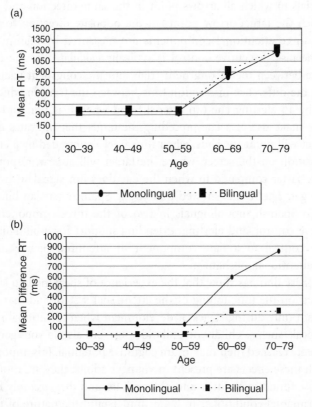

Figure 9.4: Mean reaction time (RT) by decade for monolinguals and bilinguals in the Simon task. (a) Mean RT for control condition. (b) Mean RT cost as the difference between congruent and incongruent trials (Simon effect). From Bialystok, Craik, Klein, and Viswanathan (2004). Both figures appeared in Bialystok and Craik (2010).

What kind of attentional abilities are affected by bilingualism in younger adults? This is a question that Costa, Hernández, and Sebastián-Gallés (2008) addressed in a study examining the efficiency of the attentional networks in monolingual and bilingual young adults. To this end, the authors used the attentional network task (ANT; Fan, McCandliss, Sommer, Raz, & Posner, 2002) designed to measure three different attentional components: alerting, orienting, and executive control. Of these three attentional components, the executive control abilities involved in tasks that require inhibitory control such as the Simon task have been already shown to be affected by the bilingualism experience. The aim of Costa and colleagues' study was to examine whether this bilingualism influence extends to the other two attentional components: alerting, which is involved in achieving and maintaining an attentive state, and orienting, which refers to selecting information from sensory input.

In the ANT, participants are presented with an array of five arrows and are asked to indicate the direction of the central target arrow. As in the Simon task, there are congruent trials in which all arrows point in the same direction and incongruent trials in which the target arrow points in the opposite direction to the flanking arrows. The three attentional components are measured by manipulating some aspects of the task. Executive control is typically calculated as the difference in reaction time between the incongruent trials and the congruent trials; alerting is measured as the difference in reaction time between the trials in which the target is preceded by an alerting cue (an asterisk) and when it is not; and orienting is the ability to make use of a cue preceding the target that indicates the direction that the target will point to. Thus, when the target is preceded by a cue that indicates the position on the screen where the target will appear, response times to the target are faster compared to when the cue does not signal such information about the target. The results showed that young Spanish-Catalan bilingual adults outperformed Spanish monolinguals in two of the three components of attention, executive control, and alerting, extending support for a bilingual advantage in executive control to a new component of attention, namely the alerting/monitoring attentional mechanism.

Together, these findings show that the experience of speaking two languages has positive effects on the functioning of the attentional system and that these effects are present not only during stages of development when attentional processes are not at their peak, such as childhood and older age, but also in younger adults, who have supposedly reached their maximum cognitive potential. It is important to note that although these effects are present in younger adults, they are more modest in size than those found in children and older adults, and they are only found under certain experimental conditions. To better understand the nature of the bilingual advantage and the conditions leading to this effect, Costa and colleagues gave young monolingual and bilingual adults a version of the ANT and manipulated the executive demands of the task by changing the ratio of congruent to incongruent trials (Costa, Hernández, Costa-Faidella, & Sebastián-Gallés, 2009). Thus, the authors created an easy version of the task that had low monitoring demands and a more difficult version with high monitoring demands. The easier task included predominantly one type of trial (92% congruent or 92% incongruent trials). In contrast, in the more difficult version, the two trial types were more evenly distributed (75% congruent or 50% congruent trials). The bilingual advantage was found only in the high monitoring conditions, showing that when the task relies heavily on the monitoring system, bilinguals outperformed monolinguals on both congruent and incongruent trials.

9.4.2   Bilingualism as a protective factor in delaying symptoms of dementia

In all the studies described in this chapter, the participants selected were healthy and free from cognitive impairment. But aging sometimes includes challenges such as dementia, which is characterized by significant impairment of several cognitive functions such as memory, executive function, language, and structural changes at the brain level. Given the sustained advantage of bilinguals into older age, does bilingualism continue to offer protection in such cases? A large body of research has pointed to the importance of "cognitive reserve," the protection against cognitive decline that comes from active engagement in stimulating intellectual, social, and physical activities (Stern, 2002). To examine whether bilingualism contributes to cognitive reserve, Bialystok, Craik, and Freedman (2007) conducted a study of hospital records and compared the age of onset of symptoms in 91 monolingual and 93 bilingual patients who had been diagnosed with dementia, the majority being Alzheimer's disease. Results showed that the age of dementia onset for the bilinguals was 4 years later than it was for the monolinguals – a highly significant difference. The two groups were essentially equivalent on other measures that might have influenced the result (e.g., scores on the Mini-Mental State Examination (MMSE) or occupational status) but the monolingual group had received more education (12.4 years) than the bilingual group (10.8 years), a difference that should favor monolingual subjects. This is important given that a 4-year delay of symptoms of dementia is much greater than any effect associated with drugs and represents considerable savings in health-care costs.

This result was replicated in another study (Craik, Bialystok, & Freedman, 2010) in which researchers gathered information about age of onset and other relevant factors from approximately 100 bilingual and 100 monolingual patients, all of whom had been diagnosed with probable Alzheimer's disease. Again, in this new sample, the bilingual group had their first clinic visit more than 4 years later than the monolinguals and had experienced symptoms of dementia more than 5 years later than their monolingual counterparts. As in the first study, the groups were equivalent in cognitive level and the monolinguals had the greater advantage in terms of education and occupational status. There were no differences in these results in subgroups of immigrants and non-immigrants. These studies demonstrate that bilingualism, with its high cognitive demands for establishing and managing two linguistic systems, contributes to cognitive reserve in the same way as other stimulating mental activities.

Finally, it is important to note that many experiences have been shown to modify cognitive and linguistic processing, but those demonstrations tend to be based on individuals who choose the experience because of a prior talent (architects have more spatial skills than non-architects) or develop an expertise that is part of the experience (video game players have more rapid response to perceptual stimuli than nonplayers). Bilingualism is different: for the majority of individuals who are bilingual, the experience was not chosen but imposed by circumstances. For that reason, the effects of bilingualism on cognitive and linguistic processing are not only dramatic for bilinguals but have enormous implication for understanding the human mind. Contrary to earlier views in which the capabilities of the mind were considered to be fixed, evidence for the impact of bilingualism on mental functioning across the lifespan demonstrates the essential flexibility and plasticity of the mind. Experience shapes our mind, just as our mind selects from the array of experiences in which we potentially engage. We have come a long way from the pervasive assumption that bilingualism is damaging to children's cognitive development to demonstrating a protective effect of bilingualism in coping with symptoms of Alzheimer's disease. Experience is powerful, and bilingualism may be one of the most powerful experiences of all.

Research Questions

1. It is reported that bilingualism leads to cognitive benefits across the lifespan (see Sections 9.3 and 9.4). What evidence is there for the length of time being bilingual as opposed to the age of becoming bilingual on producing these effects? How might these outcomes change if the languages are learned at the same time or at different times?
2. Why is it difficult to conclude that the effects found for language and cognitive abilities are entirely due to bilingualism? What other variables might contribute to these effects? How can you confirm the role of bilingualism experimentally?
3. The research reported in this chapter shows the effects of bilingualism on language and cognitive ability. What effects do you think there might be for individuals who speak three or more languages? How might the mechanism for such effects be the same or different as that proposed for bilingualism?

Further Readings

Bialystok, Ellen. 2001. *Bilingualism in Development: Language, Literacy, and Cognition*. New York: Cambridge University Press.

Bialystok, Ellen, Craik, Fergus I.M., Green, David W., & Gollan, Tamar H. 2009. Bilingual minds. *Psychological Science in the Public Interest* 10. 89–129.

Luo, Lynn, Luk, Gigi, & Bialystok, Ellen. 2010. Effect of language proficiency and executive control on verbal fluency performance in bilinguals. *Cognition* 114. 29–41.

Schweizer, Tom, Ware, Jenna, Fischer, Corinne. E, Craik, Fergus I.M., & Bialystok, Ellen. (in press). Bilingualism as a contributor to cognitive reserve: Evidence from brain atrophy in Alzheimer's disease. *Cortex*.

References

Barac, Raluca & Bialystok, Ellen. (2012). Bilingual effects on cognitive and linguistic development: Role of language, cultural background, and education. *Child Development* 83. 413–422.

Berko, Jean. 1958. The child's learning of English morphology. *Word* 14. 150–177.

Bialystok, Ellen. 1986. Factors in the growth of linguistic awareness. *Child Development* 57. 498–510.

Bialystok, Ellen. 1992. Attentional control in children's metalinguistic performance and measures of field independence. *Developmental Psychology* 28. 654–664.

Bialystok, Ellen. 1997. Effects of bilingualism and biliteracy on children's emerging concepts of print. *Developmental Psychology* 33. 429–440.

Bialystok, Ellen. 1999. Cognitive complexity and attentional control in the bilingual mind. *Child Development* 70. 636–644.

Bialystok, Ellen, Barac, Raluca, Blaye, Agnes, & Poulin-Dubois, Diane. 2010. Word mapping and executive functioning in young monolingual and bilingual children. *Journal of Cognition and Development* 11. 485–508.

Bialystok, Ellen & Craik, Fergus I.M. 2010. Cognitive and linguistic processing in the bilingual mind. *Current Directions in Psychological Science* 19. 19–23.

Bialystok, Ellen, Craik, Fergus I.M., & Freedman, Morris. 2007. Bilingualism as a protection against the onset of symptoms of dementia. *Neuropsychologia* 45. 459–464.

Bialystok, Ellen, Craik, Fergus I.M., Klein, Raymond, & Viswanathan, Mythili. 2004. Bilingualism, aging, and cognitive control: Evidence from the Simon task. *Psychology and Aging* 19. 290–303.

Bialystok, Ellen, Luk, Gigi, & Kwan, Ernest. 2005. Bilingualism, biliteracy, and learning to read: interactions among languages and writing systems. *Scientific Studies of Reading* 9. 43–61.

Bialystok, Ellen, Luk, Gigi, Peets, Kathleen, & Yang, Sujin. 2010. Receptive vocabulary differences in monolingual and bilingual children. *Bilingualism: Language and Cognition* 13. 525–531.

Bialystok, Ellen & Martin, Michelle. 2004. Attention and inhibition in bilingual children: Evidence from the developmental change card sort task. *Developmental Science* 7. 325–339.

Bialystok, Ellen, Shenfield, Tali, & Codd, Judith. 2000. Languages, scripts, and the environment: Factors in developing concepts of print. *Developmental Psychology* 36. 66–76.

Bialystok, Ellen & Viswanathan, Mythili. 2009. Components of executive control with advantages for bilingual children in two cultures. *Cognition* 112. 494–500.

Campbell, Ruth & Sais, Efisia. 1995. Accelerated metalinguistic (phonological) awareness in bilingual children. *British Journal of Developmental Psychology* 13. 61–68.

Carlson, Stephanie & Meltzoff, Andrew. 2008. Bilingual experience and executive functioning in young children. *Developmental Science* 11. 282–298.

Costa, Albert, Hernández, Mireia & Sebastián-Gallés, Núria. 2008. Bilingualism aids conflict resolution: Evidence from the ANT task. *Cognition* 106. 59–86.

Costa, Albert, Hernández, Mireia, Costa-Faidella, Jordi, & Sebastián-Gallés, Núria. 2009. On the bilingual advantage in conflict processing: Now you see it, now you don't. *Cognition* 113. 135–149.

Coulmas, Florian. 1989. *The Writing Systems of the World*. Oxford: Basil Blackwell.

Craik, Fergus I.M., Bialystok, Ellen, & Freedman, Morris. 2010. Delaying the onset of Alzheimer's disease: Bilingualism as a form of cognitive reserve. *Neurology* 75. 1726–1729.

Cromdal, Jakob. 1999. Childhood bilingualism and metalinguistic skills: Analysis and control in young Swedish-English bilinguals. *Applied Psycholinguistics* 20. 1–20.

Cummins, James. 1978. Bilingualism and the development of metalinguistic awareness. *Journal of Cross-Cultural Psychology* 9. 131–149.

Diamond, Adele. 2006. The early development of executive functions. In Ellen Bialystok & Fergus Craik (eds), *Lifespan Cognition: Mechanisms of Change*, pp. 70–95. New York: Oxford University Press.

Dunn, Lloyd & Dunn, Leota. 1997. *Peabody Picture Vocabulary Test-Third Edition*. Bloomington, MN: Pearson Assessments.

Durgunoglu, Aydin. 1998. Acquiring literacy in English and Spanish in the United States. In Aydin Durgunoglu & Ludo Verhoeven (eds), *Literacy Development in a Multilingual Context: A Cross-Cultural Perspective*, pp. 135–146. Mahwah, NJ: Lawrence Erlbaum Associates.

Durgunoglu, Aydin, Nagy, William, & Hancin-Bhatt, Barbara. 1993. Cross-language transfer of phonological awareness. *Journal of Educational Psychology* 85. 453–465.

Fan, Jin, McCandliss, Bruce, Sommer, Tobias, Raz, Amir, & Posner, Michael. 2002. Testing the efficiency and independence of attentional networks. *Journal of Cognitive Neuroscience* 14. 340–347.

Galambos, Sylvia & Goldin-Meadow, Susan. 1990. The effects of learning two languages on levels of metalinguistic awareness. *Cognition* 34. 1–56.

Harley, Trevor. 2007. *The Psychology of Language*. Hove/New York: Psychology Press.

Kovács, Ágnes & Mehler, Jacques. 2009. Cognitive gains in 7-month-old bilingual infants. *Proceedings of the National Academy of Sciences* 106. 6556–6560.

Miyake, Akira, Friedman, Naomi, Emerson, Michael, Witzki, Alexander, Howerter, Amy, & Wager, Tor. 2000. The unity and diversity of executive functions and their contributions to complex "frontal lobe" tasks: A latent variable analysis. *Cognitive Psychology* 41. 49–100.

Moreno, Sylvain, Bialystok, Ellen, Wodniecka, Zofia, & Alain, Claude. 2010. Conflict resolution in sentence processing by bilinguals. *Journal of Neurolinguistics* 23. 564–579.

Palmer, Michael. 1972. Effects of categorization, degree of bilingualism and language upon recall of select monolinguals and bilinguals. *Journal of Educational Psychology* 63. 160–164.

Peal, Elizabeth & Lambert, Wallace. 1962. The relation of bilingualism to intelligence. *Psychological Monographs: General and Applied* 76. 1–23.

Pearson, Barbara, Fernandez, Sylvia, & Oller, D. Kimbrough. 1993. Lexical development in bilingual infants and toddlers: Comparison to monolingual norms. *Language Learning* 43. 93–120.

Peets, Kathleen & Bialystok, Ellen. 2009. Dissociations between academic discourse and language proficiency among bilingual kindergarteners. Poster presented at the Society for Research in Child Development, Denver, CO.

Piaget, Jean. 1929. *The Child's Conception of the World*. London: Routledge & Kegan Paul.

Ricciardelli, Lina. 1992. Bilingualism and cognitive development in relation to threshold theory. *Journal of Psycholinguistic Research* 21. 301–316.

Rosenblum, Tamar & Pinker, Steven. 1983. Word magic revisited: Monolingual and bilingual children's understanding of the word-object relationship. *Child Development* 54. 773–780.

Sabbagh, Mark, Xu, Fen, Carlson, Stephanie, Moses, Louis, & Lee, Kang. 2006. The development of executive functioning and theory of mind. A comparison of Chinese and U.S. preschoolers. *Psychological Science* 17. 74–81.

Saer, David. 1923. The effect of bilingualism on intelligence. *The British Journal of Psychology* 14. 25–38.

Stern, Yaakov. 2002. What is cognitive reserve? Theory and research application of the reserve concept. *Journal of the International Neuropsychological Society* 8. 448–460.

Vygotsky, Lev. 1962. *Thought and Language*. Cambridge, MA: MIT Press.

Zelazo, Philip, Frye, Douglas, & Rapus, Tanja. 1996. An age-related dissociation between knowing rules and using them. *Cognitive Development* 11. 37–63.

Chapter 10

Neurolinguistic and Neurocomputational Models

Ping Li

Issues surrounding bilingual individuals and bilingualism have attracted the attention of not just psycholinguists, as discussed so far, but also neuroscientists, and for quite a long time. How does one brain host two languages? How does the bilingual brain differ from the monolingual brain? How does the brain change in both function and structure as a result of learning a second or third language? What are the computational processes and mechanisms underlying the use and representation of two languages? How are effects such as age of acquisition and level of proficiency reflected in the bilingual brain? Can we identify neural traces of switching from one language to the other? These are among the many fascinating questions concerning the neurolinguistics of bilingualism (or neurobilingualism) that have been asked repeatedly and examined extensively. In this chapter, we aim at providing an overview of how interesting questions like these are studied by neurolinguists using methods available at the time, although our emphasis will be placed on more recent theories, data, and tools. The neurolinguistic study of bilingualism is growing at an astonishing speed, and the purpose of this chapter is not to cover the full spectrum of the field, but to provide the reader with interdisciplinary perspectives, concepts, and methodologies, and with a view to explaining how the neuroscience of language helps to elucidate the complex interactions between the brain and multiple languages.

This chapter is organized into three sections. In Section 10.1 we give an overview of some of the neurolinguistic traditions and debates, so that the reader has a sense of where the issues came from and where they stand today. In Section 10.2 we examine the cognitive neuroscience of bilingualism, along with a brief guide to the relevant neuroimaging methodologies. In Section 10.3 we look at how neurolinguistic computational modeling complements behavioral and neuroimaging studies with insights into the interactive dynamics of the bilingual brain. We discuss these approaches with illustrative examples to show how research is done within the neurolinguistics of bilingualism.

The Psycholinguistics of Bilingualism, First Edition. François Grosjean and Ping Li.
© 2013 Blackwell Publishing Ltd with the exceptions of Chapter 1, Chapter 2, Chapter 3, Chapter 7, Chapter 10 © 2013 François Grosjean and Ping Li. Published 2013 by Blackwell Publishing Ltd.

10.1   Neurolinguistic Traditions and Debates

The study of the neural basis of cognition has led to significant discoveries in the last decades thanks to noninvasive brain imaging techniques (see the discussion in Section 10.2), but the origin of this research tradition can be traced back to at least the 19th-century ideas championed by Franz Gall (1785–1828) and his followers in the tradition of phrenology (see Leahey, 2004). Gall initiated a tradition that cognitive neuroscientists follow today, the localization of brain functions. Although he and his contemporaries were led astray by claims that the shape and size of the skull were correlated with personality traits, their idea that the brain, rather than the heart, is the seat of all mental functions had a long-lasting impact in the 19th century. In addition, Gall's conception of the brain as a compartmentalized system with individualized functions also proved useful, providing the first kind of objective measures of the so-called "mental organ" (or "mental faculty").

Subsequent neurological findings from Paul Broca (1824–1880) and Carl Wernicke (1848–1904) supported the overall idea of localization, but also clarified what specialized brain functions might look like specifically: damage to the left inferior prefrontal cortex (Broca's area) leads to speech articulation difficulties and agrammatical behavior, whereas damage to the posterior part of the superior temporal cortex (Wernicke's area) leads to comprehension difficulties and semantic impairment (see further discussion in Section 10.1.1 with regard to brain structures and damage). In the 20th century more work was done to reveal the neural bases of cognitive and linguistic behavior, notably by Wilder Penfield, a neurosurgeon and pioneer in neurolinguistics who performed a large number of brain surgeries in order to treat epileptic patients. During surgery he stimulated various parts of the exposed brain with electrodes in order to avoid removing normally functioning brain regions when taking out malignant tissues. Patients were able to report a sensation or lack of it each time an electrical stimulation was applied (e.g., seeing flashes of light when the occipital lobe was stimulated or having tingling sensations when the postcentral gyrus was stimulated). By stimulating different parts of the cortical surface, Penfield was able to pinpoint specific areas in the "living brain" for specific functions rather than relying on autopsies as did Broca and Wernicke.

10.1.1   Brain localization

Much of the early neurolinguistic research followed the lesion deficit model in the traditions of Broca, Wernicke, and other 19th- to early 20th-century neurophysiologists. According to the classic Wernicke-Geschwind neural model of language (see Price, 2000 for a review), in speech perception, the primary auditory cortex receives the information and transmits it to Wernicke's area for comprehension, and in speech production the information passes through the *arcuate fasciculus*, the fiber tracts that connect frontal-temporal cortical areas, to Broca's area for articulatory planning and finally the motor cortex for actual articulation; in reading, the visual cortex registers the visual form of the written word, transmits it to the angular gyrus for auditory encoding, and then to Wernicke's area for comprehension. Damage to each of these locations, crucially Broca's area, Wernicke's area, and the arcuate fasciculus, will result in significant impairment in comprehension, production and word repetition, respectively. Other areas such as the supramarginal gyrus in the parietal lobe may also be important for semantic representation and processing. Figure 10.1 provides an illustration of this model in the brain, with the major language pathways marked, along with key brain regions labeled, in lateral surface view (10.1a) and medial section view (10.1b).

Within this tradition of thinking based on the lesion deficit model, much of early neurolinguistics subscribed to the localization-based models of language. According to this thinking, injured regions of the brain are associated with impaired linguistic behaviors, and inferences are then made about the relation between brain structure and cognitive function. This perspective led to the useful paradigm of "double dissociation": if a lesion to brain region A is associated with impaired behavior X (A–X), a lesion to brain region B with impaired behavior Y (B–Y), and there exists no A-Y or B-X association, then it is claimed that in the normal intact brain, structure A is responsible for behavior X, and B for Y. This double dissociation paradigm assumes a close correspondence between brain structures and cognitive functions, consistent with the overall approach of phrenology in brain localization.

10.1.2   Brain organization

The Wernicke-Geschwind neural model of language has remained the dominant thinking until very recently, with the accumulation of new evidence from neuropsychology and neuroimaging (see Hickok, 2009; Price, 2000). It is now clear that the neural substrates underlying linguistic functions are much more complex than traditionally thought. There are at least four primary reasons for rejecting a purely localization-based approach to language. First, lesion to the same brain regions does not necessarily lead to the same type of symptoms. For example, damage to Broca's area could cause comprehension as well as production difficulties; all aphasic patients suffer from anomia (word-finding difficulty) and, cross-linguistically, the same type of aphasia shows very different behaviors in different languages. Second, although Broca's and Wernicke's areas are both in the left hemisphere, we now know that the right hemisphere also plays a crucial role in many aspects of language, especially with regard to acoustic and phonological processing; for example, speech perception activates the superior temporal cortex bilaterally at an early stage (see Hickok, 2009). Third, recent neuroimaging findings suggest that not only cortical but also subcortical structures are heavily involved in language processing, especially the basal ganglia (which includes the caudate and putamen) that may form a neural circuitry with the prefrontal cortex in sensory acquisition and discrimination, and in sequence learning. Finally, the neural circuitry for language in the left frontal,

(a)

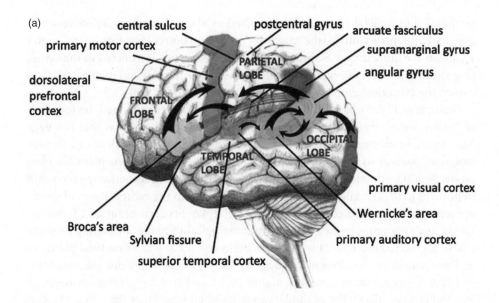

central sulcus

primary motor cortex

postcentral gyrus

arcuate fasciculus

supramarginal gyrus

dorsolateral
prefrontal
cortex

PARIETAL
LOBE

angular gyrus

FRONTAL
LOBE

OCCIPITAL
LOBE

TEMPORAL
LOBE

primary visual cortex

Wernicke's area

Broca's area

Sylvian fissure

primary auditory cortex

superior temporal cortex

(b)

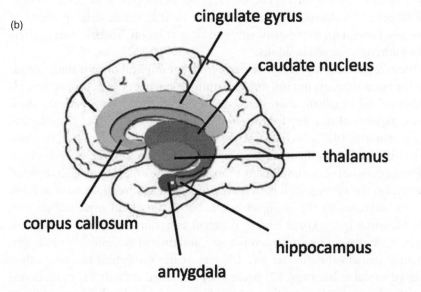

cingulate gyrus

caudate nucleus

thalamus

corpus callosum

hippocampus

amygdala

Figure 10.1: Lateral (1a) and medial (1b) views of the brain. (See Section 10.1.1 for an explanation of the flow of arrows with regard to the Wernicke-Geschwind neural model of language.) Figure 1b shows some of the critical brain regions implicated in memory (e.g., hippocampus) and bilingual language control functions (e.g., cingulate gyrus and caudate nucleus).

temporal, and parietal areas are also involved in working memory, selective attention, and inhibitory control (the "cognitive executive control" functions; see Chapter 9), and at the same time, new brain regions previously not considered in the classic language model are now revealed (e.g., anterior insula, inferior and middle temporal cortex, the posterior temporal-parietal junction; see Price, 2000).

Elman *et al.* (1996), based on arguments like the above, championed the approach of "brain organization" rather than brain localization.[1] The idea is that language and cognition may have co-evolved such that no brain region is designed just for language, counter to the brain localization hypothesis. This seems plausible both ontogenetically (development in human lifespan) and phylogenetically (evolution in history) in that language and cognition interact from the earliest stages of development, leading to the complex dynamic interplay between brain and behavior. Elman and colleagues termed this "postphrenological thinking" by highlighting the role of an interconnected network across brain regions and the structural plasticity and compensatory functions of language development (see more discussions of this in 10.2.2 regarding brain networks, and in 10.3.1 and 10.3.2 regarding connectionism and emergentism). For example, young children who suffer from brain lesions in the left hemisphere may attain normal language development by compensatory right-hemisphere involvement in language, and their language delay patterns, if there are any, depend on the severity, site, and time of lesion, which are very different from patterns observed in adults.

This brain organization perspective has significant implications for understanding how the brain supports not just one but multiple languages. In neuropsychological studies of bilingualism, there has been evidence that some patients show distinctive patterns of recovery for the two languages spoken prior to neurological insult (e.g., Paradis, 1977). Such distinctive patterns involve, for instance, one language recovering after another (i.e., successive recovery). In some cases, recovery of one language does not occur until many months after the other language completed its recovery. On the surface, such patterns are highly suggestive of separate storages of the two languages in the bilingual brain. But in the brain organization perspective, the same lesion could lead to different behavioral patterns for different languages, again depending on the severity, site, and time of the lesion. For example, one language (usually the stronger one, L1) may be less susceptible to damage than the other (the weaker language, L2) because L1 is learned earlier, or is more dominant, or has a higher proficiency than L2 and hence a higher threshold in sustaining the damage. Moreover, the L2 can become the dominant language with increased experience and proficiency, and brain injury, depending on its severity, may not alter that new dominance or proficiency. Indeed, the literature on bilingual aphasia has recorded many complex patterns of bilingual recovery that any lesion deficit model is unlikely to accommodate: for example, parallel recovery of both languages,

---

[1] The brain localization idea has been challenged since Franz Gall's time by the opposing view under various names, including equipotentiality, holism, and distributiveness. See Gardner (1985) for historical accounts of the tension and debates.

successive recovery according to dominance before lesion (dominant language recovered first), and successive recovery according to age of acquisition (i.e., L1 recovered first) (see Paradis, 1977). In some cases, the two languages may show strong competition and result in "antagonistic recovery" patterns: as one language becomes better the other becomes worse, and vice versa. These complex patterns suggest that dissociations in behavior do not necessarily map to dissociations in neural substrates, contrary to brain localization assumptions. Some neuroscientists suggest that when a language of the bilingual suffers from damage, the neural tissues associated with the language are not necessarily damaged, but the access to that language is weakened (Fabbro, 1999) or the language control mechanism disrupted (Green, 2005).

10.1.3   Language switch

A concrete but wrong example of brain localization for language is the search for neural correlates of a language switch. Bilinguals often switch from one language to another in natural conversation, especially in a bilingual speech mode (see Chapter 1). In the 1950s, Penfield and colleagues hypothesized that language switching takes time, which indicates a switching cost. This idea led them to propose that there might be a neurophysiological type of switch, one that turns off one language while turning on the other. Although much has changed since the 1950s in the neuroscience of language, the idea of an on-and-off switch for languages still strikes a familiar tone in modern theories of bilingualism.

The search for a physical correlate of a language switch ended with very mixed results. At the behavioral level, experimental studies of healthy young adult bilinguals do not yield consistent evidence for a switching cost: while some have found significant effects of language switching in terms of slowed processing speed, others showed that a switching cost or not depends on the way code-switches are produced and recognized (see Chapter 2, Section 2.3.2). At a neurophysiological level, some researchers have argued that a language switch may be localized in specific brain regions (e.g., the supramarginal gyrus), whereas others showed that patients with switching difficulty may have lesions in a variety of brain regions in the frontal, temporal, and parietal areas.

In an attempt to identify the neural basis of a language switch, Hernandez, Martinez, and Kohnert (2000) tested six Spanish-English bilinguals in an fMRI experiment (see details in 10.2.1 regarding the fMRI method). The bilinguals learned both languages before age 5 but considered English to be their stronger language. During the experiment they were asked to name a set of pictures presented successively. An auditory cue in English ("say") or Spanish ("diga") prompted them to name the picture either in English or Spanish. In the single language condition, participants named a group of successive pictures either in English or in Spanish, whereas in the language switch condition, the auditory cue switched between English and Spanish on successive pictures and the participants had to follow the cue to switch between the two languages in naming the pictures. The bilinguals were faster in the single language condition than in the language switching condition, therefore showing a switching cost. Of particular interest was the fMRI finding that among all the brain areas that were activated during picture naming, only the activation in the dorsolateral prefrontal cortex (DLPFC; see Figure 10.1) was reliably seen across all participants and, more important, the DLPFC activation was significantly stronger for the language switching than for the single language condition. This finding could be taken to suggest that the DLPFC is a candidate brain structure for a language switch at the neural level.

Interestingly, the DLPFC appears to be a "generalist" rather than a "specialist" in its cognitive functions. In the literature it has been found to be strongly activated in a variety of cognitive tasks other than bilingual switching, such as selective attention (e.g., switching between shape vs. color features of a stimulus), response selection (selecting from competing responses), response inhibition (inhibiting response tendencies that are not currently relevant), and visuospatial working memory (e.g., reporting in backward order the sequence of pictures seen) (see Abutalebi & Green, 2007 and Chapter 9 for discussions of cognitive control and bilingualism). It seems that language switching shares a common neural basis with general cognitive abilities, the "central executive control" abilities. Selecting among competing word forms, accessing corresponding word meanings in memory, and making linguistic responses all involve these control abilities. Thus, we can conclude that no single brain region is dedicated solely to language switching and that a neurophysiological language switch must be part of an interconnected cognitive executive control system.

Not only is a neural language switch nowhere to be found in the brain, but also one language may not be completely switched off when the other language is on: in the bilingual speech mode both languages may be activated nonselectively and in parallel, creating situations of multiple language competition and interaction (see Chapters 2 and 4 for a discussion). Studies of bilingual competition and interaction are made possible by modern technologies as researchers look into the *living* bilingual brain, that is, as bilingual language use takes place inside the brain, a topic we now turn to.

10.2   The Cognitive Neuroscience of Bilingualism

Until recently, neurolinguistics has relied on the examination of brain lesions for understanding how the linguistic brain works. But in recent years, neuroimaging techniques, particularly event-related potentials (ERPs) and functional Magnetic Resonance Imaging (fMRI), have allowed researchers to look into the intact living brain without making inferences about brain functions based on lesion studies. These methods have swiftly revolutionized our understanding of the relationships between language, brain, and culture. The explosion of research projects based on these methods has been unprecedented in psychology, linguistics, and cognitive science. Take fMRI as an example: the first fMRI paper on the human visual cortex was published in *Science* in 1991; in all of 1992 only 4 papers on fMRI were published, but by 2010 at least 40 fMRI studies were published *per day*! (This estimate was based on a search on Google Scholar; http://scholar.google.com/). As technological advances make these methods more reliable and accessible, neurolinguistic studies have also become more dependent on them for new insights. Neuroimaging methods have also quickly found their way into bilingualism research. We are seeing an exciting new field, the cognitive neuroscience of bilingualism, emerging rapidly and making significant headway in understanding the workings of the bilingual brain.

10.2.1 Functional neuroimaging: fMRI and ERP methods

Neuroscientists have traditionally relied on invasive technologies to probe into the neural structure underlying learning, memory, language, and the associated disorders. Some of these techniques, such as electrical stimulation, single-neuron recording, or Positron Emission Tomography (PET), while useful with animals and human clinical populations, often cannot be easily applied to healthy human subjects due to their invasiveness. Although several PET studies of bilingual language processing have been performed, most bilingual imaging studies today have used noninvasive techniques such as fMRI and ERP to track the brain's cognitive and linguistic activities.

Functional MRI has provided a very powerful tool in the last two decades for the study of brain and language. It involves the use of strong magnetic fields created by the magnetic coils of the MRI machine to measure hemodynamic changes in blood flow, specifically the blood-oxygen-level-dependent (BOLD) signals, a ratio of oxygenated vs. deoxygenated hemoglobins in given brain regions. As we engage in cognitive and linguistic behavior, neuronal cells in certain brain regions consume more energy than in others, and the energy is supplied by hemoglobins, the red proteins that transport oxygen through the red blood cells. fMRI captures these dynamic BOLD activities in various parts of the brain, presumably reflecting underlying neuronal activities related to specific processes of cognition. In general, increased BOLD signals reflect increased cognitive activities, and by comparing the different BOLD signals from cognitive tasks vs. those from a baseline task (e.g., a task in which the participant stares at a crosshair on a computer screen), fMRI researchers can infer about the role that focused brain regions play in a specific task, be it face recognition or language processing. The spatial resolution of fMRI is excellent by today's standards, in the order of several millimeters (e.g., an fMRI voxel may be 1–4 cubic mm in size). Therefore, fMRI has been particularly useful to bilingual researchers for determining where in the brain L1 vs. L2 activities take place, and whether the degree of activity is correlated with factors such as age of acquisition (AoA) and language proficiency. Figure 10.2 presents a snapshot of an MRI machine (1a) and an fMRI setup (1b).

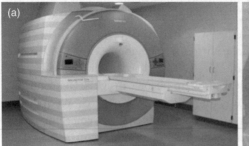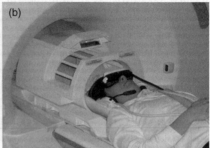

Figure 10.2: (a) A Siemens 3T MRI scanner deployed at Pennsylvania State University; (b) A participant wears goggles and headphones to be slid into the scanner. Inside the scanner the participant can make responses to linguistic material presented on MRI-compatible audio-video devices.

In addition to the functional MRI discussed thus far, researchers have also used structural MRI (sMRI) methods to detect structural differences in the bilingual brain. For example, using the VBM (Voxel-Based Morphometry) method, researchers can compare monolingual vs. bilingual participants with respect to gray matter density (the number of neuronal cells) in select brain regions. For example, Mechelli *et al.* (2004) showed in their VBM study that participants who learned a second language, as compared with monolingual participants, had increased gray matter density in the left inferior parietal cortex (near the supramarginal gyrus; see Figure 10.1) as a function of both AoA and proficiency (the earlier the L2 is learned, the higher the density; the more proficient the learner, the higher the density). These data suggest significant neural plasticity resulting from bilingualism, pointing to the fact that the bilingual brain, both in function and in structure, is shaped by specific linguistic experience and amount of experience with the languages concerned (see also Chapter 9, Section 9.5.2).

In contrast to fMRI, the ERP method measures the brain's ongoing electrical activities (electroencephalograms or EEGs) on a millisecond-by-millisecond basis, a time window within which critical cognitive and linguistic processes take place. When raw EEG signals are averaged over multiple trials of a stimulus condition, and when these signals are "time-locked" to stimulus events (e.g., presentation of a visual word), the corresponding "event-related" potentials (ERPs) that fluctuate in voltage can be extracted and analyzed. These fluctuations are designated as "components," the "brainwave peaks and valleys." ERP components vary in a number of dimensions, including polarity (positive vs. negative), latency (timing), and amplitude (level), along with distribution information (location) of the activation on the scalp. These components are typically labeled according to the latency of the waveform's peak amplitude; for example, N400 refers to a negative going waveform peaking at about 400 ms post-stimulus onset during visual or auditory presentation. Several key components implicated in language processing have been identified in the literature (see Kutas, Federmeier, Staab, & Kluender, 2007 for a review), including N400, indicating lexical-semantic integration in sentences, LAN (left anterior negativity, occurring in the same time window as N400), indicating morphosyntactic analysis, and P600, indicating syntactic analysis and repair (see Key, Dove, & Maguire, 2005 for a summary of major ERP components relevant to cognition). Together, the ERP components allow for the identification of the time course of on-line language processes in both L1 and L2.

The fMRI and ERP methods as just described are clearly complementary in their abilities to reveal brain mechanisms of language. fMRI has a high spatial resolution in terms of the regions it can pinpoint in the brain, but its temporal resolution in terms of the timing of cognitive events it can capture is quite poor, only in the order of seconds. This is because fMRI measures hemodynamic changes, which occur relatively slowly, and it usually requires a few seconds for a BOLD signal to reach its peak. By contrast, event-related potentials (ERPs) have excellent temporal resolution because they measure the electrical rather than hemodynamic activities of assemblies of neurons. On the other hand, ERP has poor spatial resolution due to the difficulty of knowing where in the cortex (which is underneath the scalp) the observed electric activity (which is recorded on the *surface* of the scalp) comes from; in other words, the site where EEG/ERP signals are recorded does not correspond to the location in the brain where cognitive processing takes place. Thus, ERP and fMRI clearly have different strengths and weaknesses, and are used to investigate different kinds of questions. Together they provide important neural data that can inform theoretical debates regarding the "where" (mostly with fMRI) and "when" (mostly with ERP) questions of language processing and representation in bilinguals. In Sections 10.2.1 and 10.2.3 we illustrate the application of fMRI and ERP to the study of the bilingual brain.

10.2.2 Distinct vs. common neural systems

A central question that has attracted the attention of investigators in bilingual imaging is whether the processing of one's native language and that of a second language involve the same (common) or different (distinct) neural systems in the bilingual brain. The debates have revolved around the role of two key variables: age of acquisition and proficiency of the second language. Age of acquisition (AoA) has been used to refer to a variety of concepts (see Hernandez & Li, 2007 for a review; see also Chapter 7), but here we use AoA to refer to the age at which L2 acquisition begins, either in the learner's L1 home environment or in an immigrant L2 environment. In the psycholinguistic literature, bilinguals are often divided into early vs. late learners according to AoA. Proficiency refers to the level the learner has reached for effective L2 communication, typically divided into high proficiency vs. low proficiency (sometimes an intermediate level is also used).

As discussed in Chapter 7, previous research has put much weight on AoA as a factor modulating the ultimate success in a second language. Earlier neuroimaging studies had likewise emphasized AoA. For example, Kim, Relkin, Lee, and Hirsch (1997) studied 12 bilingual participants who had very mixed bilingual profiles (e.g., English-French, English-Spanish, Italian-German, and Chinese-English). The participants were asked to perform a sentence-generation task, that is, to silently describe their daily experiences in L1 or L2 inside the fMRI scanner. Half of the participants were early learners (learning two languages from infancy at home) and the other half late learners (mean AoA of L2 = 11 years of age). The researchers found that the late learners showed distinct patterns of brain activation for each language whereas the early learners showed common loci of brain activation in Broca's area. No differences were shown in Wernicke's area for early vs. late learners. Although the study was well publicized, it suffered from a number of problems, particularly the lack of control in the linguistic task and lack of objective measure of the participants' L2 proficiency. Thus, it was unclear whether the observed differences should be attributed to AoA differences, as the investigators claimed, or to proficiency differences (e.g., early learners may be more proficient in the L2), or to both.

Evidence for the relative contribution of AoA vs. proficiency can be found in more recent neuroimaging studies. A number of studies have attempted to manipulate the two variables orthogonally, such that effects of AoA can be examined when proficiency level is the same for participants, and effects of proficiency examined when AoA is the same. In an fMRI study, Wartenburger *et al.* (2003) asked Italian-German bilinguals to judge the well-formedness (grammaticality judgment) and semantic contents (semantic judgment) of (a) normal sentences and (b) sentences that contained morphosyntactic violations (number, gender or case) or semantic violations. Three groups of bilinguals with varying proficiency in L2 were tested: early learners with high proficiency (EAHP), late learners with high proficiency (LAHP), and late learners with low proficiency (LALP). The results indicated that increased brain activity in L2 relative to L1 was seen in all three groups, showing that processing of the L2 is more effortful than that of L1 for all the bilingual participants. Differences were observed for the two tasks: (a) for the semantic judgment task, the EAHP and LAHP groups did not differ substantially, whereas the LALP group showed significantly more neural activity than either the EAHP or the LAHP group in the left frontal, temporal, and parietal regions; (b) for the grammaticality judgment task, late learners, irrespective of their proficiency levels, showed increased neural activity in frontal and parietal regions when processing grammatical violations. Thus, Wartenburger *et al.*'s study suggested that AoA and proficiency are both important: they may be differentially sensitive to aspects of language (syntax vs. semantics) and reflected as either common or distinct neural response patterns.

The Kim *et al.* and Wartenburger *et al.* studies are only illustrative examples of the ever-growing bilingual imaging literature that highlight the relative contribution of AoA vs. proficiency. Many other studies have tried to distinguish the role of AoA from that of proficiency in the neural representation of multiple languages (see Hernandez & Li, 2007 for a review). Several issues have been discussed in the literature. First, researchers have considered the importance of task demand in fMRI studies. For example, explicit judgment of grammaticality may lead to greater AoA differences, as shown in Wartenburger *et al.*'s study, whereas tasks that do not require explicit or conscious efforts may not. In addition, the most commonly used tasks in bilingual imaging studies, such as semantic categorization, verb generation, and silent sentence generation, may not be tapping into specific linguistic representations in L1 and L2. Whether overlapping or distinct neural systems are involved may depend on the degree to which the task places demands on general vs. specific aspects of language and memory. Second, the level of analysis may affect data interpretation: in standard fMRI data analyses, the results are based on averaged BOLD signals at a group level, and such group analyses tend to neutralize subject differences. The overlapping patterns of activation in L1 and L2 might have been exaggerated by group analyses, in which individual differences may be washed out. With a more individual-subject-based approach, specific L2 areas may be identified.

A final issue that has been considered is the impact of cross-language overlap or similarity. Cross-language overlap refers to the common features shared by the two languages of the bilingual. In previous discussions (see Chapter 9, Section 9.2.2) we saw how language overlap may affect other aspects of bilingualism. Larger cross-language overlap could lead to greater overlap in brain regions during processing, whereas smaller overlap could be associated with distinct neural response patterns in the bilingual's two languages. For example, using the lexical decision task, Chan *et al.* (2008) identified distinct neural patterns in bilinguals' responses to nouns and verbs in English vs. Chinese, showing that the differences in how grammatical classes are marked in the two languages affect the areas and degrees of neural activity. In fMRI studies of English and many Indo-European languages, verbs activate prefrontal regions whereas nouns activate temporal-occipital regions. fMRI evidence from Chinese, however, showed no such dissociations (Li, Jin, & Tan, 2004). Chan *et al.*'s study indicated that their Chinese-English bilinguals who lived in Hong Kong were able to respond to the language-specific properties of L1 and L2 differently. In contrast, a recent study by Yang, Tan, and Li (2011) that examined late Chinese-English bilinguals who grew up in mainland China showed that the brain activation patterns for nouns vs. verbs were undifferentiated not only in Chinese but also in English for the late bilinguals, suggesting the use of native language mechanisms for the processing of second language stimuli.

Taken together, it is clear that there is no simple answer as to whether common or distinct neural systems underlie the representation or processing of the bilingual's two languages. A host of variables including AoA, proficiency, task demands, levels of analysis, cross-language overlap, among others, may modulate the functional activities in the bilingual brain. It would indeed be surprising if the bilingual brain did not use both common and distinct neural systems to support the comprehension and production of multiple languages. In this regard, it is worth mentioning that in recent years researchers have embarked on a new direction by studying brain networks (or "connectivity"), examining not just activation of individual brain regions, but also the spatial and temporal relationships between multiple brain regions during cognitive and linguistic processing. In a recent review,

Bressler and Menon (2010) provided a framework for analyzing brain networks for cognition, in which a set of subnetworks in the frontal, temporal, and parietal brain regions are responsible for attention, memory, and cognitive control, and these subnetworks are interconnected and coordinated such that different subnetworks may play different roles; for example, internally generated, "mind wandering" mental states may evoke a brain subnetwork different from that of externally driven, cognitively demanding tasks. The study of connected and coordinated neural networks, rather than isolated brain regions of interest, has the potential to reconcile some of the debates between brain localization and brain organization (discussed in Sections 10.1.1 and 10.1.2) and will undoubtedly stand at the forefront of the neurolinguistics of bilingualism as well as cognitive neuroscience in general in the years to come.

10.2.3   Electrophysiological signatures of bilingualism

In contrast to fMRI studies that highlight distinct vs. common neural systems on a spatial dimension, ERP studies have focused on bilingual processing on a temporal dimension. ERPs can be used to examine both quantitative differences (e.g., in terms of timing of events) and qualitative differences (e.g., in terms of types of processing involved) within the same experimental task. ERP studies provide the electrophysiological signatures of bilingual processes often through the comparison of the bilingual's performance in L1 vs. L2, or in L2 as compared with native speakers' performance in that language. In addition, while most studies test bilinguals with natural linguistic materials from the L2 (words and sentences), others have used artificial language learning paradigms. The last decade has also seen a rapid growth of ERP studies of L2 learning and bilingual language processing (see Van Hell & Tokowicz, 2010 for a review; see also Chapter 7).

ERP findings can complement fMRI findings in a number of ways. For example, ERP research demonstrates that early bilinguals process semantics similarly in the two languages, but process morphosyntax either similarly or differently depending on various factors. Consistent with fMRI findings, several ERP studies of grammatical processing in bilinguals highlight the role that language overlap plays in affecting bilingual ERP response patterns. For example, Tokowicz and MacWhinney (2005) asked English-Spanish bilinguals to make grammaticality judgments to sentences that varied in the overlap of syntactic functions. ERP data were collected as participants made judgments about the sentences first in Spanish (L2) and then in English (L1). In both languages number agreement is required for subject and verb, but number agreement for determiner-noun is marked only in Spanish (*la casa* vs. *las casas*) and not in English (*the house* vs. *the houses*). Interestingly, the ERP patterns for these two types of number agreement differed significantly: while a P600 component (which indicates syntactic analysis and repair processes) was evident for grammatical violations in the subject-verb agreement sentences, it was not seen in the determiner-noun agreement cases in the learner's L2. Thus, cross-linguistically similar features, as assessed by ERPs, are processed similarly in the two languages (i.e., both eliciting P600) while cross-linguistically dissimilar features are not (e.g., determiner-noun agreement without P600).

Language-specific features that are not shared across the languages may pose significant challenges to L2 learners. Bilinguals may use L1 processing routines to handle L2 (consistent with fMRI data as discussed in Section 10.2.2), sometimes even after years of experience with the L2, as demonstrated by Chen, Shu, Liu, Zhao, and Li (2007) who examined Chinese-English bilinguals with high proficiency in the second language (English). Using the ERP method, they tested the bilinguals' ability to detect subject-verb agreement violations in the second language (e.g., *the price of the cars are too high*). Unlike in Western languages, subject-verb agreement in sentences is not required in Chinese. Chen *et al.* collected ERP data from both Chinese-English bilinguals and from native-speaker participants processing the same English sentences that contained either correct subject-verb agreements or agreement violations. Their data indicated distinct ERP response patterns for the bilinguals and the native speakers. Native English speakers showed a typical LAN component (which indicates early morphosyntactic analysis) followed by a P600 component in response to agreement violations, whereas this pattern was absent in the Chinese-English bilinguals. Interestingly, the behavioral performances of the native speakers and that of the bilinguals were very similar, indicating that the bilinguals could detect the ungrammatical sentences in behavioral responses, and that they were indeed proficient in the second language. The fact that only brain responses as measured by ERPs showed group differences suggests that on the one hand, neural measures are highly sensitive, and on the other, when processing syntactic features that are absent in one's native language, the learner may use neurocognitive mechanisms from the native language to process the second language, consistent with our fMRI data discussed earlier (e.g., Yang, Tan & Li, 2011).

The advantage of ERP data is also demonstrated by Thierry and Wu's (2007) study, in which monolingual English speakers and late proficient Chinese-English bilinguals were asked to decide whether English words presented in pairs were related in meaning or not. The novel aspect of this study is that half of the English word pairs (e.g., *train* vs. *ham*), when translated into Chinese, contained shared Chinese characters (e.g., 火车 *huoche* vs. 火腿 *huotui*) that were concealed and unknown to the participants when reading in English. If bilinguals automatically activate the L1 when they are processing the L2, we should expect faster response times and reduced ERP amplitude in N400 from the Chinese-English bilinguals but not the monolingual English speakers, due to the repetitions of L1 word pairs like *huoche* (train) and *huotui* (ham) in Chinese. Thierry and Wu found the predicted ERP effect but not the expected response time effect, confirming that bilinguals are translating the English words to Chinese even when reading or listening only in English, and that ERPs can reveal unconscious processes not evident in the behavioral data.

In recent years ERP researchers have begun to design longitudinal studies to track developmental neural changes associated with the learning of a second language.

Although time-consuming and expensive, such studies are necessary for fully understanding the adaptive changes triggered by the learning of new languages and the competition created by the representation of multiple languages. A good example is McLaughlin, Osterhout, and Kim (2004), who tested American students learning French at three different time intervals (sessions) in a college classroom setting: students had received an average of 14 hours, 63 hours, and 138 hours of classroom instructions at the three sessions of testing, respectively. The participants' ERP responses to written French word pairs, as well as their behavioral responses, were recorded. There were three types of word pairs: word-pseudoword pairs (*mot-nasier*), semantically unrelated (*maison-soif*), semantically related (*chien-chat*). Only the second of the pair was the target word to which the participants needed to make a lexical decision response ("is the letter string a word or not?"). As mentioned earlier, the N400 is an ERP component that indicates semantic congruity or integration, and for native speakers, the word-pseudoword pairs should elicit the largest N400 amplitude, followed by semantically unrelated pairs, and then by semantically related pairs. McLaughlin *et al.* wanted to see if the L2 learners' N400 patterns would change as a function of learning more French over the three sessions of testing. Their results showed that compared with a control group of participants who had not learned French during the same period, the French learner participants' N400 responses showed progressively larger amplitudes for the pseudowords than the words across the three sessions, and for the words in the semantically related condition than in the semantically unrelated conditions in the second and third sessions. These data suggest that the ERP components, particularly the N400, are sensitive to learning successes over a developmental time.

What's more striking about McLaughlin *et al.*'s study was their finding that short-term training produced rapid developmental changes, only reflected in ERP responses and not in behavioral responses. With only an average of 14 hours of initial training (their first session), individual participants' N400 patterns were correlated with the number of hours of L2 instruction, but the behavioral measures were not. These findings, interestingly, contrasted with those of the Chen *et al.* (2007) study in which grammatical learning was tested: the Chinese-English bilinguals showed no P600 after many years of learning, even though their behavioral responses matched those of native speakers. In both cases, though, the ERP method provided additional insights into the L2 processes, with contrasting patterns for grammar vs. semantic learning (see Chapter 4 for several other ERP studies of bilingual lexical and sentence processing that complement behavioral studies).

10.3   Neurolinguistic Computational Modeling

In the mid-to-late 1950s, the "cognitive revolution" occurred along with the birth of artificial intelligence, cognitive science, psycholinguistics, and related areas in the study of the mind (see Gardner, 1985; Leahey, 2004 for a historical tour). A critical impetus to this revolution was the advent of computers and the accompanying computational thinking. The idea that we can treat the human brain as a computing system and make inferences about how the mind works was very appealing. The key to this comparison is the system's capacity for information processing, particularly in manipulating symbols. In other words, the brain, as well as the computer, can be viewed as a type of symbol processor, or symbolic "information processing system." Computational modeling that relies on symbolic information processing has since become a very powerful methodology in cognitive science and psycholinguistics.

In spite of the significant progresses in the tradition of symbolic information processing, researchers have come to realize that there are fundamental differences between computers and brains. For example, computer programs are written in codes that need to be executed serially, whereas the brain's "software" involves simultaneous activities of a large number of neurons to compute information in parallel. The joint actions of multiple neurons are coordinated both spatially (i.e., *which* neurons become active) and temporally (i.e., *when* neurons become active). Moreover, these patterns of neural activity, unlike static computer programs, dynamically change in response to external stimuli and to the learning individual's specific experiences. Connectionism, also known as artificial neural network, is based on considerations of these ideas, that is, parallel processing, coordinated patterns of activity, and networks of neural connections. In the last 30 years connectionism has become one of the most influential theoretical frameworks for modeling human cognitive and linguistic behaviors. Because connectionist models are neurally inspired, we call them "neurocomputational models."

10.3.1 Connectionist models as neurolinguistic computational models

Connectionism stands in stark contrast to the classic computational view of the human mind that draws upon properties of digital computers with regard to discrete (symbol-based), modular (domain-specific), and serial (one-step-at-a-time) processes. Connectionist models attempt to understand how neural computation is conducted in the brain by simulating the cognitive and neural processes of language, memory, and learning.

Typically, a connectionist model is made up of two fundamental components: simple processing elements (*nodes, units,* or *artificial neurons*), and connections among these processing elements (hence the term "connectionism"). A distinction is sometimes made to distinguish "localist" models from "distributed" models. Localist models rely on node-to-word correspondences to represent the lexicon (or other linguistic components), such that the form or the meaning of a word is assigned a single numerical value, and a given node's activation is unambiguously associated with the presence of the numerical value that represents the word. By contrast, distributed models assume that information is not localized in specific nodes and thus rely on patterns of activation across many nodes in the network,

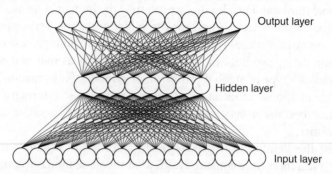

Figure 10.3: A standard feed-forward connectionist network. The network consists of nodes at three layers: Input layer, Hidden layer, and Output layer. The Input layer represents input patterns, the Output layer represents patterns produced by the network in response to the inputs, and the Hidden layer forms internal representations that allow the network to correctly map the received inputs to desired outputs.

particularly through the inter-connections between nodes, as in real biological synapses.

A standard connectionist network consists of three layers of nodes: Input layer, Hidden layer, and Output layer. The Input layer receives information from input patterns (e.g., representations of alphabetic features), the Output layer provides output patterns produced by the network (e.g., classifications of alphabets according to shapes), and the Hidden layer forms the network's internal representations as a result of the network's learning (e.g., the visual similarities between "O" and "Q"). Figure 10.3 provides a diagrammatic sketch of the typical three-layer connectionist network. In this type of model, information flows from the input layer upward to the output layer, and as such it is also called a "feed-forward" model (in contrast to models that use "feedback" or "recurrent" connections between different layers). In the standard three-layer feed-forward models, the hidden layer plays a key role in developing intermediate representations for the input and output relations; without this layer, correct input-output mapping may be impossible, given the often complex, nonlinear relationships that exist between inputs and outputs such as those for the sound-meaning mappings in language.

Moreover, these connections take on different values of strength (i.e., weights), which are adjusted and updated during learning. Weight adjustment is dynamic and adaptive, dependent upon the learning task and learning algorithms. It is this adaptive nature that makes connectionist networks particularly suitable as neuro-linguistic computational models.

Different connectionist models use different algorithms to adjust weights to achieve learning. The most widely used algorithm in cognitive and linguistic studies is "backpropagation" (Rumelhart, Hinton, & Williams, 1986), according to which the discrepancy between the desired output and the actual output (the "error") is used as teaching signals to adjust the weights. Specifically, at the beginning of learning, the weights holding between different nodes at different layers are randomized, but as the input-output pairs are continuously presented to the network at each cycle of learning, the errors between the actual output and the desired output are calculated, which are then propagated back to the network so that "blame" can be assigned to those connections and nodes that have contributed to the errors. The amount of adjustment is made relative to the amount of errors produced, such that the connections that contribute to larger errors are adjusted more strongly than the connections that contribute to smaller errors or no errors at the output.

10.3.2 Computational modeling of bilingualism

While neurolinguistic computational models have flourished (see MacWhinney & Li, 2008, for a review), most of them so far have focused on monolingual rather than bilingual processing. Among the few computational models for bilingualism, most are based on connectionist architectures (see Thomas & Van Heuven, 2005, for a review). Here we briefly discuss some of these models.

The BIMOLA model (Lévy & Grosjean, 2008) and the BIA model (Dijkstra & Van Heuven, 1998) were two early computational models of bilingualism that have been developed to account for spoken word recognition and visual word recognition, respectively. These models are discussed in detail in Chapters 2 and 4. It is worth noting here, however, that BIA and BIMOLA are both localist models, and both rely on the interactive activation principles. They were designed to account for proficient adult bilingual speakers' lexical knowledge and processing, and therefore are not connectionist learning models. As these models extend their principles to cover the bilingual learner more generally, they should incorporate learning principles to capture important factors such as bilingual proficiency and other learner profiles in development. Connectionist learning models of bilingualism (mostly distributed models) have been developed, for example, by Thomas (1997), French (1998), Li and Farkas (2002), and Zhao and Li (2010), as discussed below.

A critical notion in connectionist networks is *emergentism*, which is that cognitive or linguistic representations (e.g., words, concepts, grammatical structures) are emergent properties. In this view, higher-level mental representations emerge naturally as a result of lower-level simple processes such as the interaction between a large number of processing units (neurons) in a network. In an early attempt in this direction, Thomas (1997) simulated bilingual processing with a Bilingual Single Network (BSN) model to learn the orthography-semantics mapping in word recognition. The BSN uses a standard three-layer network with the backpropagation algorithm to transform a word's orthography (Input Nodes) to a word's semantic representation (Output Nodes) through the network's internal representations (Hidden Nodes). The model was trained on a simplified artificial vocabulary from two languages (L1 and L2), either in a balanced condition (equal amount of training) or unbalanced condition (L1 trained three times as often as L2). The modeling results indicated that under both conditions the network was able to develop distinct internal representations for L1 vs. L2 in the hidden layer activation patterns, although in the unbalanced condition the L2 words were less clearly represented as compared with those in the balanced condition. In addition, the network also explored language-general orthographic similarities of L1 and L2 words, thereby capturing cross-language coactivations as in the BIA model.

The BSN model, despite its simplification in representation, showed that connectionist models are able to account for both language independence and language interaction within a single network. In the same vein, French (1998) tested a bilingual SRN (BSRN) model trained on artificially generated sentences of the N-V-N structure in English and French. The network was exposed to mixed bilingual input as in Thomas (1997), with the two artificial languages intermixed at the sentence rather than the word level (i.e., sentences having a certain probability of switching from one to the other language). Their model adopted the network architecture of Elman (1990), the *simple recurrent network* (SRN), which adds a context layer to the standard three-layered network discussed in Section 10.3.1. This context layer is linked to both the input layer and the hidden layer, and it keeps a copy of the hidden-layer activations, which is then sent back to the network along with new inputs at the next time cycle of learning. This procedure allows the SRN to develop a powerful dynamic memory for temporal sequences such as lexical context due to the recurrent loops between the context layer, hidden layer, and the input layer.

As in the original SRN model, French's (1998) BSRN model was trained to predict the next word given the current word input in the sentence. In the original SRN model, distinct linguistic representations can emerge from the network's ability to learn lexical context in which individual lexical items occur. In the bilingual SRN model, distinct patterns of representation emerged for each language: words from the two languages became separated in the network's internal representations (the hidden layer activations). The modeling results supported the hypothesis that the bilingual input environment itself (mixed bilingual sentences in this case) is sufficient for the development of distinct mental representations for each language, requiring no separate or predetermined processing mechanisms for different languages.

One significant issue with these connectionist models is the use of highly simplified, artificially generated input representation as proxy for linguistic material. Although such "synthetic" inputs are easy to construct and can greatly streamline the modeling process, it raises the question of whether results from the models can make direct contact with the properties of natural linguistic input that the actual learner experiences. Realizing this limitation, Li and Farkas (2002) proposed a self-organizing model of bilingual processing (SOMBIP), in which training data derived from actual linguistic corpus were used. The SOMBIP was based on the self-organizing map architecture (SOM; Kohonen, 2001). In the SOM network, nodes are organized on a map-like structure that captures the similarities of the input: each time a new input is learned, the weight values of the output nodes are changed to resemble the weight values of the inputs. This process forces the nodes on the map to become "specialists" for specific inputs, so that at the end of learning the multidimensional statistical structure in the input is reflected in the output as similarity distances in the two-dimensional topographic map, or technically as neighborhoods of ordered nodes. In the SOMBIP model, two SOM maps, one learning phonology and the other semantics, are connected. Unlike BSN and BSRN models, SOMBIP uses phonological representations based on articulatory features of phonemes, and semantic representations based on co-occurrence statistics in child-directed parental speech, which gives SOMBIP more linguistic and developmental realism. Like BSN and BSRN, SOMBIP learned mixed bilingual input (216 English words and 184 Chinese words) simultaneously and the model produced patterns highly consistent with those of BSN and BSRN in that distinct lexical representations for Chinese and English were observed in the simultaneous learning of two languages. SOMBIP also provides a different way to assess proficiency by having the network exposed to fewer sentences in L2, simulating a novice learner having limited linguistic experience. This more natural way of modeling proficiency, interestingly, yielded comparable results to those from the BSN: the "novice" network's representation of the L2 was more compressed and less clearly delineated, as compared with the "proficient" network.

The SOMBIP model later evolved into the DevLex (Developmental Lexicon) model in an attempt to provide a general mechanistic account for both monolingual and bilingual learning and processing (see Li, Farkas, & MacWhinney 2004; Li, Zhao, & MacWhinney, 2007). Zhao and Li (2010) simulated a DevLex-II bilingual model. This model, in contrast to the BSN, BSRN, and SOMBIP models that received bilingual inputs simultaneously, learned L1 vs. L2 inputs sequentially to simulate the age of acquisition effects: (a) early L2 learning involved onset time of L2 input slightly delayed relative to L1 while (b) late L2 learning involved L2 input significantly delayed relative to L1. In addition, DevLex-II was also scaled up to learn up to 1000 real words (500 words from each language), the largest bilingual vocabulary in a connectionist model so far.

Figure 10.4 presents a snapshot of the modeling results. These results show that AoA plays an important role in modulating the overall representational structure of L2: in early L2 learning, the network could organize the L2 lexical structure well (as assessed through measures of lexical space and accuracy in form-meaning mapping), though not as well as in the simultaneous learning situation as in SOMBIP, whereas in late L2 learning, the network was unable to establish an independent lexical space for the L2. Such "age" effects in L2 learning may reflect the changing learning dynamics and neural plasticity of the learning system. In particular, if L2 onset occurs at a time when the L1 has been consolidated, as in late L2 learning, the learned structure in L1 will constrain what can be learned, and the plasticity of the network may also decrease because of the network's commitment to the L1. Interestingly, these patterns are comparable, though not identical, to the modeling patterns due to proficiency manipulations (in BSN and SOMBIP), indicating that "age" (or maturation) per se is not the answer to the AoA effect (see Hernandez, Li, & MacWhinney, 2005; Li, 2009 for further discussion of competition, entrenchment, and plasticity in bilingual networks).

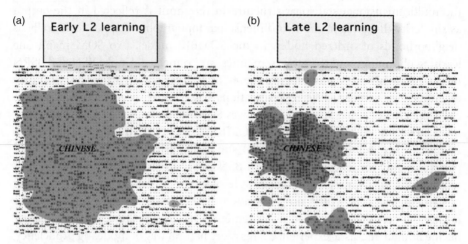

Figure 10.4: Organization of lexical representation as a function of (a) early vs. (b) late learning of L2 in the DevLex-II model. Shaded areas indicate Chinese (L2) representations. Labels of Chinese and English as well as the shading were added by the author for visual clarity. No labels were provided to the model during training. Similar simulation results are obtained when Chinese is the L1 and English the L2. See Zhao and Li (2010) for details.

10.3.3   Importance of modeling and evaluation of models

One distinct advantage with computational modeling, as can been seen from the discussion in 10.3.2, is that it allows us to manipulate variables of interest much more flexibly and to study their interactions in a more systematic way. In many cases it is difficult or impossible to directly manipulate these variables in empirical studies through parametric variations (e.g., to orthogonally cross all levels of one variable with all levels of another variable). For example, one cannot easily manipulate the time, frequency, and size of linguistic input in naturalist language learning situations, or to cross different levels of time (early vs. late) with different frequencies of words (high vs. low) during the course of language learning. In computational modeling, this type of manipulation is not only possible, but necessary. In addition, because computational modeling attempts to provide mechanistic accounts of empirical phenomena, it forces researchers to describe the phenomenon to be studied more precisely, and to specify the hypotheses and predictions more explicitly and more rigorously so that the phenomenon can be implemented in the model in terms of input-output mapping relationships and the hypotheses can be verified or tested. For example, in the DevLex-II model described in Section 10.3.2, the modeler needs to consider how to define what successful word learning means (e.g., correct input-output mapping), how word form and word meaning are represented, how they are organized with other words, and how they compete among a larger pool of phonologically or semantically similar items.

The advantage of using computational models to study bilingualism is even more obvious. Bialystok (2001) used an interesting metaphor: if bilingualism is a smorgasbord at a dinner table, some people eat several things at once (e.g., salad, meat, dessert all together), others eat one at a time (at varying speed), and still others come late and take only a bite of the dessert. Such volatile situations present great difficulties to empirical studies for the control of relevant variables (e.g., time and amount of L1-L2 learning, L2 input quantity and quality), while computational modeling provides a tool for systematically manipulating the two languages in terms of L2 onset time, L2 input frequency, amount of L1 vs. L2 input, order of L1 vs. L2 learning, and so on. In other words, different ways in which the linguistic smorgasbord is served and taken can be computationally instantiated in connectionist models.

One important issue to bear in mind is that computational models need both to be informed by empirical data and to inform empirical studies. This means that researchers need to understand what empirical patterns and what hypotheses are out there, but not be satisfied with the model's ability to simply emulate the data or fit the data. Instead, they should make predictions as to what the data would look like under one hypothesis vs. another, thereby effectively evaluating competing hypotheses and informing theories of language processing and bilingualism. In other words, a good model should be evaluated not only against empirical data (i.e., on how well it displays patterns observed in empirical studies), but also against its ability to generate testable predictions and new ideas, thereby inspiring future research.

Research Questions

1. How do different neuroimaging techniques (e.g., ERP and fMRI) inform us of different aspects of bilingual language processing and representation? What are their relative strengths and weaknesses with regard to the research questions asked?
2. With new perspectives from recent neurolinguistic and psycholinguistic studies of bilingualism, why is it less meaningful to look for simple answers to questions like single vs. separate storage of bilingual lexicon, or common vs. distinct bilingual representations?
3. Among the various computational models of bilingualism, there are localist vs. distributed models, and processing vs. learning models. What are the advantages and disadvantages of each type of model? How might some of them be combined to form new powerful models?
4. The understanding of the complex and dynamic relationships between brain, language, and bilingualism through both neuroimaging and computational perspectives is exciting. Do you see areas, topics or issues that lend themselves to the joint efforts of both neuroimaging and computational modeling? Discuss areas or topics that might be good examples for such efforts.

Further Readings

Abutalebi, Jubin, Cappa, Stefano F., & Perani, Daniela. 2005. What can functional neuroimaging tell us about the bilingual brain? In Judith F. Kroll & Annette M.B. De Groot (eds), *Handbook of Bilingualism: Psycholinguistic Approaches*, pp. 202–225. New York: Oxford University Press.

Hickok, Gregory. 2009. The functional neuroanatomy of language. *Physics of Life Reviews* 6. 121–143.

MacWhinney, Brian & Li, Ping. 2008. Neurolinguistic computational models. In Brigitte Stemmer & Harry A. Whitaker (eds), *Handbook of the Neuroscience of Language*, pp. 229–236. New York: Elsevier.

Rodríguez-Fornells, Antoni, Cunillera, Toni, Mestres-Missé, Anna, & de Diego-Balaguer, Ruth. 2009. Neurophysiological mechanisms involved in language learning in adults. *Philosophical Transactions of the Royal Society of London* 364(1536). 3711–3735.

References

Abutalebi, Jubin & Green, David. 2007. Bilingual language production: The neurocognition of language representation and control. *Journal of Neurolinguistics* 20. 242–275.

Bialystok, Ellen. 2001. *Bilingualism in Development: Language, Literacy, and Cognition*. Cambridge: Cambridge University Press.

Bressler, Steven L. & Menon, Vinod. 2010. Large-scale brain networks in cognition: Emerging methods and principles. *Trends in Cognitive Sciences* 14. 277–290.

Chan, Alice H.D., Luke, Kang-Kwong, Li, Ping, Yip, Virginia, Li, Geng, Weekes, Brendan & Tan, Li-Hai. 2008. Neural correlates of nouns and verbs in early bilinguals. *Annals of the New York Academy of Sciences* 1145. 30–40.

Chen, Lang, Shu, Hua, Liu, Youyi, Zhao, Jingjing, & Li, Ping. 2007. ERP signatures of subject-verb agreement in L2 learning. *Bilingualism: Language and Cognition* 10. 161–174.

Dijkstra, Ton & Van Heuven, Walter J.B. 1998. The BIA model and bilingual word recognition. In Jonathan Grainger & Arthur M. Jacobs (eds), *Localist Connectionist Approaches to Human Cognition*, pp. 189–225. Mahwah, NJ: Lawrence Erlbaum.

Elman, Jeffrey. 1990. Finding structure in time. *Cognitive Science* 14. 179–211.

Elman, Jeffrey L., Bates, Elizabeth A., Johnson, Mark H., Karmiloff-Smith, Annette, Parisi, Domenico, & Plunkett, Kim. 1996. *Rethinking Innateness: A Connectionist Perspective on Development*. Cambridge, MA: MIT Press.

Fabbro, Franco. 1999. *The Neurolinguistics of Bilingualism*. Hove, UK: Psychology Press.

French, Robert. 1998. A simple recurrent network model of bilingual memory. In Morton A. Gernsbacher & Sharon A. Derry (eds), *Proceedings of the 20th Annual Conference of the Cognitive Science Society*, pp. 368–373. Mahwah, NJ: Lawrence Erlbaum.

Gardner, Howard. 1985. *The Mind's New Science: A History of the Cognitive Revolution*. New York: Basic Books.

Green, David W. 2005. The neurocognition of recovery patterns in bilingual aphasics. In Judy F. Kroll & Annette M.B. de Groot (eds), *Handbook of Bilingualism: Psycholinguistic Approaches*, pp. 516–530. New York: Oxford University Press.

Hernandez, Arturo & Li, Ping. 2007. Age of acquisition: Its neural and computational mechanisms. *Psychological Bulletin* 133. 638–650.

Hernandez, Arturo, Li, Ping, & MacWhinney, Brian. 2005. The emergence of competing modules in bilingualism. *Trends in Cognitive Sciences* 9. 220–225.

Hernandez, Arturo, Martinez, Antigona, & Kohnert, Kathryn. 2000. In search of the language switch: An fMRI study of picture naming in Spanish-English bilinguals. *Brain and Language* 73. 421–431.

Hickok, Gregory. 2009. The functional neuroanatomy of language. *Physics of Life Reviews* 6. 121–43.

Key, Alexandra, Dove, Guy, & Maguire, Mandy. 2005. Linking brainwaves to the brain: An ERP primer. *Developmental Neuropsychology* 27. 183–215.

Kim, Karl H., Relkin, Norman R., Lee, Kyoung-Min, & Hirsch, Joy. 1997. Distinct cortical areas associated with native and second languages. *Nature* 388. 171–174.

Kohonen, Teuvo. 2001. *Self-organizing Maps* (3rd edn). Berlin & New York: Springer.

Kutas, Marta, Federmeier, Kara D., Staab, Jenny, & Kluender, Robert. 2007. Language. In John T. Cacioppo, Louis G. Tassinary, & Gary G. Bernston (eds), *Handbook of Psychophysiology* (3rd edn), pp. 555–580. New York: Cambridge University Press.

Leahey, Thomas H. 2004. *A History of Psychology: Main Currents in Psychological Thought* (6th edn). Upper Saddle River, NJ: Pearson Prentice Hall.

Léwy, Nicolas & Grosjean, François. 2008. The Léwy and Grosjean BIMOLA model. Chapter 11 of Grosjean, François. 2008. *Studying Bilinguals*. Oxford/New York: Oxford University Press.

Li, Ping. 2009. Lexical organization and competition in first and second languages: Computational and neural mechanisms. *Cognitive Science* 33. 629–664.

Li, Ping & Farkas, Igor. 2002. A self-organizing connectionist model of bilingual processing. In Roberto R. Heredia & Jeanette Altarriba (eds), *Bilingual Sentence Processing*, pp. 59–85. Amsterdam: North-Holland/Elsevier Science.

Li, Ping, Farkas, Igor, & MacWhinney, Brian. 2004. Early lexical development in a self-organizing neural network. *Neural Networks* 17. 1345–1362.

Li, P., Jin, Z., & Tan, L. (2004). Neural representations of nouns and verbs in Chinese: An fMRI study. *NeuroImage* 21, 1533–1541.

Li, Ping, Zhao, Xiaowei, & MacWhinney, Brian. 2007. Dynamic self-organization and early lexical development in children. *Cognitive Science* 31. 581–612.

McLaughlin, Judith, Osterhout, Lee, & Kim, Albert. 2004. Neural correlates of second-language word learning: Minimal instruction produces rapid change. *Nature Neuroscience* 7. 703–704.

Mechelli, Andrea, Crinion, Jenny T., Noppeney, Uta, O'Doherty, John, Ashburner, John, Frackowiak, Richard S., & Price, Cathy J. 2004. Structural plasticity in the bilingual brain. *Nature* 431. 757.

Paradis, Michel. 1977. Bilingualism and aphasia. In Haiganoosh Whitaker & Harry A. Whitaker (eds), *Studies in Neurolinguistics*, pp. 65–121. New York: Academic Press.

Price, Cathy J. 2000. The anatomy of language: Contributions from functional neuroimaging. *Journal of Anatomy* 197. 335–359.

Rumelhart, David E., Hinton, Geoffrey E., & Williams, Ronald J. 1986. Learning internal representations by error propagation. In David E. Rumelhart, James L. McClelland, and PDP Research Group (eds), *Parallel Distributed Processing: Explorations in the Microstructure of Cognition* (Vol. 1), pp. 318–362. Cambridge, MA: MIT Press.

Thierry, Guillaume & Wu, Yan Jing. 2007. Brain potentials reveal unconscious translation during foreign-language comprehension. *Proceedings of the National Academy of Sciences of the United States of America* 104(30). 12530–12535.

Thomas, Michael S.C. 1997. Connectionist networks and knowledge representation: The case of bilingual lexical processing. Unpublished doctoral dissertation, Oxford University, UK.

Thomas, Michael S.C. & Van Heuven, Walter J.B. 2005. Computational models of bilingual comprehension. In Judith F. Kroll & Annette M.B. de Groot (eds), *Handbook of Bilingualism: Psycholinguistic Approaches*, pp. 497–515. New York: Oxford University Press.

Tokowicz, Natasha & MacWhinney, Brian. 2005. Implicit and explicit measures of sensitivity to violations in second language grammar: An event-related potential investigation. *Studies in Second Language Acquisition* 27. 173–204.

Van Hell, Janet G. & Tokowicz, Natasha. 2010. Event-related brain potentials and second language learning: Syntactic processing in late L2 learners at different L2 proficiency levels. *Second Language Research* 26. 43–74.

Wartenburger, Isabell, Heekeren, Hauke R., Abutalebi, Jubin, Cappa, Stefano F., Villringer, Arno, & Perani, Daniela. 2003. Early setting of grammatical processing in the bilingual brain. *Neuron* 37. 159–170.

Yang, Jing, Tan, Li-Hai, & Li, Ping. 2011. Lexical representation of nouns and verbs in the late bilingual brain. *Journal of Neurolinguistics* 24. 674–682.

Zhao, Xiaowei & Li, Ping. 2010. Bilingual lexical interactions in an unsupervised neural network model. *International Journal of Bilingual Education and Bilingualism* 13. 505–524.

Index

The Psycholinguistics of Bilingualism, First Edition. François Grosjean and Ping Li.
© 2013 Blackwell Publishing Ltd with the exceptions of Chapter 1, Chapter 2, Chapter 3, Chapter 7,
Chapter 10 © 2013 François Grosjean and Ping Li. Published 2013 by Blackwell Publishing Ltd.